STOCKPORT

Developmental Psychology

Crucial Study Texts for Psychology Degree Courses

Titles in series

To order, please call our order line 0845 230 9000, or email learningmatters@bebc.co.uk, or visit our website www.learningmatters.co.uk

Developmental Psychology

Dianne Catherwood and Rachel Gillibrand

(illustrations: Dianne Catherwood)

First published in 2004 by Crucial, a division of Learning Matters Ltd.

British Library Cataloguing in Publication Data
A CIP record for this book is available from the British Library.

ISBN 1 903337 14 3

Cover design by Topics – The Creative Partnership
Project management by Deer Park Productions
Text design by Code 5 Design
Typeset by PDQ Typesetting, Newcastle under Lyme
Printed and bound by Bell & Bain Ltd, Glasgow

Learning Matters Ltd
33 Southernhay East
Exeter EX1 1NX
Tel: 01392 215560
Email: info@learningmatters.co.uk
www.learningmatters.co.uk

Contents

Introduction and overview

(Dianne Catherwood)

Why study child and adolescent development?

Have you ever wondered why and how you got to be the person you are? For instance, why are you studying psychology instead of lion-taming or accountancy or the mating habits of toads? When we arrive in this world as newborn babies, it may seem that there are infinite possibilities for the direction our lives can take, but are we really free to become anything we want to be: arsonist or fireman, rock star or opera singer? What are the factors that determine our fate? Maybe you will never know for sure why your life has taken a certain path, but by studying developmental psychology, you may be able to get a good idea. Developmental psychology helps us to understand why and how we end up being who we are. It is the study of how human behaviour and capacities emerge and possibly change with age and it helps to identify the forces that can shape our lives.

In this book we will focus on development in childhood and adolescence. Of course development does not end with adolescence and there are ongoing challenges and changes right across the lifespan. However, these early phases of life provide the foundation for development thereafter and so we will be considering them in detail. In the next chapter we will begin by discussing broad issues, theoretical perspectives and themes in regard to human development, especially how nature (our genes) and nurture (our environment) work together to produce individual human beings. Then in the following chapters, human development will be considered from conception through the prenatal and neonatal phases of life, followed by discussion of physical, perceptual, cognitive, social, emotional and linguistic development across childhood and adolescence.

You might be doubtful about the value of studying children and teenagers. To you, children might seem like alarmingly noisy and helpless creatures (and many parents might describe their adolescent offspring the same way). However, by studying these early phases of life, we can gain an idea of the 'starting point' or raw materials for human abilities and behaviour and of how these basic capacities are shaped or moulded thereafter.

The other good reason for studying children's development is an 'applied' one. For better or worse, judgments and predictions are made about children's abilities. Although the complex forces acting on human experience can make such judgments and predictions challenging, understanding early development offers a chance to do this in an informed way and to offer advice on the healthiest ways to raise and educate children.

The format of this book

This book aims to present quintessential information about the theoretical issues, debates, models and research on the main aspects of development across childhood and adolescence. The aim is also to provide support for students in respect to identification of key aspects of the material covered. The format reflects these aims by presenting the information in a very concise way with identification of learning outcomes at the start of each chapter and crucial concepts, crucial studies and quick tests throughout the chapters. In addition at the end of each chapter a crucial example of assessment will be provided along with sample readings. A full reference list is provided at the end of the book.

Chapter 1
The big questions about human development: broad issues, theories and approaches

(Dianne Catherwood)

Chapter summary

In this chapter, the broad themes, debates and theoretical perspectives in regard to human development will be considered, along with the main types of methodological approaches to studying development. The focus will be on nature (the genes we inherit from our ancestors) and nurture (our experiences within our environment) and the relationship between these. A detailed explanation will be given about genes and how they influence human development, followed by the effect of experience on development. Finally the patterns of interaction between these two factors will be considered using the concept of heritability (the extent to which individual differences in a particular group of people can be explained by differences in genes).

Learning outcomes

After reading this chapter, you should be able to:

Outcome 1: Explain the broad issues and debates about human development.
For example, you will be able to explain the debate on how nature and nurture shape human characteristics.

Outcome 2: Appreciate historical and contemporary theoretical perspectives on human development.
For example, psychodynamic, ethological, behaviourist, social learning, information processing, neural network and dynamic systems approaches.

Outcome 3: Explain the main methodological approaches used to study child and adolescent development.
For example, you will be able to describe the cross-sectional, longitudinal and cross-sequential methods.

The three questions at the end of the chapter respectively test you on these learning outcomes.

Section 1

What are the big questions about human development?

In this section the broad themes or issues that underlie much of developmental psychology will be briefly described.

Perhaps the most important issue or debate about human development is whether nature (our genes) or nurture (experience) plays the larger role in shaping our lives. This issue will be examined in depth in this chapter but will also be a theme throughout the other chapters in this book. Another broad issue that will be explored in relevant chapters is whether we basically remain the same person throughout life with stable characteristics or whether these change as we develop. A third question that will be addressed in the book is whether human development occurs gradually or whether it proceeds in leaps and bounds, in stages which are essentially different from each other. A related topic is whether there are critical periods for the growth of certain capacities (e.g. language) with no possibility of development once that period has elapsed. All of these issues have generated controversy, with a range of differing views being proposed. The way in which this has occurred for particular aspects of development will be covered in relevant chapters of the book, but a brief overview of some of the main theoretical views on the nature of development is provided in the following section.

CRUCIAL CONCEPTS

The most important issues in regard to human development include:

- The debate about the relative role of **nature** (genes) and **nurture** (experience).
- Whether development proceeds **continuously or in stages** and involves **critical periods** of growth.
- Whether human characteristics are **constant or undergo change** across the lifespan.

Quick test

What are some of the most important issues in respect to the study of human development?

Section 2

Are there theories about human development?

In this section a summary will be provided of key ideas, views, models and theories regarding human development.

All psychological research is based on and gives rise to theorising that may take a variety of forms, ranging from broad or loosely-connected ideas to very specific and detailed schemes and models. Developmental psychology is no exception in this respect.

There have been recent attempts to provide all-encompassing theories of development, most notably the **dynamic systems perspective** (e.g. Wachs, 2000). This approach stresses the interrelationships amongst all the aspects of development (bodily as well as psychological) and also identifies the complexity of development by proposing that different aspects of development may be following different pathways and timetables. In general however, developmental theories tend to have a more selective focus and in the main, contemporary developmental psychology does not follow any one theory but rather draws on many perspectives which may each contribute to overall understanding. For this reason, no single theoretical model will be followed in this book, but instead each particular topic or aspect of development will be considered in regard to any useful perspectives.

A preliminary overview of older and more recent theoretical frameworks is provid
It should be stressed that none of these offers a single correct view about develo
that these are not necessarily opposing views since each has a somewhat diff

Amongst the earliest efforts to develop large-scale theories of development we.
psychoanalytic approach of Freud (1935) and the **psychosocial** model of Erikson
(1963) that attempted to explain how the human personality develops in a series of stages
across the lifespan as the result of conflicts between innate needs and the demands of
society (see Chapter 6 for further reference to these views). **Ethological** viewpoints
(notably of Lorenz, 1952 or Bowlby, 1969) also focused on basic innate needs, emotions
and behaviours (such as aggression, attachment, play) but with an interest in how these
would emerge in or adapt to particular contexts for development (see Chapter 6 for further
detail on these views).

Other broad theoretical approaches were particularly concerned with how environmental
factors shape human development. These views included (a) **behaviourist** perspectives
that stressed the ways in which new patterns of behaviour could be learned by association
between environmental stimuli and responses (Watson and Rayner, 1920) or reinforcement of responses by environmental outcomes (Skinner, 1966) and (b) **social behaviourist** views that focused on the ways in which children learn by imitation of the
responses of others (Bandura, 1989). Other perspectives stressed the way in which the
individual acquires knowledge or the values, beliefs and customs of the society or culture
through interaction with others (e.g. Vygotsky's *socio-cultural model*,1987). The **ecological systems theory** (Bronfenbrenner and Evans, 2000), describes the 'layers' of
environmental contexts for children's development, ranging from the immediate sur-
roundings (microsystems) through to the broadest cultural setting (macrosystem). (See
Chapters 6, 7 and 8 for further reference to theoretical views of this type.)

Other theoretical frameworks are especially concerned with how the child develops
abilities that allow understanding about the world. One of the earliest attempts to chart
the course of this development was the **constructivist** approach of Piaget (1929; 1952)
who proposed that cognitive capacities develop through both maturation and action on
the world in a series of four stages from infancy to the end of adolescence (see Chapter 5
and 8 for more details). More recent **knowledge-based** (Chi,1978) and **information
processing** (Siegler, 1996) perspectives focus on basic brain processes for dealing with
information. These approaches describe the development of mastery over attention,
encoding, representation, 'working' and long-term memory as well as the growth of more
explicit understanding in particular domains or areas of knowledge (Karmiloff-Smith,
1992) (see Chapter 5 for more details). Some versions of these approaches propose that
this development occurs in stages (e.g. Case,1992) but the general view is that such
development proceeds more or less continuously, although the pace and direction may be
governed by the individual context for growth (see Chapter 5 for more detail).

CRUCIAL CONCEPTS

Broad theoretical perspectives regarding human development include:
- **psychoanalytic** (Freud) and **psychosocial** (Erikson);
- **ethological** (Lorenz, Bowlby);
- **behaviourist** (Watson and Rayner, Skinner) and **social learning** (Bandura);
- **socio-cultural** (Vygotsky);
- **ecological systems** (Bronfenbrenner);
- **constructivist** (Piaget);
- **information processing** (Siegler, Case);
- **knowledge or domain-based** (Chi, Karmiloff-Smith);
- **dynamic systems** (Wachs).

Quick test

Briefly describe some of the main theoretical approaches or perspectives on human development ranging from the earliest to the most recent.

Section 3

Approaches to studying development

There are a number of general approaches or methods used in developmental research to determine if or how abilities or behaviour change with age. These will be broadly described in this section.

Developmental research varies according to the number of children involved. It can be intensive case studies of single children or alternatively (and more commonly) studies of groups of children. It can also be **idiographic** (concerned with explaining patterns of development for individual children) or **normative** (concerned with explaining typical or average patterns of development for all children).

Developmental research also varies depending on whether the aim is to determine the causes of children's behaviour or simply to describe it. The latter usually involves either **observational** approaches in which children's behaviour or capacities are recorded in one particular context (often naturally occurring) or **correlational** approaches in which possible links between two or more aspects of development are examined. Alternatively (and most commonly) developmental research involves an **experimental** approach in which children's behaviour is observed or recorded under two or more predetermined conditions for a variable of interest (such as for different age groups or with different types of tests or contexts) in order to determine cause and effect relationships.

Developmental research also varies according to the timescale involved. The **cross-sectional approach** involves studying samples of children at different ages at the same time and comparing their performance or abilities. This provides a relatively quick or efficient means for deciding if age differences exist. Sometimes this approach is done more implicitly than explicitly. For example studies of newborns might examine abilities that are readily apparent in older children and adults (e.g. colour vision) but not directly compare the babies with older people.

One disadvantage of the cross-sectional approach is that it doesn't allow for individual development to be charted. The **longitudinal approach** does this by studying either single children or the same group of children over time and perhaps assessing or observing them on several occasions over the course of the study. Some studies like this have been running for many years and have tracked the participants' development from birth to adulthood (e.g. the New York *Study of Temperament*, Plomin and Dunn, 1986). However, the drawback of such studies is that they can be demanding of resources (time, money, etc.) and the participants may withdraw over time, leaving a potentially biased sample in the study. **Microgenetic** studies involve an abbreviated form of this approach and are used to record children's development in a particular trait or skill over a more limited period of time (Kuhn, 1995).

The other method, the **cross-sequential** approach, combines the cross-sectional and longitudinal approaches by involving samples that represent a cross-section of age groups and then studying these participants over time.

All of these approaches have played a major role in one way or another in providing understanding about how, why and when human development occurs.

CRUCIAL CONCEPT

Methodological approaches to studying human development:

- include single **case studies** as well as **group studies**;
- can be **idiographic** or **normative**;
- can be **observational**, **correlational** or **experimental**;
- can be **cross-sectional**, **longitudinal** (including **micro-genetic studies**) or **cross-sequential**.

Quick test

Describe the main methodological approaches to studying human development.

Much of the research and theorising on child and adolescent development is focused on the question of why we develop the way we do and specifically whether nature or nurture plays the larger role. These might sound like rivals, but in fact they are partners and both contribute to the development of the human being. Let us look more closely at these unlikely bedfellows.

Section 4

Nature: the role of heredity in human development

In this section, we will describe genes and how they can affect human development. You probably know that your body and brain are made up of tiny cells. Inside every single one of these, are our genes: material that controls how the cell grows and works and copies itself. It is due to genes that we only grow nose cells for our noses, feet cells for our feet and so on – otherwise we could look like a creature from Frankenstein's lab, with ears on our elbows or eyeballs on our toes. Be thankful for your genes!

What are genes? The code for life

Genes are bound together in long strands called chromosomes made of material called DNA (deoxyribonucleic acid) that looks like a twisted ladder. A gene is just one segment or chunk of this ladder. In each human cell there are tens of thousands of different genes arranged along 23 chromosomes (and there are actually two versions of each gene since, except in sperm and ova cells, chromosomes come in pairs, one from Mum and one from Dad). If you could see a DNA ladder, you would notice that it has 'rungs' made out of pairs of substances called nucleotides (adenine, thymine, guanine and cytosine). These rungs are our genes. Genes are different lengths and in human cells can have anything between 1000 to 2 million rungs. Each gene has its own unique arrangement of nucleotide pairs or rungs and it is this pattern that provides the 'code' or template of the gene for building or copying cells of the human body or brain (Pinel, 2000).

The exact way that this happens is still being studied, but the basic action of genes is broadly understood. To help you get some idea of the way that genes work, you should consult diagrams of genes and DNA in biological psychology texts (e.g. see Pinel, 2000), but it might also be easier to visualise genes if you think about them as if they were like children's toy-bricks. Let's play! Imagine that you have green, yellow, red and blue bricks and the yellow and blue can lock together sideways and the red and green can too. These would be like the four types of nucleotides (since adenine and thymine pair off, as do guanine and cytosine). Now imagine you have made lots of yellow-blue and red-green pairs and you build a very tall ladder with each pair of bricks forming one rung of the ladder. The rungs can be arranged in different ways along the length of the ladder (e.g. you might have a yellow-blue rung then a red-green then green-red then blue-yellow and so on). A gene would be one section of our ladder with its own series of rungs.

CRUCIAL CONCEPT

A **gene** is a segment of a chromosome or DNA found in each human cell and the arrangement of the gene material (nucleotides) provides a template for building and copying the cell.

Mitosis: How you grow new cells

To grow a new human being or to keep refreshing an existing one, we need to be able to make copies of the cells in the body. Making a carbon copy of a cell is called mitosis and it works like this: the cell starts to swell and duplicate all its chromosome pairs, ending up with 92 chromosomes rather than 46: or the equivalent of two cells in one. Then the cell splits in half to make two new cells, each with its copy of the full set of 46 chromosomes (23 pairs) that were in the original.

Unzipping our genes

How does all of this duplicating and copying actually work? It's all about the unzipping of genes (and maybe of 'jeans' too!). To help you understand, imagine you had completed a jigsaw puzzle and then you pulled it apart in the middle and separated the two halves. You'd then have two incomplete puzzles, but you could make new pieces that fit into the shapes of the pieces that you *did* have in each half. You would then end up with two complete puzzles that were copies of each other. This is an analogy to the way in which chromosomes and genes work to make copies of a cell or make it grow.

The ladder of genes or DNA can unzip or split in half lengthwise (at the point where the nucleotides or our toy bricks are joined to each other in pairs) and then each half of the ladder pulls in new material from the cell to make a whole new ladder that is a direct copy of the old one: so, hey presto – you now have two ladders instead of just one. Or when a particular gene has to make a cell grow rather than a whole new copy, the relevant section of the gene ladder just pulls apart or is exposed temporarily so that other material inside the cell (messenger RNA) can make a copy of the missing half. The RNA then dashes off elsewhere in the cell and sets off a whole chain of copying and collecting that ends up with nucleotides in the cell being pulled together in the appropriate shape.

CRUCIAL CONCEPT

Mitosis is a process by which the chromosomes (or DNA strands) in human cells make copies of themselves and then the cell splits, making two cells, each with a full copy or set of chromosomes and genes.

Bosses and workers

So the gene action makes an ear cell in the ear or a brain cell in the brain if all goes to plan, but the genes that do the actual building work are the same in all cells, so how do these different types of cell grow?

The answer is that there is another type of gene in the cells that acts like a boss or a switch (**operator genes**) to tell the builders (**structural genes**) when to start or stop work. In some cases the bosses can hold the workers in check for years and will only throw the on-switch at a set 'maturational' time in the human lifespan (e.g. the onset of puberty is affected by signals from operator genes). Bosses can also be affected by environment and may not throw the switch if conditions are not good (e.g. poor diet may affect cell growth in this way: Darnell, 1997).

CRUCIAL STUDIES

A massive research effort called **The Human Genome Project** (Genome International Sequencing Consortium, 2001) has recently mapped the locations and codes (the rungs) of the genes on human chromosomes. Some studies have now begun of the links between these genes and human traits and abilities. For example, a gene has been found for switching on testosterone in the male foetus promoting male sexual growth (Goodfellow and Lovell, 1998) and other genes have been found that influence the growth of neural connections in the brain (Li, van Aelst and Cline, 2000).

Gifts from Mum and Dad

Genes are passed on from parent to child (see next chapter) and each human cell has two versions (called **alleles**) of each gene: one on the chromosome inherited from mother and one on that from father. The alleles can be the same or different and they can interact in complicated ways. If they are different, they may simply add together and the result will be a mixture (e.g. as can occur with skin colour genes). But sometimes, one will be the **dominant** gene and the other **recessive** (i.e. one will be the active gene and the other will be carried silently).

For example, dark hair genes dominate blonde hair genes, so people who inherit a dark-hair gene from one parent and a blonde-gene from the other will inevitably have dark hair, though they will still carry the blonde gene in their cells and could pass it on to their children. If they had a child with another person who had a blonde gene (even if this person has dark hair too and was also only carrying the blonde gene), then they could well have a blonde child.

CRUCIAL CONCEPT

Alleles are the two versions of each gene inherited respectively from each parent.

How can genes affect human behaviour and capacities?

It has been known for a long time that genes can affect physical features like hair colour. But can genes affect behaviour or complex abilities like memory or musical skill? The answer seems to be that genes may affect some basic aspects of human behaviour but may not control complex capacities in a simple direct way.

Genes can, however, influence brain cells just as they do body cells. For example genes may affect how many neurons grow in particular areas of the brain and how many connections are made amongst these neurons (Li, et al., 2000) (see Chapters 2 and 3). In this way genes could conceivably influence the basic capacity of the brain for processing information and so have some impact on learning, memory and problem-solving abilities.

Studying the links between genes and behaviour

A long history of selective breeding studies with animals has confirmed that genes can affect animal behaviour such as learning.

CRUCIAL STUDY

In one classic study (Tryon, 1934, in Pinel, 2000) two distinct groups of rats were bred by selective mating: one group that were very good at finding their way through mazes (maze-bright) and another group that were not (maze-dull). Even if the babies of these two groups were cross-fostered after birth (i.e. maze-bright babies were reared by maze-dull parents and maze-dull babies by maze-bright parents), the maze-bright offspring still made fewer errors in the mazes than the maze-dull offspring: strong evidence that genetic factors were at work in their learning abilities.

It is more difficult to study the effects of genes on behaviour in humans in any direct sense. Most people would object to being part of selective breeding studies not of their own choosing! In any case, most human capacities are complex and involve multiple components that in turn may draw on different genes to different degrees (polygenic) and may involve environmental factors too (see next sections). Thus it is unlikely that there is a simple direct link between some overall behaviour and genes.

For example, champion tennis-playing may depend not only on good reflexes, but also physical fitness and the motivation to win. Each of these factors may draw on genes and environment in varying ways. Even in animal breeding studies, the link between observable behaviour and genes has been shown to be complex. One early study (Searle, 1949 in Pinel, 2000) found that their maze-bright rats were better learners than their maze-dull ones, not because they were more intelligent, but because they were less emotional. So the relevant factor (tendency to low emotionality) was not necessarily obvious.

One approach to determine the role of genes in human behaviour is to study newborn babies (neonates). Because they have little experience of the world, their behaviour may be more likely to show the effects of genetic factors at work. As will be seen in the next chapter, neonates arrive in the world with many reflex abilties (such as being able to suck and swallow) as well as remarkably complex capacities to take in and remember information from the sensory world around them (Slater and Lewis, 2002). These findings provide support for the idea that many basic human abilities may be shaped by innate or genetic forces in the first instance.

However, we cannot say for certain that neonatal behaviours only reflect the action of genes or that environment has played no role, since even in the womb, human development is vulnerable to the external environment (see next chapter for details).

Genotype and phenotype

Nonetheless, even if an ability or feature is directly due to genes, it still has to emerge or develop within a certain environment. For example, you may have the genetic potential (genotype) for being tall, but a malnourished diet in childhood may mean that your actual height (phenotype) is short.

─────────────────── CRUCIAL CONCEPT ───────────────────

Phenotype is the actual behaviour or feature that develops and this may differ from the **genotype** (genetic template or potential) because of the interaction of genes with environmental factors.

Quick test

1. What are genes and how do they affect the growth and copying of human cells?

2. What is the difference between genotype and phenotype and what is the relevance of this difference for human development?

Section 5

Nurture: the role of experience and the environment in human development

In this section, environment is defined and an explanation is given of the ways in which this can affect development. The environment for human development takes in the physical, cognitive, linguistic, social and emotional conditions a child experiences. The physical factors encompass not only basic aspects of life such as type and adequacy of nutrition, but also the sensory-perceptual stimulation offered by the child's situation. As well, a child develops within a particular interpersonal, family and cultural environment that provides emotional and social experiences, as well as exposure to language and other forms of information or knowledge.

Such environmental factors can impact on children's development in positive or negative ways. Physical growth will proceed well if children have adequate nutrition but any deficiencies in this respect can have serious results (see Chapters 2 and 3 for details on this issue). For example, low levels of protein in children's diet can cause kwashiorkor, a condition in which children develop large bellies and become very listless.

Likewise, children's cognitive and language development is enhanced by a stimulating and encouraging home environment (Espy, Molfese, and DiLalla, 2001). Emotional and social development is also influenced by early family interactions and parenting practices (see Chapters 6 and 8 for more details on this issue). For example, parents who are very accepting and responsive to children's needs but also use reasonable and consistent discipline (i.e. have an authoritative style) are more likely to raise children with higher self-esteem and greater social competence than are parents who are either permissive or overly controlling (Baumrind and Black, 1967).

Children's experiences can have a major impact on the course of their development. The physical environment directly affects the growth and functioning of the body and brain. But how do the other aspects of a child's experiences have a lasting effect on development of behaviour and abilities? Experience of the world arouses the human brain and can leave a lasting effect in the form of memory. The brain is a physical organ like others in the body and it can be physically changed by experiences and can retain an impression from them (see Chapters 2, 3, 4 and 5 for more details on this).

CRUCIAL CONCEPT

Learning and memories acquired through **experience** depend on biochemical and other physical changes in the neurons of the brain and so input from the environment can affect human development in a direct way.

Section 6

Nature *and* nurture: the interaction of genes and environment in human development

Both genes and environment can interact to affect many aspects of human development. In this section, the way in which this can occur will be considered.

The interaction between genes and environment can take a number of forms. The environment can (a) magnify or increase genetic tendencies, or (b) suppress or inhibit them or (c) change the way in which a genotype appears in actual behaviour. This pattern of interaction of genes and environment can vary for different traits and can also vary for the same trait in different people.

This close interaction between genes and environment has been shown in many research examples in both humans and other animals. Animal evidence includes studies showing that visual abilities which depend in the first instance on the action of genes can be lost through a restricted early visual environment (e.g. Blakemore, 1976).

CRUCIAL STUDY

Another study (Cooper and Zubek, 1958) bred maze-bright and maze-dull rats, but then reared the rat babies from both groups either in enriched environments (with lots of toys and tunnels to explore) or in poor environments (a bare wire cage). The rats were then tested for maze-learning skills. The type of rearing had little effect for the bright babies: they did well regardless of type of rearing, presumably because of the effects of their genes. But type of rearing had a marked impact on the dull babies. They did very badly after the poor childhood, but performed as well as the bright babies after the enriched childhood, so the rich environment was able to overcome their poor genotype.

This study shows the variation in the ways environment and genes can interact. Environment was of low importance for the bright-gene rats, but it was crucial for the dull-gene rats. Such studies might offer suggestions about human development. For example, a child may be born with genes that contribute to good musical ability. If the environment offers support, then the genotype may flourish in a musical phenotype, but in an unsupportive environment the child may not develop to full genetic potential or alternatively the genotype may find expression in a novel form (e.g. writing computer programs for musical scores). Alternatively a child with a weaker genetic disposition for musical skill may nonetheless be raised in a musically nourishing environment and develop musical competence as the result.

However, it is not a simple matter to predict the outcome of such gene-environment interactions, because many forces operate on children's development at any one time. In our music example, even a child with supportive genes and environment may ignore music and choose to play football instead in order to win the approval of peers. In the complex web of human existence, genetic dispositions for one aspect of behaviour may be overridden by other factors that could be due to genetic or environmental forces or some interaction of both.

But does this mean that there are no genetic limits or bounds to human development and that given the right environment, we can essentially develop in any way at all? One view on this issue (Wahlsten, 1994) is that genes may allow a 'reaction range' and the environment determines the final outcome within this range, so there is plenty of room for experience to have an influence but within limits set by genes.

The relationship between genes and experience is a fluid one. The same output (phenotype) may spring from different genotypes and on the other hand, the same genotype may give rise to different phenotypes. The environment can increase, decrease or even alter the way in which a genotype appears in the actual phenotype or behaviour, though possibly within genetic limits or a 'reaction range'.

Whatever the exact form of the links between genes and environment, it is certain that there *is* such an interaction for many of our important attributes and abilities. Many studies confirm the interplay between nature and nurture in human development.

Even negative genotypes can be overcome by environmental factors as shown in the case of the hereditary or genetic disorder called PKU (phenylketoneuria). This affects brain growth and impairs children's mental abilities but such effects can be minimised by control of diet: an environmental factor (Diamond, Prevor, Callender and Druin, 1997). Moreover, evidence of human gene-environment interactions is not limited just to physical development. Babies are born with the ability to perceive a vast range of the sounds that make up the languages of the world. However, with increasing exposure to their own language environment, babies show rapid development of *that* language, but lose the ability to perceive sounds from foreign languages (Eimas, 1975): a case of genetic potential being both enhanced and limited by the environment.

So it is likely that nature and nurture contribute to most aspects of human development in some way, but exactly how much does each contribute in relative terms? For the reasons explained above, it is not easy to give a definite estimate that will apply to every person on the planet for all eternity. The estimate could change from one person to the next depending on how genes and environment work together for each person. Even for the same psychological attribute, it may vary across different groups of people in the same society (e.g. for men and women or for different age groups) and it is likely to vary across groups who live in different kinds of societies or environments. Why?

CRUCIAL CONCEPT

Even if all human beings were clones of each other with exactly the same genes, we could still develop different attributes and abilities due to the **unique environmental experiences** that each of us would invariably have.

This conclusion is based partly on concordance studies of identical twins raised together who are often very similar (concordant) in psychological traits but nonetheless are still not identical – reflecting the impact of their individual experiences (Plomin, 1994). Thus even for traits that have a genetic basis, and even if identical genotypes are involved, environmental differences can act to produce different phenotypes.

Heritability: explaining human differences in a particular context

Although it is difficult to specify the exact contribution of nature or nurture for any particular individual, it is possible to give a more definite estimate of how much the differences amongst people in a particular group can be explained by differences in their genes (or, conversely, differences in their environment). Such calculations are called heritability estimates. These figures are based on findings from kinship studies that compare the similarity in particular traits amongst people of varying genetic similarity to each other and who live in basically the same type of environment in regard to the factor of interest (e.g. Scarr and Weinberg, 1983).

---CRUCIAL CONCEPT---

Heritability estimates tell us to what extent the differences in a trait for a group of people **at a given time and place** can be explained by genetic differences. Such estimates can vary over time and place and do not provide a fixed estimate of how much genes or environment account for a trait in everyone.

Numerous types of **kinship studies** have provided data for heritability estimates. The general idea is that if the similarity in some attribute increases with genetic similarity, then gene differences play a larger role in explaining differences within the group under study. One version (**family studies**) compares pairs of family members of varying relatedness (e.g. parent-child with 50% similarity in genes *vs.* grandparent-grandchild with only 25% similarity). Another version (**adoption studies**) compares adopted children to their adoptive parents and to their natural parents while a third variation (**twin studies**) compares identical twins (with 100% gene overlap) with fraternal twins (50% gene overlap). The final variation (**adopted twin studies**) involves twins reared apart. One of the most famous of such studies has been the Minnesota Twin Study of twins separated at birth (Bouchard, 1994). Heritability estimates are based on the extent of correlation between individuals on the trait of interest. For example, if identical twins (100% genetically similar) show a higher correlation on scores for some personality variable like shyness than is the case for fraternal twins or siblings (50% genetically similar), then this suggests that genes carry a greater weight for that variable.

What are the findings from such studies? The heritability estimates vary depending on the manner of calculation but there is some consensus for main attributes. For example, height and weight have relatively high scores of about .8 (Wilson, 1986), which means that most of the differences in height or weight for the populations in the studies are due to genotype differences rather than differences in diet or other environmental factors. Estimates of 'intelligence' (as it is measured in certain tests of IQ) vary, but on average are about .5 (Scarr, 1997), which means that about half of the variation in IQ amongst the people in the studies can be attributed to genotype differences. Similar estimates have been found for some measures of personality variables such as negativity and aggression (Braungart, Plomin, DeFries and Fulker, 1992).

It must be stressed again that these estimates only tell us about the relative importance of genes in explaining differences amongst people in a particular environment at a particular time. Even for the same group, the estimate may change if the environment changes and it may be quite different for another group of people living in different circumstances.

For example, weight has a heritability of about .8 in the studies so far (meaning genes account for 80% of variation in weight in the communities studied and environment for about 20%). However, if people in those communities were to change their environment in some way (e.g. if each person decided to eat a very different diet from everyone else), then environmental factors (diet) could account more for any resulting weight differences. The heritability estimate may then be smaller than .8 (because genes could then be less important than environment in explaining why one person is heavier than another).

CRUCIAL CONCEPT

One of the main **limitations** of heritability estimates is that they cannot tell us about the reasons for differences in traits or abilities amongst people from **different environments**.

The classic example used to make this point involves a gardening analogy (Lewontin, 1976). Imagine a handful of seeds of mixed genes are divided and put into two gardens (garden A or B). Garden A gets the best care, but garden B is neglected. When the plants grow, there may be variations in height. Since the plants within each garden received exactly the same environment (good in A *or* bad in B), any differences in height within each garden must be due to their genes. However the plants in garden A might on average be taller than those in B. Why? It may be because A plants had better genes or a better environment, or both – although if the range of genes is similar in each garden then we could conclude it was environment (because the gene differences between the gardens would be averaged out).

There are clear parallels here for considering human characteristics. For example, this same logic applies to considerations of any apparent developmental gains shown by economically advantaged children over disadvantaged children. Such differences may be due to genetic factors or environmental differences or both (although, as for the plants example, if the range of genes is similar in each group then the differences are most likely due to environment). In any case, as shown in this chapter, even if differences are due solely to genetic influences, this still allows the possibility that improving the environment for disadvantaged children will enhance their development, since genetic influence may well be modifiable by experience (Cooper and Zubek, 1958). As explained in this chapter, having a genetic basis does not necessarily mean a feature is static or fixed or impervious to environmental forces.

Quick test

What is heritability? What research methods are used to estimate it and what are the limitations on its usefulness in regard to explaining differences amongst people?

To sum up, the main points to note about the role of genes and environment or nature and nurture in human development are:

- Both factors contribute in flexible ways to human development so that the same genotype may produce different phenotypes and vice versa, the same phenotype may stem from different genotypes.

- The relative role of genes and environment can vary within individuals for different traits.

- The relative role of genes and environment can vary across individuals and across groups for the same trait.

- There may be a 'reaction range' or potential for environmentally-influenced variation in individual development within limits imposed by genes.

- Kinship studies and heritability scores can tell us about the differences amongst people with the same environment but not about individual cases or group differences.

Section 7

End of chapter assessment

How will you be assessed?

Here are some examples of the type of question you may be asked to answer either in the form of an assignment or as an exam question. You will be able to use these questions to assess your own progress against the Learning Outcomes at the beginning of the chapter. Outline answers are provided to indicate how you could tackle each of the questions.

Questions

1. Write a 2,000 word essay on the following question:

   How do 'nature' and 'nurture' contribute to children's development? (This relates to Learning Outcome 1.)

2. Write a short essay (300 words) comparing the various methods used to investigate human development. (This relates to Learning Outcome 2.)

3. Write an essay (2,000 words) describing and comparing some of the broad theoretical perspectives on human development. Your answer should cover both older and contemporary views. (This relates to Learning Outcome 3.)

Answers

1. Your answer should:

   - Explain the issue here: that is, whether children's development is shaped by experience or genes or both.

   - Define nature in terms of the actions of genes in the cells of the human body and brain, with an explanation that genes are segments of DNA or chromosomes in human cells that act as a template for copying and rebuilding the cell (you can also explain about operator and structural genes, alleles and polygenic traits).

   - Raise the issue of whether or how genes might affect actual behaviour or abilities (here you could refer to animal research such as the study by Tryon, 1934, that demonstrated the impact of genes on learning ability or the work with human neonates that suggests some abilities may be innate).

   - Then define nurture in terms of the lasting effects of experience and environmental factors such as physical and family contexts for development.

   - Discuss how the environment can have lasting impact on development and give examples from research into early physical, social, cognitive and language development.

   - Then explain that nature and nurture invariably interact (describe the concepts of phenotype and genotype, reaction range, and indicate that environment can magnify, suppress or alter genetic dispositions).

   - Critically discuss whether there are sound estimates of how much nature and nurture each contribute to development (explain the concept of heritability estimates, indicating how these are derived from kinship research and say how much these are for certain characteristics such as IQ or weight, taking care to explain that these apply only to a particular group at a particular time and place).

   - Sum up the case so far and finish by saying that both nature and nurture contribute to development but do so in highly individualistic and fluid ways.

2. Your answer should describe the cross-sectional, longitudinal, cross-sequential and microgenetic approaches and weigh up their pros and cons. This discussion should cover the points that the cross-sectional approach is the most 'economical' in terms of resources but does not allow for individual development to be charted, while the longitudinal and micro-genetic approaches cover the latter objective more satisfactorily, but are more demanding on resources and the cross-sequential approach offers a compromise between these methods.

3. Your answer could:

- Begin with a brief outline or history of the range of theoretical positions you will be covering and perhaps identifying some of the major similarities and differences amongst them (such as whether they propose that development occurs in stages and whether nature or nurture is the primary force in human development or whether some interaction occurs between these factors).

- Describe the main proposals of the psychodynamic approach (using the work of Freud and Erikson as examples) indicating that these views propose that development occurs in stages across the lifespan as the result of conflict between innate needs and societal demands.

- Discuss ethological viewpoints (Lorenz, Bowlby) and explain how these focus on basic innate needs but with a concern as to how these are adapted to fit particular environments.

- Cover 'learning' and 'behaviourist' perspectives and explain that these emphasise the way in which development can be shaped by environmental experiences involving associations amongst stimuli and responses (Watson), or by reinforcement (Skinner) or imitation (Bandura) of responses.

- Move to accounts that emphasise the context for development such as Vygotsky's socio-cultural model or Bronfenbrenner's ecological systems theory.

- Discuss the Piagetian viewpoint that children develop cognitive capacities in four stages as a result of both maturation and action on the environment, resulting in both assimilation of new information and accommodation or change in exisiting knowledge.

- Finally you could move to more contemporary accounts of cognitive development in terms of knowledge-based (Chi) and information-processing (Case) accounts, that respectively emphasise the effect of acquiring information on cognitive growth and of developing basic cognitive capacities such as working memory. You could explain that some versions of these approaches maintain that development occurs in stages (Case) while others do not (Chi).

Section 8

Further reading

You should try to read the references provided in this chapter (see the full reference list at the end of this book). However, the following sample of readings may provide a starting point for the three main topics in this chapter.

For further detail on the history and methods of developmental psychology:

Berk, L. E. (2003). *Child Development*. London: Allyn and Bacon.
Butterworth, G. and Harris, M. (1994). *Principles of Developmental Psychology*. Hove: Lawrence Erlbaum.

Slater, A. and Muir, D (eds.) (1999). *The Blackwell Reader in Developmental Psychology*. Oxford: Blackwell.

For debates on the nature–nurture issue:

Sternberg, R. J. and. Grigorenko, E. L. (1997). *Intelligence, Heredity and Environment.* New York: Cambridge University Press.

Chapter 2
Genesis: conception, prenatal development, birth and neonatal abilities

(Dianne Catherwood)

Chapter summary

This chapter charts the earliest phases in the development of the human being – from conception through the three phases of the prenatal period (germinal, embryonic and foetal) to birth. It then looks at the condition and abilities of the neonate or newborn.

Learning outcomes

After reading this chapter, you should be able to:

Outcome 1: Understand the main developmental changes and processes in the three phases of prenatal life: germinal, embryonic and foetal.

Outcome 2: Understand the processes of childbirth.
For example, the chemical signals from the foetus and the three stages of labour and associated risks to the baby (especially anoxia).

Outcome 3: Appreciate the physical state and psychological capacities of the neonate.
This should include knowledge of the Apgar assessment scale, neonatal states of sleeping and waking, reflex capacities, average physical characteristics and perceptual and cognitive competencies.

The three questions at the end of the chapter respectively test you on these learning outcomes.

Now, let's make a baby!

Section 1

Making a whole human being from two halves: sex, conception and the germinal phase

This section describes how a human being is made. Then we'll track the development that occurs in the first two weeks of human life (the **germinal phase**) (see Figure 2.1 for a summary).

Making a baby, or when sperm met ovum

This story usually begins with sex: an evolutionary device for allowing two separate bundles of genes to get together and make a whole human being. Today human life can be made outside the body by in-vitro methods or by artificial insemination, but mostly it is created in the more old-fashioned way with a sperm and an ovum cell making a personal acquaintance during sex. Once upon a time though, sex was a brand-new evolutionary invention. Before that, animals simply cloned themselves. It is thought that some bacteria then tried hiding inside others, thus becoming (respectively) the first sperm and ovum and eventually swapping genetic material to create sexually-reproduced offspring (Margulis and Sagan,1997). This allowed the advantage of novel genetic mixtures but brought a whole new challenge of getting sperm and ovum together.

Sperm and ova are special types of body cells called **gametes**. Conception involves the conjoining of these cells, thereby uniting their genetic endowment. At conception, each of the two gametes have all the 23 human chromosomes but not pairs of these as do other body cells that have one from Mum and one from Dad in each pair (although ova have 23 pairs before fertilisation and only shed the extra set after entry by a sperm: see details below).

Gametes are made in a process called **meiosis**. They start by making copies of a cell in the usual way through **mitosis** (see Chapter 1 Section 2 to review this), but then go through a second extra step of cell division. This results in each sperm or ovum shedding one member of each of its chromosome pairs (leaving 23 singles rather than 23 pairs, some from Mum and some from Dad). This means that sperm and ova only have 'half' a cell each and so need to get together to make a whole human being. Furthermore, when gametes are made, they can swap or cross over genes from Mum's chromosomes to Dad's and vice versa – and so they increase the genetic diversity on the chromosomes.

Sperm are chromosomal bachelors!

If sperm and ova did not shed their extra chromosomes before they joined up with each other, human cells would keep adding more and more chromosomes with each generation and would not be able to function properly. Ova and sperm do differ in their development however. Ova begin to grow before a girl is born (with about 400 prenatally-made ova surviving into adult life), but do not finish shedding their extra chromosomes in meiosis *unless* they are fertilised by a sperm. For males, the process of making sperm is continuous after puberty and each sperm completes its meiosis or chromosome-shedding before it fertilises an egg. This means that sperm only have 23 single chromosomes: bachelor boys! On the other hand, ova have a complete set of 23 pairs, but will shed half of these only when fertilised by a sperm. Now that's 'love'! Maybe the ova are just being appreciative. After all, sperm do have a tough time: millions of them start out on their perilous quest but only a few hundred make it to the fallopian tubes where an ovum might be waiting (if sex is occurring during the fertile or ovulation phase of a woman's menstrual cycle). Only one sperm might be able to join its genes with those in the ovum to start a new human being.

Figure 2.1 shows the sequence of fertilisation of an ovum by a sperm, leading to the shedding of extra chromosomes from the ovum to make a zygote with 46 chromosomes: 23 from Mum and 23 corresponding ones from Dad (the example only shows one such pair of Mum-Dad chromosomes). This is followed by ongoing mitosis (duplicating of the chromosomes and then splitting of the cell) to produce a multi-cellular ball or blastocyst with an embryonic disc at one end that will form the embryo and then the foetus.

Figure 2.1 A human being arrives! Development from conception to birth.

A new individual sets out on life's journey: the human zygote

After fertilisation, there is now a single cell called a **zygote** that has two sets of the 23 chromosomes (with their genes) that are necessary to make a human being, one set from each parent. A new human life has been introduced to the universe. The zygote begins to make a copy of itself (by mitosis: see Chapter 1 Section 4) so that it then has two cells. This first copying takes some time (about 30 hours) but it soon gets easier and then continues relentlessly to build the new baby. But the odds of survival are not good and it is estimated that only about 1/3 of all zygotes will make it alive and kicking to the finish line of birth 266 days later. You are indeed lucky to be alive!

Occasionally there is double copying at this early phase. A zygote can make a whole extra copy to produce two identical zygotes that will grow into **monozygotic** twins. Also it can happen that two ova are fertilised by different sperm at the same time to make non-identical zygotes which will develop into non-identical or fraternal (**dizygotic**) twins.

CRUCIAL CONCEPT

Conception involves the union of **gametes** (ovum and sperm) and of their 23 single **chromosomes** resulting in a new human cell called a **zygote** that has a full complement of 23 pairs of chromosomes. The zygote then begins to make copies of itself by **mitosis.**

Girls and boys

One pair of chromosomes in the new zygote may be of particular interest to the new parents since this pair determines the sex of the baby. In females the members of the 23rd chromosome pair are similar (both large X chromosomes) but in males they are different (one X and a stumpy one with less genetic material called Y). The Y chromosome carries genes that control male sexual development (see Chapter 1).

Since sperm only have half the chromosomes of other cells, some sperm end up with an X chromosome and others with a Y. Thus the type of sperm that fertilises the ovum decides if the baby will be a boy or girl (Goodfellow and Lovell, 1993).

Baby's first trip

By day four of life there is a bunch of about 70 cells in the zygote and by the end of week four there are millions. By about the fourth day, the zygote is now a **blastocyst**, a hollow, fluid-filled ball with an **embryonic disc** or plate of cells inside at one end that will form the human being and a skin (**trophoblast**) that will form the protective **amniotic sac** for the baby along with its **placenta** and **umbilical cord** that allow passage of oxygen and nutrients. After about a week, it makes the trip to burrow into the uterine wall, still furiously copying itself as it goes along.

About a third to a half of all blastocysts fail to be implanted in the uterus – possibly because they are abnormal in some way. However, if all goes well, the baby can now grow in earnest. (See Moore and Persaud, 1998 and Sadler, 2000 for more detail on this phase of development.)

CRUCIAL CONCEPTS

By the fourth day, the zygote has made about 70 copies of itself by mitosis, forming a hollow fluid-filled ball called a **blastocyst** with an **embryonic disc** of cells at one end that will form the human being.

Quick test

Describe the main events in the development from zygote to blastocyst.

Section 2

The embryo: building all the main body parts and the beginnings of behaviour

This section follows the next distinct phase of development from week three to week eight after conception, when the blastocyst becomes an **embryo**. (See Table 2.1 for a summary of the main events in this phase.) This is the fastest and most vulnerable phase of prenatal development, with all of the main internal and external structures of the human body being formed and hence being susceptible to abnormalities. Estimates are that about 20% of all embryos are miscarried.

The human being emerges

CRUCIAL CONCEPTS

The embryonic disc (the plate of cells inside the blastocyst ball) now forms three layers that make it look like a sandwich: the **ectoderm** or top layer of the sandwich (which will develop into the nervous system, sensory organs, skin, teeth, hair), the **mesoderm** or the filling in the sandwich (which grows into heart and blood vessels, muscles, bones, sex organs) and the **endoderm** or under-layer of the sandwich (that becomes the digestive system, lungs, urinary tract, glands) (Rosenzweig, Leiman, and Breedlove, 1999).

Cell copying (mitosis) and growth continues under genetic control, but is affected by environmental forces even at this point in development, since cells are more likely to grow if their neighbours are also growing (Jacobson, 1966). By week four, the embryo resembles a tiny tube of cells and by the end of this embryonic phase, it has a human-like appearance, is about one inch long and its mass has increased by about two million per cent. By now the embryo can respond to touch and can turn its head and move (Prechtl, 1988), although the movements cannot yet be noticed by the mother.

The major milestones in this phase are listed in Table 2.1. Perhaps of most interest to psychologists is the rapid growth of the brain and nervous system.

Embryo: 3–8 weeks	Foetus: 9–38 weeks
Week 3–4: nervous system and brain begin to grow from neural groove and tube/ heart beats with basic blood supply/muscles, ribs, backbone, limb buds appear/ digestive system appears	3rd month: basic brain organisation/moves limbs, body and face/ sexual differentiation
	4th month: lower body growth/stronger reflexes and movements
Week 5–6: head and brain grow rapidly/upper limbs grow and lower limbs appear	5th month: 100 billion neurons in place in brain and connections to rest of body/fingernails and toenails/more active/responds to sound and light/swims-kicks-turns/may show sleep–waking cycles
	6th month: eyes and lids fully formed/hair/ some breathing movements/grasp reflex
Week 7–8: stumps of fingers and toes appear/ eyes open; all main body structures have begun to form	7th month: 'age of viability' at 22-26 weeks though still needs oxygen and temperature support
	8–9 months: rapid weight gain/fatty tissues/ increase in organ activity/antibodies from mother

Table 2.1 Major physical changes in the human embryo and foetus
(Berk, 2003; Moore and Persaud, 1998; Nilsson and Hamberger, 1990;
Rosenzweig et al., 1999; Sadler, 2000).

How to grow a brain

The brain and nervous system begin to grow out of the top layer of the embryonic disc by about day 18 after conception (see Rosenzweig, Leiman and Breedlove, 2000, for a clear diagram of this). Due to the uneven ways the cells grow, a groove appears across this layer, with ridges of cells either side. The disc has an oval shape by now and the groove looks a bit like a river valley with high cliffs along its length. This 'valley' is the **neural groove**: the basis of the human brain and nervous system. Next, the walls of the groove start to grow so high that they close around on themselves at the top, and the groove now looks like a tunnel running through the length of the embryonic disc. This tunnel is the **neural tube** and it contains the cells that form the neurons and supporting tissue of the brain and spinal cord. The top or front end of the tube then grows more cells forming the bulge that will become the human brain, while the interior of the tube forms the spinal cord (Rosenzweig et al., 1999).

Sometimes the neural tube doesn't close fully and this results in a serious defect called spina bifida that leaves a gap in the spinal column after birth, but mostly it goes to plan. By the end of week four, the tiny brain already shows three distinct areas corresponding to main brain regions. Week five brings the appearance of the brain areas responsible for basic functions such as breathing, temperature control and heart function, followed closely by the beginnings of the forebrain, the region of the brain involved in all higher-order functions (see Chapter 3 for more details) (Rosenzweig et al., 1999; Thompson, Gedd, Woods et al., 2000).

Quick test

Describe the main developmental events in the period of embryonic development.

Section 3

The foetus: getting ready for the world

This section keeps following the development of the baby (or **foetus** as it is now called) in the last 30 or so weeks before birth. At the start of this period most of the major organs and structures of the body are formed and in place and it now remains for them to grow bigger and more complex. Most babies survive this phase. Some of the landmarks of this period are summarised in Table 2.1. During this time the foetus looks more human (helped by the realignment of the eyes to the front of the face as well as by the thickening of the skin and growth of bones). The body proportions also alter so that the head changes from being half the foetal length to about ¼ at birth.

In this period, the foetus grows rapidly in overall size from being less than an ounce and only two inches in length to an average of about seven to eight pounds and 20 inches in length at birth, although there is of course considerable variation in body size and weight. Growth eventually slows down – probably only because there is no room left to move in the final weeks before birth.

───────── CRUCIAL CONCEPT ─────────

The foetus also becomes obviously male or female, if all goes to plan. At the end of the embryo phase, the sex or gonadotropic hormones switch on and begin to influence growth of the sexual organs and genitals. These grow from the same tissue in males and females and will continue to develop as female, unless testosterone begins to flow through the baby's system by about the 10th week after conception causing the organs to become male (Goodfellow and Lovell, 1993). The female foetus develops the basic cells for all the ova (eggs) that she will carry over her lifespan.

The foetus makes contact with the world: prenatal perception and learning

As well as these changes, there are marked developments in foetal behaviour and responsiveness that show the increasing complexity of the brain and nervous system. The brain has its major divisions by now and has probably formed all of the neurons (nerve cells) it will ever have, though the connections amongst these neurons continue after birth and indeed all through life in response to experience (see Chapters 3 and 5 for more details). The most remarkable changes in the foetal period of life are the increasing responsiveness to external stimulation and the ability to remember or learn about information from the outside world. The universe of the foetus might seem a secluded, dim place full of sounds from the mother's organs, but many aspects of the external environment do penetrate this world and the foetus increasingly reacts to and may even remember these.

Most external sounds can be detected in the uterine world and, by 20 weeks, the foetus responds to them (especially if loud enough), being particularly able to hear the sounds of the mother's voice and even the theme tunes of television programmes (Hepper, 1996; Wilkin, 1993). Moreover there is evidence that the foetus is able to retain such auditory information in memory.

Foetuses as young as 22 weeks have been shown to **orient** to simple tones (by reacting with movement and decreased heart rate) and then eventually ignore or **habituate** to the sounds, with a recovery of response to a new sound. It is even possible to train or condition the foetus to associate two separate stimuli (**classical conditioning**) such as a tone paired with a tactile stimulus (Hepper, 1996; Hepper and Leader, 1996). These are signs that the foetus is capable of at least simple learning and memory.

What is even more remarkable is that this foetal memory and learning for auditory information may even be retained after birth.

CRUCIAL STUDIES

Studies of newborn babies show that they have a preference for their own mother's voice (over that of an unfamiliar woman) (DeCasper and Fifer, 1980), indicating that the foetus can remember properties of the mother's voice. There is even evidence that the foetus can retain the speech patterns in a Dr Seuss story (Decasper and Spence, 1986) or of a nursery rhyme (DeCasper et al., 1994) read by the mother during pregnancy (see Chapter 4 for more details). Perhaps more sobering is that the foetus may even retain memory for auditory input from the mother's television programmes! Neonates whose mothers had watched *Neighbours* during the pregnancy became more alert and stopped moving when presented with the theme tune from the programme at two to four days of age (while babies whose mothers did not watch the programme in pregnancy did not show this reaction), with this apparent memory persisting for up to three weeks after birth even without further exposure to the tune (Hepper, 1988; 1996).

The foetus also reacts to touch by about eight weeks and seems to have a sense of taste, showing more swallowing if a sweet substance is introduced into the amniotic fluid than if a more unpleasant (but harmless) substance is added (Liley, 1972). There is also some reaction to light, since a foetus younger than six months will try to shield its eyes with its hands if a light is introduced into the mother's abdomen in certain diagnostic procedures (Nilsson and Hamberger, 1990). The foetus may also show cycles of sleeping (and waking) and these may be related to basic temperament after birth (as judged by mothers) in that calmer babies may have had more regular cycles of sleeping in the foetal phase than fussier babies (DiPietro et al., 1996). Voluntary movement increases in general and the mother usually becomes aware of these movements from about 18 weeks or so: the first real signal to the world that an independent individual has arrived.

The foetus shows increasing responsiveness to stimulation from the external environment along with the capacity for simple learning (especially of music and speech sounds) and may show cycles of activity and rest.

Quick test

Summarise the main developmental events in the foetal period of life.

Section 4

Problems: life does not always go to plan

It might seem that the foetus goes from strength to strength, but in some cases this is not the story and about 6 or 7% of all newborns have congenital defects. These defects are due to either (a) **genetic factors** or (b) **teratogens** (harmful environmental factors). In this section we will consider some common examples of these problems.

Chromosomes can get it wrong

Genetic defects can occur because during the process of making new cells there can be 'errors' resulting in chromosomal or genetic aberrations in the new cells. One of the most common examples of such errors is the condition known as Down's Syndrome, in which children are born with an extra chromosome in Pair 21. The problem arises when the ovum fails to shed its extra chromosome for Pair 21 during fertilisation (see Section 1 of this chapter) and the new cell has three such chromosomes instead of the usual two.

This produces havoc when the genes try to go to work to copy and build the cells of the body and a range of problems appear: including physical abnormalities such as facial defects, heart, eye and ear problems and cognitive, language and motor impairments too. The condition is mostly linked to the age of the mother (and probably to the age of her ova which were formed before she was born), with the risk rising from 1 in 1,900 at age 20 to 1 in 30 at age 45 (Halliday, Watson, Lumley, Danks and Sheffield, 1995). The chromosomal DNA may weaken with age and hence the pairs of chromosomes fail to separate properly or in a less serious variation, may fragment and leave pieces of an extra chromosome in the new cell (Hodapp, 1996).

Some chromosome defects are sex-linked because they involve genes carried on the X-chromosome in the 23rd pair (see Section 1 above). This is not so much a problem for female babies who have two X-chromosomes on that pair and can use the dominant and unaffected gene instead. However, males do not have this option and so may inherit the faulty condition, as is evident in abnormalities in colour vision.

Teratogens: disease, drugs and other dangers

The developing baby is not only subject to perils from within its own body but also from other hazardous agents or teratogens from the outside environment. These can include: (a) infectious diseases, (b) effects from maternal ingestion of toxic chemicals (drugs) as well as (c) dangerous factors from the wider physical environment in which the mother lives such as noxious agents in the mother's air, food and water. The damage depends on considerations such as the frequency and timing of exposure, but for most teratogens, the critical period is during the embryonic phase of growth when the major organs and body systems are developing (see Section 2).

One of the most common cases of the effects of disease is that of Rubella measles which can result in blindness, hearing loss, heart abnormalities and brain damage in the child (Enkin, Keirse and Chalmers, 1989). Another serious concern arises from certain prescribed and illegal drugs taken by the mother. Perhaps the most widely-abused legal drug is alcohol and maternal consumption of a few glasses of alcohol per day has been linked to foetal alcohol syndrome, associated with poor growth, facial abnormalities, small head size and learning or cognitive disabilities (Guerri, 1998).

The developing infant is also vulnerable to any environmental toxins that may accumulate or pass through the mother's body. One of the earliest documented cases of this problem is the example of a community in Japan (Minimata) in which mercury pollution was linked to mental and physical abnormalities in children (Tuchmann-Duplessis, 1975).

Perhaps the most critical environmental hazard for many infants is malnutrition which can inhibit implantation of the zygote in the early germinal phase of pregnancy. Poor diet can especially affect development of the brain in the last few months of foetal life when the cortex of the brain (site for many higher-order brain functions) is rapidly developing (Morgane et al., 1993).

CRUCIAL CONCEPTS

Prenatal development may be impaired by **genetic or chromosomal aberrations** in the process of mitosis (as occurs in Down's Syndrome) as well as by effects of **environmental hazards** or **teratogens** (maternal disease, malnutrition or ingestion of toxic chemicals or drugs, as well as effects from environmental pollutants such as lead).

Quick test

Describe some of the main teratogens that may affect prenatal development.

Section 5

Birth: the neonate makes an exit and a grand entrance

In this section we will consider some of the risks in being born and briefly cover the main stages of labour: it takes a lot longer in reality!

If all has gone to plan, then at around 38 weeks, or by the 266th day after conception, the baby will be ready to make the grandest appearance of life: birth is imminent. The mother will now go into **labour**: a physically demanding event in which the uterus will contract and the cervix (entrance to the uterus) will open to allow the baby free passage to the outside world. But what triggers this extraordinary event? It is thought that labour is initiated by a complex chain reaction of hormonal signals released by the placenta and the infant's adrenal glands (at the top of the kidneys). 'Stress' hormones from the latter also help prepare the baby for the challenge of birth by clearing fluid from the lungs and generally increasing alertness (Lagerkrantz and Slotkin, 1986).

During pregnancy, the placenta releases progesterone, a hormone that keeps the uterus relaxed and the cervix closed, but it also makes increasing amounts of another substance: CRH (corticotropin-releasing hormone). This plays a major role in the timing of labour and causes build-up of two hormones (oestrogen and oxytocin) in the mother's body that help the uterus contract and the cervix to dilate (Smith, 1999). The baby is also involved, since CRH causes the baby to produce hormones such as adrenaline that help prepare the baby for breathing and reacting outside the womb (Emory and Toomey, 1988). These hormones also cause more oestrogen to be made and so encourage labour.

Hard labour

The length of labour varies and is typically about 12 hours for a first baby and half that for later babies (Niswander and Evans, 1996), but it routinely proceeds in three clear stages. In

Stage 1 (the longest), rhythmic contractions of the uterus begin, becoming stronger and more frequent and accompanied by the increasing dilation of the cervix (from matchstick- to baby-width). Stage 2 (from about 1–2 hours) involves the maternal desire to push and the baby is born – usually head first. Stage 3 (about 5 minutes) involves the delivery of the placenta.

CRUCIAL CONCEPT

Birth or **labour** consists of three stages (stage 1: rhythmic uterine contractions; stage 2: maternal desire to push and delivery of the baby; stage 3: expulsion of the placenta) and is thought to be the result of a complex circuit of hormonal signals involving both the mother and baby.

The birth process is universal of course, although attitudes and practices surrounding birth vary considerably across cultures and generations. For example, the presence of the father is considered to offer positive benefits to the progress of labour (Parke and Beitel, 1986) but, while it is welcomed in some cultural contexts, it is forbidden in others (Read, 1968).

Labour doesn't always go to plan and there can be complications, with the risk of loss of oxygen supply to the baby (**anoxia**) and possible brain damage, but most infants arrive safely in the world. The next section considers the reaction and state of the newborn after being catapulted from the safe, warm womb into the bright, cold external world.

Quick test

Sum up the main stages of labour and explain the factors that control it.

Section 6

Assessing the physical condition of the neonate

This section will cover the way in which the physical maturity and health of the neonate is checked and the problem of low birthweight will be discussed.

All things considered, most babies appear to survive the birth process in good shape and spirits. Those stress hormones may help. Neonates seem to have more than 30 minutes of quiet alertness just after birth as they survey the landscape with wide-open eyes (Klaus, Kennell and Klaus, 1995). During this time their physical condition and state will be monitored and even scored: the judgments start at birth!

The physical state of the neonate is usually checked at one minute and five minutes after birth against the **Apgar scale** that gives the baby a score on a 3-point scale as follows (after Apgar, 1953):

Score	Heart rate	Breathing	Reflexes	Muscle tone	Skin colour
0	none	none	none	none	grey/blue
1	<100 bpm	shallow, irregular	slow or moderate	weak or moderate	grey extremities/ 'rosy' body
2	100-140bpm	regular, cries	clear	flexed limbs, strong movements	'rosy' all over (allowing for ethnic variation)

A total score of 7 or better is taken to reflect good physical condition, while a total between 4-6 indicates that the baby may need support to breathe and so on, and a total of 3 or below is the signal that the baby is in difficulty and needs emergency aid. The biggest indicator that the neonate is 'at risk' is low birthweight which may be associated with immaturity in the lungs and other organ systems of the body.

CRUCIAL CONCEPT

The neonatal physical condition is checked by rating on the **Apgar scale** that provides a score out of 3 for: heart rate, breathing, reflexes, muscle tone and skin colour. A total of at least 7 indicates good condition while a score of 3 or less indicates risk.

The average neonate is about 7½ pounds and 20 inches long, though boys are slightly bigger on average than girls and there is a wide range for both sexes (length is affected by uterus size before birth but by genes thereafter). Babies can most readily survive if born at or beyond the **age of viability** of seven months (see Table 2.1), provided birthweight is not below 2,500g (5½ pounds). Such low-weight babies account for two thirds of all deaths following birth and are three times more likely to have neurological deficits that may impair subsequent cognitive, language, emotional and social development (Mayes & Bornstein, 1997). However, low birthweight may be due to being either pre-term (prematurely born) or small-for-gestational age (SGA), or both. Babies who are pre-term but of the expected size for their phase of development are likely to catch up in later development (Brooks-Gunn, Gross, Kraemer, Spiker and Shapiro, 1992).

Quick test

Describe the physical condition of a healthy neonate and explain how this is assessed.

Section 7

What can a newborn do? Behavioural and psychological capacities of a neonate

In this section the behavioural and psychological capacities of the neonate will be described (and see Chapters 3, 4 and 5 for more details on neonatal perceptual and cognitive capacities).

Neonates arrive with a remarkable range of capacities that involve organised processing in the brain and nervous system, including abilities for attending and reacting to the world as well as learning about it. These abilities include both reflex reactions that do not engage higher centres in the brain as well as more voluntary responses that do call on complex brain functions.

The state of things

Are neonates able to react to the world at all or do they immediately fall into a deep slumber? – perhaps in an understandable effort to avoid the reality of life on the outside! As noted above (Section 6) most newborns show a state of quiet attentiveness for the first half hour or so after birth. After that, they show varying states of alertness, with cycles of sleeping and waking as do all human beings.

CRUCIAL CONCEPTS

Neonates show six different states (Wolff, 1966): **deep sleep** (motionless with regular breathing), **light sleep** (possibly with irregular breathing and rapid eye movements as for adults when they are dreaming), **drowsiness, quiet alertness** (awake and focused on external stimuli and events, with little movement), **alert activity** (awake but 'fussy' and restless, reacting in a startled way to stimuli) and, finally, a state painfully familiar to new parents: **crying** (often linked to physical discomfort such as hunger).

Contrary to the impressions of harried new parents, newborns sleep about 16–18 hours a day, though they do this in shorter bursts and with a higher percentage of REM sleep than for adults (Louis, Cannard and Challamel, 1997); (perhaps they are dreaming of their lost uterine paradise, though of course no-one knows if newborns 'dream'). Sleep does not come under the control of one of the brain 'sleep hormones' (e.g. melatonin) for a number of months and so the sleep of young babies is not governed by cycles of light and dark. However, there is variation in their states of arousal and these are important signs that the baby's nervous system is functioning as it should.

Reflex moves

Neonates can move their heads and kick their feet voluntarily if on their stomachs, but in general have weak control over their body and limbs. However, they do display many **reflexes** (reactions not requiring control from the higher cortical centres of the brain). Some of these provide early abilities that will fade and have to be re-established later under more conscious control. Examples of such abilities are the **stepping and swimming reflexes**, as well as the **palmar grasp reflex** (which is so strong at first that the newborns can support their own weight by grasping an adult's fingers).

The maturity of the nervous system is monitored at birth by checking on neonatal reflexes. Likewise, the disappearance of most of these reflexes within the first year of life is also used as an index of how well the baby's nervous system is developing, since unusual persistence of reflexes may indicate abnormalities in this regard. An example is the **Babinski reflex** which occurs when the inside of the foot is stroked, leading to flexing of the big toe, fanning out of the other toes and twisting inward of the foot. If this is absent it could indicate defects of the lower spine but if it persists after a year or so, it may reflect defects in the motor nerves to the brainstem. Some reflexes disappear in the early months of life (such as the stepping, swimming and palmar grasp examples), while others (such as the Babinski) may persist for the first year and there are even a few reflexes that continue across the lifespan (such as the eye-blink reflex).

While some reflexes such as sucking and swallowing have obvious advantages for the newborn, others have somewhat more obscure utility. One such example is the **Moro reflex** in which the baby flings out all limbs and opens the hands (but with fingertips closed) in reaction to a loud noise and then quickly pulls the limbs back to the midline of the body. This may have been especially important in our evolutionary past by providing a way to help the newborn baby cling to the mother's body.

CRUCIAL CONCEPTS

The neonate has **reflex reactions** which for the most part disappear a few months to a year after birth. However, if such reactions are not present at birth, it may be a sign of neurological disorder. These reflexes include the **stepping, swimming, palmar grasp, eye blink, swallowing, Moro** and **Babinski reflexes**.

Neonates want to know about the cosmos too

Decades of research into infant perceptual, motor and cognitive abilities (Slater, 1998; Slater and Lewis, 2002) have confirmed that even newborns are actively engaged in acquiring and processing information from the world around them. They have little control over their limbs and so are limited in their movement (motor) abilities, but within these constraints are voracious in their appetite for information.

Neonates show a clear ability to attend to aspects of the world of interest to them. There is a marked difference in their reaction to threatening stimuli (e.g. loud noises) as opposed to those that provide information or knowledge without threat. They show a **defensive reaction** to the former (e.g. with increased heart rate and negative emotional response, etc.) but display an **orienting reaction** to the latter (with a decline in heart rate, visual fixation to the stimulus and calming of the body movements) (Finlay and Ivinskis, 1984; Sokolov, 1963). Even minutes after birth, infants display head-turns and visual fixation to visual stimuli (such as a moving facial pattern: Morton and Johnson, 1991) or interesting sounds (Morrongiello, Fenwick, Hillier and Chance, 1994) and will track a moving object if it is large enough for them to see (although not too smoothly) and will even try to scan for objects in the dark (Haith, 1980). All of these behaviours suggest an active effort to engage with, attend to and (within their bodily limits) explore the world in a selective way. They are keen scholars or at least confirmed stickybeaks!

This ability of **selective attention** is fundamental to acquiring understanding about the world. Without this curiosity and ability to zero in on particular items, the world would pass by unnoticed and could not be carved up into manageable slices of information: it would be just one big jumble of fleeting, unintelligible sensations.

But does this mean that newborns are actually taking in information about the items that draw their attention? Indeed are their senses (eyes, ears, touch, taste, smell) even working to any useful degree and if they are, can neonates remember or learn about the items they experience? We will answer the first of these questions in detail in Chapter 4 (sensory-perceptual development) and the second question in detail in Chapter 5 (cognitive development) but, for the moment, the following summary gives a brief idea of the rich capacity of neonates to both perceive and retain impressions of the world.

The newborn has a weak visual system as far as seeing details, but is able to see basic colours and many shapes and forms of interest, with a particular fascination for human faces. The other perceptual systems are also well developed and although neonates may be less sensitive to low-pitch sounds, they can hear most common sounds and show particular sensitivity in respect to the human voice and speech. Newborns are responsive to touch, appear to distinguish between pleasant and unpleasant smells and amongst salty, sour, bitter and sweet tastes with a preference for the latter. In sum, although the infant perceptual systems may not be fully mature, they are more than competent to register the sensory environment in an organised way. The studies that support these claims will be discussed in detail in Chapter 4.

In addition, there is ample evidence to indicate that these impressions from the senses are not necessarily momentary but may be able to be retained by the infant in memory and recognised on a later occasion. Even newborns can learn. Indeed learning and memory seem to be operational to some extent even before birth, as shown by the evidence from studies of foetal learning discussed in Section 3. The studies that support conclusions about neonatal learning will be further discussed in detail in Chapter 5.

Many experiments and studies have indicated that the human neonate arrives with the basic capacities for perceiving, attending to and remembering many aspects of the sensory world in a coherent or sensible way.

It has been an epic, amazing and often perilous journey from the making of the zygote to the arrival of a neonatal human being who can attend, perceive and learn. But the story of human development does not end here. In fact in many ways it is just beginning. Let us continue to follow the trail.

Quick test

Briefly outline some of the main behavioural capacities of the human neonate.

Section 8

End of chapter assessment

How will you be assessed on this?

Here are some examples of the type of question you may be asked to answer either in the form of an assignment or as an exam question. You will be able to use these questions to assess your own progress against the Learning Outcomes at the beginning of the chapter. Outline answers are provided to indicate how you could tackle each of the questions.

Questions

1. Write an essay outlining the main patterns of development from conception to birth and explain the risks during this period of development. (This relates to Learning Outcome 1.)

2. Write a short essay (300 words) on the main events during birth and discuss whether the average neonate is adversely affected by the birth process and how this possibility is evaluated. (This relates to Learning Outcome 2.)

3. Write an essay on this topic: Is the human newborn basically helpless and unresponsive to the world? (This relates to Learning Outcome 3.)

Answers

1. Your answer should describe the main developmental events:

    (a) during conception (particularly the union of genetic material or chromosomes from ovum and sperm during the formation of the zygote);

    (b) in the germinal period from 0 to 2 weeks (multiplication of cells by mitosis to form the blastocyst by day 4 with the embryonic disc);

    (c) in the embryonic phase from 3-8 weeks (refer to the differentiation of the embryonic disc into the ectoderm, mesoderm and endoderm layers indicating what bodily structures will develop from each of these, and describe the way in which the brain and nervous system grows from the neural tube and indicate that all the main body structures have begun to form in this phase);

    (d) in the foetal period from 9 to 38 weeks (referring to the physical milestones listed in Table 2.1 and the main evidence of foetal behavioural capacities described in Section 3).

    Then you should indicate (a) the genetic and (b) the environmental hazards (maternal infectious disease or malnutrition, maternal ingestion of toxic chemicals such as drugs or noxious agents in the physical environment) that can affect prenatal development, indicating the most critical period for these.

2. Your answer should cover the main stages of labour, explaining the hormonal factors that trigger and control this process and possibly arouse the infant to cope with the stress of birth. Then you should describe the physical condition of the healthy neonate (refer to the Apgar score) and indicate the basic state of alertness after birth.

3. To answer this question fully you will need to read Chapters 4 and 5 as well as this one. Your essay should cover the main behavioural and psychological capacities of the neonate (see Section 7 in this chapter) including:

- reflexes (referring to stepping, swimming, palmar grasp, sucking, eye blink, Moro and Babinski reflexes as examples and saying why these are important indicators of the state of the infant nervous system);
- states of arousal (describing the six states as proposed by Wolff, 1966);
- voluntary movements, including orienting, defensive and and attentional responses;
- perceptual capacities (see Chapter 4 for more details); and
- learning and memory capacities (see Chapters 4 and 5 for more detail).

Section 9

Further reading

The full set of references used in this chapter is provided at the end of the book but, as a starting point for further reading, you could consult the following articles and books that provide a sample of information on prenatal and neonatal development.

Berk, L. E. (2003). *Child Development*. London: Allyn and Bacon.
DeCasper, A. J. and Spence, M. J. (1986). Newborns prefer a familiar story over an unfamiliar one. *Infant Behavior and Development,* 9: 133–150.
Moore, K. L. and Persaud, T. V. N. (1998). *Before We Are Born.* Philadelphia: Saunders.
Slater, A. and Lewis, M. (2002). *Introduction to Infant Development*. Oxford: Oxford University Press.

Chapter 3
Physical development across childhood: growth of brain, body and motor skills

(Dianne Catherwood)

Chapter summary

In this chapter the basic structure and function of the brain will be explained. Brain development from birth to the end of childhood will be described. The patterns of growth in the body will be covered, including the development of movement (or motor) abilities.

Learning outcomes

After reading this chapter, you should be able to:

Outcome 1: Understand the main aspects of brain growth after birth.
This includes **synaptogenesis** (the rapid development of the connections amongst the neurons in the brain), **neural 'pruning'** (the competition amongst connections) and **myelinisation** (the insulation or coating of the tail or axon of the neuron).

Outcome 2: Understand the main patterns of physical growth across childhood.
This studies bodily proportions and dimensions (including sex differences in this regard).

Outcome 3: Understand the main trends and milestones in both gross-motor and fine-motor development in childhood.

The three questions at the end of the chapter respectively test you on these learning outcomes.

Section 1

Neurons and the brain: the tools for registering and recording human experience

In this section the basic aspects of the neuron and the main structures and systems of the human brain will be briefly described. This will include a description of 'micro-level' neural processes as well as the broader systems of the brain. Understanding this section will be necessary for following the material in Section 2 and in Chapter 5.

To new students of psychology, the brain can seem like a rather unpleasant-looking organ with a bunch of alarming Latin names to describe its form but, on closer acquaintance, it is a thing of beauty. In any case, like it or not, the brain is responsible for our sensations, thoughts, feelings, hopes, dreams, actions: in short, it IS us! So, let us get acquainted! (Further detail and support for the following summary can be obtained from any recent textbook on biological psychology such as Pinel, 2000 or Carlson, 2001).

The humble neuron makes us human

The brain is really a collection of neurons (nerve cells), along with some other types of cells to nourish and support the neurons. Neurons come in all shapes and sizes, but all of them work a little like switches that can pass signals on to one another when they are turned on.

Neural impulses or signals involve the movement of simple chemicals like sodium in and out of the neuron. This generates a positive 'charge' that runs along the neuron tail or **axon** from its head to its feet. Signals travel fastest in neurons that have a fatty coat called **myelin**. The tops of neurons look like trees with many branches called **dendrites**. Signals can be passed from neurons on to the head of another neuron or on to one of its dendrites across a tiny gap called a **synapse**. In this way messages can speed through chains or networks of neurons. The more dendrites a neuron has at its head and the more feet or **terminals** at its bottom, the more connections it can have with other neurons.

CRUCIAL CONCEPT

Neural **signals** or **impulses** depend on the movement of chemicals such as **sodium** in and out of the neuron and are carried along the tail or **axon** of the neuron. The signal is then passed on to other neurons (especially to the branching **dendrites** at the top of the neurons) across tiny gaps called **synapses**.

Meet your brain

If you remember from Chapter 2, the brain grows like a bulge on the end of the spinal cord in the early stages of life in the womb. The brain and spinal cord are the **central nervous system** and are connected to the rest of the body by the **peripheral nervous system**. The brain is just a collection of neurons that grow into rather oddly shaped bundles. From the outside it looks like a large soft greyish walnut. The walnut part is really the outer skin or cortex of the brain and is the main location for many complex aspects of brain activity. There are many other clusters or groups of neurons inside: a bit like the seed inside an apricot (to continue with the food analogies). See any recent biological psychology textbook (e.g. Pinel, 2000, or Carlson, 2001) for views of the brain and neurons.

CRUCIAL CONCEPTS

The brain consists of billions of interconnected neurons in different structures or bundles:

- The **hindbrain** (including the **cerebellum** for control of balance) and **midbrain** (which along with the **pons** and **medulla** in the **hindbrain** forms the **brainstem** for controlling breathing and heartbeat and alertness).
- The **forebrain** which contains the **thalamus** (a relay station for signals from the senses), the **hypothalamus** (involved in eating and sexual response and forming part of the **limbic system** that is active in memory consolidation and emotional arousal), **basal ganglia** (important for movement initiation) and the **cerebral cortex** (active in many aspects of perception, emotion, cognition).

The cortex is a very thin sheet of billions of neurons but is the main site for storing our memories and for most of our complex functions. It communicates with the rest of the brain and with the body and has four lobes or regions, each with a degree of specialisation. These are:

- The **frontal lobes** (involved in movement, experience of emotion and control or inhibition of behaviour necessary for planning or decision-making).
- The **parietal lobes** (that decipher touch and taste sensations and register the spatial location of objects).

- The **occipital lobes** (with the occipital or visual cortex, the primary location for analysing signals from the eyes and visual pathways).
- The **temporal lobes** (for processing of auditory signals and the structure of language).

The two sides or left and right **hemispheres** of the cortex are connected by a band of nerve fibres called the **corpus callosum**. The hemispheres are not symmetrical in function. For example, in most people the left hemisphere is dominant in many aspects of language and hand movement (in the opposite right hand). However, other functions such as perception of the rhythm of speech or of emotional expression in faces is handled better by the right hemisphere.

Quick test

Describe the main components of neurons and briefly explain how the neural signal is produced and passed on to other neurons. Next, list the main structures and functional regions of the brain.

Section 2

How the brain develops in childhood

In this section the main patterns of brain growth in childhood and the roles of nature and nurture in this process will be described.

How mature is the human brain at birth?

The human newborn arrives in the world with a brain that is firing on all cylinders in some respects but is relatively undeveloped in others. The brain systems and networks involved in the infant's ability to perceive many aspects of the sensory world are functioning well, as is the important capacity to learn and store information in memory (see Chapters 2, 4 and 5). From these basic competencies, the brain goes from strength to strength in a short space of time. However, many aspects of the brain are relatively immature and require months or even years for full function to be achieved. For example, the brain regions that control movement and those involved in producing language undergo considerable development after birth. Why is the human brain developed in some ways but not others at birth? One good reason may be that this allows the infant the basic competence to explore and learn about the world without being limited to rigid patterns of behaviour. Thus the human brain is pliable in many ways, allowing adaptation to environmental conditions.

The neonatal brain does not look too different from that of an adult except that it is only about a quarter of the weight of an adult brain (Thatcher, Lyon, Rumsey and Krasnegor, 1996). The main structures are present and all of the 100 billion neurons are there, having been produced in the eighth to sixteenth week of foetal life at the astonishing rate of about 250,000 a minute. No more neurons will be formed across the human lifetime. However, there are two marked differences between the newborn and the adult brain.

Making connections

One main difference is in the number and complexity of synapses or connections amongst the neurons. The newborn brain only has about one sixth of the number of connections found in the adult brain. However, in the months after birth there is **synaptogenesis**: a massive overproduction of synapses due to rapid increases in the number and length of dendrites at the tops of neurons and of terminal branches at their feet. By about 12 months of age, the infant brain has twice as many synapses as the adult brain (Huttenlocher, 1990).

This overproduction leads to redundancy or doubling-up in the connections in the system and this situation does not last. Eventually there is a reaction to this overabundance and neurons then compete with each other for the right to the connection with others.

After synaptogenesis in a brain region, there is a **pruning** back of the number of connections in accord with the 'use-it-or-lose-it' rule: neurons compete for connections and only those used the most will survive (Eisenberg, 1999). However, synaptogenesis and pruning do not occur uniformly across the brain. The earliest regions to show these processes after birth are the cortical regions involved in the primary or initial analysis of information or signals from the senses.

For example, there is a rapid increase in the density of neural connections in the visual cortex after birth, peaking at about eight months of age and then falling to adult levels by the end of childhood (Johnson, 1993). Synaptogenesis occurs in the language areas of the brain in later infancy as language comes into play (Thatcher, 1991) and the last regions of all to undergo the process are the frontal lobes which show increasing synaptic growth throughout childhood and indeed the lifespan if there is stimulation of the neurons from new experiences (Johnson, 1998).

CRUCIAL CONCEPTS

Synapotogenesis is the rapid overproduction of connections or synapses amongst the neurons in the infant brain in the months after birth (due to the increase in the number and length of **dendrites** at the head of neurons and **terminal branches** at their feet). This process is followed by competitive **pruning** back of these connections. These developments occur first in the sensory areas of the brain and continue in the frontal lobes across childhood.

Getting faster: the process of myelinisation

The other main change in the brain after birth is an increase in the number of neurons that have an insulating coating of **myelin**.

Myelin is a fatty sheath that makes the impulse travel faster along the neuron and hence helps the brain and rest of the nervous system to function more efficiently. **Myelinisation** (or **myelination**) begins before birth but increases rapidly throughout early childhood, slowing thereafter into adolescence (Casaer, 1993). It begins in the spinal cord, then moves to the hindbrain, midbrain and finally the forebrain, corresponding to the increasingly efficient use of these brain regions.

In general as for synaptogenesis, the primary sensory areas show the most rapid development, becoming myelinated in the early months of postnatal life (Huttenlocher, 1990). Myelinisation of the cortical neurons involved in control of the arms and trunk begins about one month of age, while those for controlling the legs and finer motions of the fingers and hands myelinate later (Tanner, 1990) The frontal lobes begin to myelinate in infancy but in this region the process continues throughout childhood to adult life.

CRUCIAL CONCEPT

There is increasing **myelinisation** (insulation) of neurons in the infant brain after birth, starting with the brain stem and ending with the forebrain regions. This improves the efficiency (rate) of neural transmission.

The brain starts to 'lateralise'

As explained in Section 1, the human brain has two hemispheres that are not identical in function. This **lateralisation** of brain function begins after birth. For example, even in neonates there is left hemisphere bias in speech perception (Davidson, 1994) and control of some movements (Grattan, De Vos, Levy and McClintock, 1992) and the right hemisphere may be more involved in the response of young infants to the spatial configuration of facial patterns (Catherwood, Cramm and Foster, 2003; de Schonen and Mathivet, 1990). However, this process continues over childhood and the communication between the two hemispheres also continues to develop. The latter is improved by the myelinisation of the corpus callosum, the bundles of nerve fibres that connect the hemispheres. This begins by the end of the first year of life, being most rapid between three to six years of age and slowing into adolescence (Giedd et al., 1999).

Development of brain tissue is reflected in changes in brain activity

There are numerous ways the actual function or activity in the human brain can be observed and these are being increasingly used to study the development of brain function in childhood.

One common method is the electroencephalogram (EEG) which records general patterns or 'waves' of activity in regions of the brain via electrodes (or most recently for infants a cap of electrodes) placed on the head. Such methods have indicated a close link between brain growth (in terms of myelinisation and synaptogenesis) and brain activity in children. For example, crawling ability or experience is linked to changes in the child's motor cortex and this is reflected in the patterns of EEG activity in the motor cortex area (Bell and Fox, 1996). EEG records have also been used to examine whether the infant brain shows coordinated patterns of activity. One sign that brain regions are working in a coordinated way may be patterns of synchronous EEG waves within or across brain areas that come faster than 30 a second (gamma-band waves). Adults are thought to show these patterns when the brain is binding parts of an object being viewed (its colour and shape, etc.). Such patterns have been found for infants eight months or older while viewing an illusory shape, suggesting that brain activity can potentially be coordinated at this age (Csibra, Davis, Spratling and Johnson, 2000).

Plasticity and critical periods in brain development

In general, the brain is more plastic and can recover better from the same type of injury in childhood than in adulthood, since the functions of the damaged regions can be taken over by other areas of the brain. There may be a 'critical period' in recovery from brain injury up to about five or six years of age. After that it becomes more difficult to regain function because the brain may simply run out of spare capacity and may become 'crowded' (Banich, 2003).

CRUCIAL CONCEPT

There may be a **critical period** in the development of the basic functional organisation of the brain in the first five or six years of life, as suggested by data on recovery from brain injury. During that time, the brain seems more plastic in its organisation so that damaged functions can be taken over by other areas.

What causes the brain to mature?

Does increasing use of the brain after birth cause it to develop or is it the opposite case: the brain can be used more because it has developed or matured under genetically-controlled instructions? The answer is neither one nor the other: the growth and use of the brain are tightly intertwined. Genetic factors play a role, but even genetically identical or cloned brains in other animals such as grasshoppers (Goodman, 1979) do not develop in physically identical ways, since the environment invariably interacts with genetic factors.

This interaction of nature and nurture is clear in regard to the development of the dendrites that provide a basis for neural connections. Genes have been found that directly affect the growth of dendrites (Li et al., 2000), but it is also well established that experience promotes growth and strengthening of dendrites as shown for laboratory animals reared in enriched conditions compared to those raised in impoverished conditions (Turner and Greenough, 1985).

The close relationship between genes and experience in brain development may be seen in cases of **amblyopia,** a visual impairment that results in one of the eyes being misaligned, giving double vision. If the condition is uncorrected, the neurons in the visual cortex receiving messages from the affected eye will eventually be dominated by those linked to the healthy eye and will die away, causing blindness in the turned eye (Epelbaum, Millerett, Buisseret and Dufier, 1993). Visual development depends on genetic factors, but the quality of visual input from the environment is clearly important.

Nature and nurture work in an interactive fashion in brain development. Both genetic factors and experience affect brain maturation in the form of myelinisation and the growth of dendrites and synapses.

The same close interaction between genetic factors and environment can be seen in the development of the rest of the body.

Quick test

Summarise the main aspects of brain development after birth and explain how nature and nurture affect this development.

Section 3

Growth in the body

In this section the development of the body across childhood will be described, including growth patterns in height, weight, body proportions and muscle-to-fat ratio.

Bodily growth is quite apparent in children although it proceeds at different paces for individuals and is faster in late childhood for girls relative to boys (as it also is prenatally) (Juul, 2001). Growth occurs because of increases in both the number of body cells and size of existing cells (Vasta, Haith and Miller, 1992).

Growth in height and weight is rapid over the early years of childhood with one-year-olds being 50% taller and three times heavier on average than at birth and two-year-olds 75% taller and four times heavier (Tanner, 1990). Development in height and weight slows throughout middle childhood until the growth spurt that occurs prior to puberty, about

10-11 years for girls and some two years later for boys, so that for a period of time girls are taller and heavier than boys of the same age (Juul, 2001).

There is also change in the proportions of the body over childhood since body parts grow at different rates (Thelen, 1995). For example, the head is one quarter of the body length at birth but one fifth at one year and about one eighth by adulthood. Another noticeable change is in regard to the legs which are about a quarter the length of the newborn's body but half in an adult, a factor that may contribute to the development of balance as the child begins to walk.

Another change occurs in the muscle-to-fat ratio of the body. Muscle grows gradually across childhood, but there are marked changes in fat accumulation. Newborns have a high percentage of body fat and this continues to accumulate until about nine months old. After that the trend reverses and children become slimmer until middle childhood, though girls usually have slightly higher body fat ratio than boys (Siergovel et al., 2000) and obesity can have an early onset in some children at around four to five years of age (Eichorn, 1979).

There is a rapid increase in height and weight in the early years of childhood with a slowing during middle childhood and a spurt prior to puberty.

Both nature and nurture influence this process. Evidence of genetic factors comes from studies of twins. Identical twins show increasingly similar weights and heights across childhood, whereas non-identical twins show increasingly different weights across childhood, suggesting that both genes and environment can affect body growth (Falkner and Tanner, 1986). Environmental influences include diet or nutrition and also exposure to disease and infection – all factors that are linked to socioeconomic status.

Increasing physical strength in childhood is linked to growing control over the body and its movement. The latter is considered in the next section.

Quick test

Summarise the main patterns in the development of physical growth in childhood.

Section 4

Moving on: the development of motor control

In this section, the general patterns of development of both gross-motor (limb) and fine-motor (hands and fingers) control will be described, with identification of major milestones and discussion of the role of nature and nurture in motor development.

Broad trends in motor development

The neonate has minimal control over the muscles of the body and is limited in self-propelled movements, but motor control develops rapidly in early life with increasing stability and awareness of movement in the child. There are two broad patterns of growth. The first principle of motor development is that it proceeds in a **cephalo-caudal direction**, meaning that control over the body develops from the head to the feet. The other principle is that it is **proximo-distal**, with control developing from the midline or trunk of the body then out to the extremities (hands and fingers).

Patterns of gross-motor development

Typical patterns of gross-motor development are summarised in Table 3.1, but it must be stressed that this a guide only and there are individual variations in this development. The newborn arrives with a variety of reflex movements of the limbs and body (see Chapter 2) and these subside as cortical brain control takes over many aspects of movement. This allows a rapid sequence of growth that may proceed from lifting of the head *to* sitting without support *to* crawling then ultimately *to* standing and walking alone. However, there are individual variations in the timing and phases of this pattern.

Approximate age	Gross-motor skill
1-4 months	reflex leg movements (stepping, kicking); lifts head if prone on stomach, sits with support
2-4 months	uses arms for support if prone
5-9 months	sits without support
5-10 months	pulls self to standing position
5-11 months	coordinates arm and leg motions: crawls
10-17 months	stands alone then walks alone
18-30 months	runs, jumps, throws and catches ball with rigid upper body
4-5 years	smoother movement, increasing body rotation in throwing
5-6 years	increase in running speed, skips well, uses whole body to throw ball well
7-12 years	increasing speed, accuracy, fluidity of movement

N.B. There may be considerable individual variation in this pattern of development.

Table 3.1
Milestones in Gross-Motor Development
(Bayley, 1993; Berk, 2003; Cole and Cole, 2001)

─────────────── CRUCIAL CONCEPTS ───────────────

Motor development in general proceeds in both **cephalo-caudal** (head to toe) and **proximo-distal** (midline to extremities) directions. Initially infants show a variety of reflex movements with these subsiding as cortical control is exercised.

Patterns of fine-motor development

The primary focus for fine-motor development is the growth of control over the hands and fingers especially in the act of reaching for and grasping objects. This skill is critical to infant exploration of the properties of objects, an essential basis for all knowledge and understanding about the physical world (see Chapters 4 and 5).

Fine-motor control over the hands and fingers occurs rapidly in the first year of life from the uncoordinated swiping motions of neonates to the fine manipulation of fingers and thumb seen in one-year-olds. Neonates show **pre-reaching**, poorly coordinated swiping at objects, but by about five months infants can accurately reach for an object even in the dark (McCarty and Ashmead, 1999). By about four to six months of age reaching comes increasingly under visual control and guidance and infants begin to adjust the shape of their reaching hand to that of the desired object (von Hofsten, 1979; Newman, Atkinson and Braddick, 2001), but young infants may hold objects in a clumsy **ulnar** grip, rigidly trapping the object between fingers and palm. Older infants of about 4–7 months use a more controlled **palmar** grip with more involvement of the fingers in holding the object into the palm. Around 7–8 months the thumb comes into play and by about 9–10 months infants are using a more mature **pincer** grip involving coordination of thumb and fingers. By 12 months children are so adept at this that they can pick up pins and other undesirable objects from the floor!

Further fine-motor development occurs throughout childhood (and indeed the lifespan) as new skills are demanded by the environment. For example, children who are learning to write will initially hold their pencils in a palmar grip with this evolving into a more finely-controlled **tripod** grip (thumb and index holding the pencil against the second finger).

CRUCIAL CONCEPT

Initially infants display poorly coordinated reaching for objects but by about four to six months, use of the hands comes increasingly under visual guidance. The grasping of objects also undergoes refinement with increasing coordination of the fingers and thumb.

Quick test

Explain the broad patterns of motor development in childhood and outline the main milestones in (a) gross-motor and (b) fine-motor development.

Section 5

Nature and nurture in motor development

In this section, the relative roles of nature and nurture in shaping motor development will be considered.

Motor development was initially thought to be under the control of genetic factors that caused maturation of skills in a fixed sequence and at a fixed rate, but more recent evidence has indicated that both genes and experience are important (Goldfield and Wolff, 2002). Early motor capacities may be more reliant on genetic factors since they are under spinal or sub-cortical control (reflexes). However, more skilled movements involving higher cortical brain centres seem subject to the effect of experience and practice. There is evidence for this claim from cultures that deliberately stimulate babies' limbs to this end (Hopkins and Westra, 1988) and motor development of infants reared in institutions has been shown to benefit from moderate amounts of stimulation (White and Held, 1966). The Dynamic Systems approach explains the situation by suggesting that each new skill is the product of the development of the brain and spinal cord, the growth of the body as well as the goals or motivation of the child and the stimulation offered by the environment (Thelen and Smith, 1994).

A range of both genetic and environmental factors interact with the child's own cognitive and motivational state to promote the exercise and development of motor skills and capacities.

Summary: from neonate to self-propelled human being

This chapter has covered the vast developmental distance travelled by children in the early years of life from the physically dependent neonate to the upright and mobile child able to explore and investigate the world in an independent way. The next chapters will focus on how the child makes optimal use of this physical prowess and skill to interact with the world of people and things.

Quick test

Discuss the ways in which nature and nurture interact in fine-motor and gross-motor development in childhood.

Section 6

End of chapter assessment

How will you be assessed?

You may be asked to write essays or short answers as in the following examples.

Questions

1. Describe the main events in brain growth after birth. (This relates to Learning Outcome 1.)

2. Write a short essay (300 words) on the pattern of childhood physical growth in both girls and boys and the factors underlying this. (This relates to Learning Outcome 2.)

3. Write an essay on the main patterns of motor development in childhood and discuss whether these are due to nature or nurture. (This relates to Learning Outcome 3.)

Answers

1. Your answer should describe the extent of the physical and functional maturity of the newborn brain and then go on to describe the main patterns of growth in terms of synaptogenesis, neural pruning and myelinisation, stressing that no new neurons are made after birth. You should describe the rate of development for each of the major brain areas, explaining that the primary sensory areas develop first and the frontal lobes last. You need to talk about lateralisation and the development of the corpus callosum. Finally you should discuss the relative roles of genes and experience in this development.

2. Your answer should include information about:
   - the rapid growth in height and weight over the early years of childhood followed by (a) the slowing of growth in middle childhood and (b) the pre-pubertal spurt (around 10-11 for girls and 12-13 for boys);
   - the change in body proportions over childhood;
   - the change in muscle–fat ratio (and sex differences in this);
   - the mutual influence of nature and nurture on this development (citing the evidence for identical twins).

3. Your answer should:

- explain the state of both gross- and fine-motor control at birth with a description of the reflex movement capacities discussed in Chapter 2;

- explain about the broad patterns of development in motor control (cephalo-caudal and proximo-distal);

- describe the main milestones for gross-motor development (see Table 3.1);

- describe the main milestones for fine-motor development, covering the issue of visual control of reaching and the development of hand grips;

- finally, consider the evidence in Section 5 that indicates that both nature and nurture play a role in these patterns of development (refer to the concept of maturation, evidence on acceleration of motor competence by parenting practices and describe the dynamic systems perspective on the range of factors involved in motor development).

Section 7

Further reading

You should consult the full list of references for this chapter provided at the end of the book, but the following sample may be a good starting point to extend your reading for the issues and material covered in this chapter.

Johnson, M. H. (1993). *Brain Development and Cognition: A Reader*. Oxford: Blackwell.

Newman, C., Atkinson, J. and Braddick, O. (2001). The development of reaching and looking preferences in infants to objects of different sizes. *Developmental Psychology,* 37: 561–572.

Pinel, J. J. (1999). *Biopsychology*. London: Allyn and Bacon.

Thelen, E. (1995). Motor development: A new synthesis. *American Psychologist,* 50: 79–95.

Chapter 4
Making contact with the world: sensory-perceptual development

(Dianne Catherwood)

Chapter summary

James (1890) thought that babies perceive the world as a 'blooming, buzzing confusion', like a scattered jigsaw puzzle, and that sensory-perceptual abilities mature over the early years of childhood. This chapter will explain why this idea is no longer accepted. Recent research shows that many basic aspects of sensory and perceptual processing are working in a coherent way at birth or by the end of the first year of life. Important findings on the early development of visual, auditory, tactile (touch), olfactory (smell) and gustatory (taste) perception will be covered. The early integration of sensory-perceptual capacities will also be described.

Learning outcomes

After reading this chapter, you should be able to:

Outcome 1: Understand the main patterns of sensory-perceptual development from birth onwards.
This indicates early competencies in all the sensory-perceptual systems of vision, audition, touch, taste and smell, with ongoing refinement in some aspects across childhood.

Outcome 2: Explain the basic details about contemporary research methods used to study the development of perception.
These include preferential looking methods, habituation and familiarisation methods, high-amplitude sucking procedures.

Outcome 3: Understand why the traditional ideas about early perception have been discarded.
This is due to a wealth of research findings showing early perceptual competence.

The question at the end of the chapter tests you on these learning outcomes.

Section 1

Basic definitions and rationale

We begin with some basic definitions of 'sensation' and 'perception' and explain why it is important to know about the development of these capacities.

CRUCIAL CONCEPTS

Sensation is the reaction of special cells in the body to stimulation from the environment (light, sound waves, etc.). It alerts us that 'something is out there'. **Perception** is the additional response in the neural pathways and in regions of the brain that gives a more complete or coherent impression of what that 'something' is.

There are five main sensory-perceptual systems: visual, auditory (hearing), tactile-haptic (touch), olfactory (smell) and gustatory (taste). In each of these, perception is said to be **coherent** because it provides **structure** to the flow of stimulation from the outside world. It does this by keeping different sensations separate from each other but also by binding sensations together into a whole where necessary.

CRUCIAL TIP

To get a better picture of these concepts, think about our reaction when we see a face. We can perceive the different features (eyes and so on) but can also see the face as a whole pattern. Try to imagine life without both these aspects of perception. Picture how the world could be just a confused jumble or kaleidoscope of scattered sensations and fragmentary impressions.

Quick test

1. Define the terms 'sensation' and 'perception' and the difference between them.
2. Why is perception 'coherent'?

Section 2

The main viewpoints on sensory-perceptual development

In this section, we briefly describe older ideas about sensory-perceptual development and then explain how these ideas have been overturned by more recent experimental research, especially studies of very young infants.

CRUCIAL CONCEPTS

The main differences amongst viewpoints on sensory-perceptual development relate to the relative stress on **nature** (innate, genetic mechanisms) or **nurture** (effects from learning and experience).

The big question is whether you arrive in the world with all your sensory-perceptual systems at full throttle, or whether it takes time for these to develop. Early ideas stressed nurture (or learning), while recent views emphasise nature (or innate processes) or how this interacts with experience.

What are the 'traditional' ideas about perceptual development?

CRUCIAL CONCEPTS

The earliest accounts (James, 1890) suggested that the infant perceptual world was a **blooming, buzzing confusion** – like the scrambled kaleidoscopic view we asked you to imagine above. Sensory-perceptual abilities were thought to be developed through experience and learning. A related view was that of Jean Piaget (1929, 1952, 1958) who proposed that perceptual abilities were **constructed** through experience and maturation in a series of six sub-stages during a **sensorimotor stage** of development (birth to about two years).

In Piaget's view, very young infants were not thought to have coherent perception. They were seen as incapable of either distinguishing the separate features of objects such as colour or seeing links between different views of the same thing: an infant in a Piagetian universe would seem to have hundreds of different mothers and fathers!

Contemporary views

Piaget's ideas on sensory-perceptual development have been largely overturned. In the late 1960s, better methods for studying infant perception were developed by researchers such as Robert Fantz (1964). These methods allow an experimental approach (i.e. control and variation of factors that might influence the infant's response) but rely on natural responses of infants such as showing visual interest or preference (see Section 3 for further explanation). Piaget used a case study approach to record the reactions of young children (including his own). This did not allow him to vary factors to see if the child would respond better under other circumstances. Piaget's ideas were also developed before any substantial understanding of brain processes and relied on notions of hypothetical brain 'structures'. More recent work has been able to focus on basic perceptual processes closer to the actual workings of the brain. The general contemporary view is that Piaget's work was valuable in showing how infants come to learn from their environment, but learning and cognition (memories, hypotheses, etc.) are not necessary for the basic processes of sensation and perception to appear in the first place.

CRUCIAL CONCEPT

From recent perspectives, perception is not considered to develop in the Piagetian sense and even newborns are thought to have **coherent perception** for many basic aspects of the world. They can perceive separate features of objects such as shape and are able to perceive objects as 'wholes'.

Contemporary views do not totally rule out the potential effects of experience. Even innate mechanisms may not develop fully in an inadequate environment (e.g. you may have the genes to be six feet tall but if your diet is poor, then you may not reach your full height – the difference between genotype and phenotype discussed in Chapter 2). It has been shown that children's vision may be affected by environmental factors (Simons, 1993) and studies with other animals have confirmed that perceptual abilities present at birth can be either strengthened or weakened by early experiences. There may be critical periods or limited timespans in development for sensitivity to such changes (Held and Hein, 1963) and although experience may affect perceptual capacities, it is not the basis for creating those systems in the first place.

Quick test

1. Describe and contrast Piagetian and contemporary viewpoints on sensory-perceptual competence in early infancy.

2. Compare the relative weight given to nature and nurture in these views.

In the following sections we cover some of the main contemporary research methods and results for each of the sensory-perceptual systems in turn. We focus mostly on the development of vision because, for most human beings, vision becomes the dominant sensory-perceptual system by about four or five months of age.

Section 3

The development of visual perception

The material in this section will (a) provide some background information on the visual system and on the physical maturity of this system at birth, and (b) summarise the methods and findings for core aspects of visual development (visual acuity, shape, colour and depth perception) especially in infancy.

The nuts and bolts: the basic visual kit

Vision is the reaction of part of the nervous system to the light that bounces off or comes from the world around us. The visual system includes: (a) eyeball(s) to collect light; and in each eye (b) an iris and pupil to control the amount of light entering the eye, (c) a lens capable of focusing light by accommodation (bulging for close things, flattening for far), (d) a retina or coating of the inner eyeball with (e) rod-shaped receptors that react to dim light and (f) cone-shaped ones mostly in the fovea or central part of the retina that react in brighter light, allowing us to see finer detail and colour, (g) neural pathways or links from the retina to the brain and finally (h) the visual (occipital) cortex at the back of the brain (comprised of groups of neurons that do the final analysis of the visual message).

Do we arrive in the world with a full visual kit?

Newborns (neonates) have most of the basic visual equipment, although it takes about a year for some of the main parts of the visual system to mature with some lingering development across childhood (Hainline, 1998). In particular, the fovea of the newborn is less densely packed with cones and is covered by layers of cells that will eventually move out of the way to improve the clarity of central vision. Also the lens will improve its ability to focus at a range of distances. It used to be thought that the baby's lens was rigidly fixed to focus on objects at about 20cm but it is now known even newborns can potentially focus objects 75cm away (Hainline, 1998), but may not do so. The lens and brain need to work together for correct focusing and it takes some fine-tuning before this partnership works smoothly. One major development is the increasing myelinisation of the visual pathways and cortex that reaches adult levels by about two years of age, as well as the increasing growth of synapses in the visual system, reaching adult levels by about nine months of age (Atkinson, 2000).

In general though, the main nuts and bolts are all there. However, this does not necessarily mean they work well – any more than simply knowing that a car has all its engine parts will tell us if it runs well. Let us take a closer look at how vision actually works in babies.

Visual acuity: seeing the fine print

One way of measuring the power of people's vision is to test their acuity – their ability to see fine detail. You may have had your acuity tested with a Snellen chart with rows of letters of diminishing size. There would have been a row where you couldn't read the letters clearly (e.g. saying that an F was an E). This gives one measure of your acuity. This is usually compared to the estimates for an 'average' adult . If you have 20/20 vision, you can see as well as the average person at 20 feet (or 6/6 if you are measuring in metres). If your vision is weaker than average then the number on the right side will be bigger than 20. For example, if you have 20/600 vision, this means that what you see at 20 feet is about the same as what an average observer sees at 600 feet. But how can we measure acuity for babies who cannot talk, let alone read letters on a chart? There is a way around this problem.

Testing infant visual acuity

Even a newborn baby's acuity can be measured by a version of the **preferential looking** method (Atkinson, 2000; Dobson and Teller, 1978) that relies on the basic idea that babies (like the rest of us) would prefer to look at something rather than nothing. (See Figure 4.1.) The baby is held or seated facing a panel in a quiet room. In the panel are two round holes, one to the left of the baby's line of sight and one to the right and in between these is a tiny viewing hole that allows a tester to watch the baby's eyes. Another tester now places a card over each of the holes in the panel, one of these being just a blank grey card and the other a black and white striped pattern. Imagine you are that baby, seated in a boring room when all of a sudden a striped pattern appears in view. It is likely that if you could *see* the pattern, you would look at it with relief. One of the testers waits to check. This tester does not know which side of the panel has the stripes and so is not biased. If the baby looks towards the stripes then it is a fair bet that she or he can see the stripes, or else the pattern would seem no different to the blank side of the panel. The baby is initially shown patterns with thick stripes and then finer and finer ones – just as the letters in the Snellen charts get finer and finer. (The stripes are varied from left to right randomly to stop the baby 'guessing'.) Eventually there will be a pattern too fine for the baby to make out the stripes (just as there is a row in the Snellen chart in which adults make errors) and the baby will not show a clear preference for the striped pattern (and will most likely protest loudly). This is taken as the limits of the baby's acuity just as the lowest readable line of the Snellen chart is for adults.

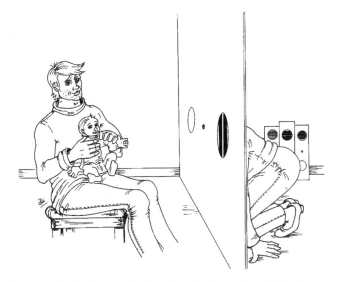

Figure 4.1 Testing infant visual acuity with the preferential looking test

An even more sensitive test involves measuring VEPs (visually-evoked potentials). In this method, EEG waves (reflecting states of brain alertness, etc.) are monitored while the baby looks at striped patterns. This can reveal a response even when the baby does not show obvious looking preferences.

CRUCIAL CONCEPT

Using preferential looking and VEP methods it has been estimated that the **visual acuity** of newborn babies is about 20/600 and improves rapidly to be comparable to adult levels by about nine months of age – though precise ages and estimates vary somewhat with different methods (Atkinson, 2000; Gwiazda and Birch, 2001) and there are further small improvements across childhood.

So does this mean that babies cannot see when they are born? Not at all. It is true that newborns couldn't see the fine print on their birth certificates, but that is not a problem if you cannot read! They can see the really important objects in their world (like nipples and teats) and should be able to see the main features of people's faces 50cm away (Atkinson and Braddick, 1981). They even show preferences for looking at certain types of visual patterns such as faces (Pascalis and Slater, 2003). Newborns can see the basic shapes of the things important for their survival (people and food) and vision improves so fast that by the end of the first year of life, babies see about as well as adults. But does this mean that they see in a coherent or sensible way? Or is the infant visual world as chaotic as the picture painted by James and Piaget? The answer to this question has come through the use of the following methods.

Habituation and familiarisation methods

These methods involve repeatedly presenting an infant with some stimulus or item (to the point of boredom) and then observing any change in response when a different item is suddenly introduced (see Figure 4.2). The items can be presented in any perceptual modality although, for vision, they are usually images or pictures shown on a screen or panel and the 'response' is the amount of looking or visual fixation that the baby shows to the item (this can easily be timed).

Figure 4.2 Testing infant discrimination of shape with the habituation-recovery method

If babies are thoroughly bored with the first item (called the '**familiar** stimulus') and can perceive the change or difference when the next item (called the '**novel** stimulus') appears, then they may show renewed interest. For example, for studies of visual perception, they may look longer at the novel item. If they cannot see the difference, then they continue to act bored – or irritated: infant researchers need ear plugs! By reverse logic then, if babies do show 'recovery' or greater interest in the novel item on the test phase, the difference between the familiar and novel items must have been detected: a sign of coherent perception.

In the habituation version of this method, the first item is presented until the infant's response drops to some pre-set level (e.g. half of the level of response shown on the first exposure). The familiarisation approach is more 'economical', with the presentation of the first item for a set period of time or number of trials. The test phase in either approach can involve presenting the old and new items together or one after the other (with the order of the old and new being random or otherwise balanced out to avoid order or carry-over effects).

CRUCIAL CONCEPT

The **habituation/recovery** and **familiarisation** methods involve repeatedly presenting infants with a stimulus and then observing any change in response (fixation duration) when a novel stimulus is presented. Increase in fixation to the novel stimulus is taken as indicative of discrimination of the old and new stimuli.

These basic approaches have been used for over 30 years to assess whether infant perception works in a coherent way – that is if infants can distinguish between different perceptual features as well as being able to bind these together when needed. They are very powerful methods – provided infants do show a preference for the novel item, but cannot necessarily offer any conclusions if that does not happen. However, many studies have obtained positive results, so let us examine what these indicate about infant perception of the basic visual features of shape and colour.

When does coherent visual perception of shape develop?

One of the main requirements for perceiving shape in a sensible way is that you are able distinguish between shapes – or you may find yourself trying to put your dog in the oven and taking your frozen pizza for a walk! When does this shape perception emerge?

CRUCIAL STUDIES

The earliest demonstration that infants of only a few months of age can distinguish one shape from another was provided by Fantz (1964) who presented babies with different patterns (faces, bullseyes, etc.). The babies showed preferences for particular stimuli over others, especially for the faces, indicating that they could distinguish the patterns. Numerous studies have now indicated that newborns who are habituated to one shape will show recovery of visual interest to another (novel) shape – for example, babies habituated to a rectangle would show recovery to a square and vice versa (Slater, Morison and Rose, 1983). (See Figure 4.2.) Although there is ongoing discussion about how the infant visual system manages this feat, this type of evidence is consistent with discrimination of basic shapes in newborns.

When does colour perception develop?

Next time you see a rainbow think about this. 'Colour' does not exist outside the visual system. We only see colours because of the way our visual system reacts to light. Light is said to travel in 'waves' and depending on the frequency of these, different neural pathways are triggered in the human visual system and so we 'see' different **hues** – the basic component in colour (to which we can roughly match the names blue, green, yellow and red).When do we begin to see the world in this technicolour way? Are babies stuck in a black-and-white universe or do they see colour too?

CRUCIAL STUDIES

One simple test of this involved showing newborn babies two checkerboard patterns that were identical, except that one had black and white checks and the other black and coloured checks (Adams, 1987; Adams and Courage, 1998). Newborns showed a visual preference for the coloured patterns, although this was not apparent for violet-blue and there have been doubts about newborn ability to distinguish all colours. However, two-month-olds seem to be capable of doing this, so colour vision may be present to some degree at birth but develops rapidly thereafter (Teller, 1998). Other studies (Teller and Bornstein, 1987) have used the habituation method (see Figure 4.2). Babies of three months were habituated to lights of one hue (e.g. blue) and then shown a different hue (e.g. red). They showed renewed interest in the new hue (regardless of which hue was used first), indicating that they could see the main hue differences. Further studies have indicated that even at two months of age infants are able to distinguish the basic hue types or categories, provided the items are big enough and the hue examples are clearly different (Hainline, 1998; Teller and Bornstein, 1987).

CRUCIAL CONCEPT

In general the conclusion to date is that at birth **basic shape discrimination** is functional and at least some **colour vision** is operational.

Vision in our 3-D world: development of depth perception

We exist in a 3-D world – or at least our perceptual systems register three dimensions although the physicists tell us that there may be 11 out there! To allow us to move safely around this world, our visual system uses many cues to perceive depth or distance. For example, if you look at a carpet, the pattern or texture will look bigger or thicker the closer it is to you. Classic studies have assessed if infants are able to perceive such pattern/texture cues to distance or depth.

CRUCIAL STUDIES

To study the development of depth perception, infants have been tested on an apparatus called the **visual cliff** (Gibson and Walk, 1960). This consists of a table with a transparent surface or top. The illusion of depth in the form of a 'visual cliff' is created by attaching a patterned material (usually checked) to the under-surface of one half of the table-top and leaving the other half clear, but placing the same patterned material on the floor under the clear side of the table. The difference in the size of the pattern on the shallow and deep side creates a very strong illusory impression of a drop (the 'cliff') An unsuspecting infant is placed on the 'shallow end' of this table surface while the parent calls from the 'deep end'. The basic idea is to see if the baby will crawl over to the parent or will see the illusory depth cues and baulk at the 'edge' of the apparent precipice. Babies old enough to crawl (around seven months or so) stop at the cliff and act fearfully as also indicated by a rise in heart rate.

However, it would seem that motor development may affect sensitivity to depth cues. Two-month-olds showed a drop in heart rate if placed on the deep side of the visual cliff, suggesting that the depth cue was noticed by these young infants but not in a way that led to fear, which would have produced a rise in heart rate (Campos et al., 1978). Another study showed that babies who were relatively inexperienced at crawling were reluctant to reach across an edge to retrieve an object while they were in a sitting position, but nonetheless moved towards the edge when they were crawling (Adolph, 2000). These findings are consistent with the conclusion that self-propelled movement experience contributes to the sensitivity to depth, or at least the potential danger signalled by depth cues to the edges of objects.

CRUCIAL CONCEPT

From the **visual cliff** and related studies, it would seem that infants may perceive at least some cues to depth (such as changes in texture) before they begin to crawl, but that movement experience increases the sensitivity to depth cues or at least the potential danger signalled by such cues.

Quick test

1. How good is infant visual acuity at birth and how do we measure this?

2. Describe the habituation and familiarisation methods. How have these changed our understanding of infant perception of (a) shape and (b) hue (colour)?

3. What do studies using the 'visual cliff' tell us about perceptual development?

Section 4

The development of auditory perception

This section will describe (a) the physical and perceptual maturity of the auditory system at birth, (b) the main methods used to study early auditory perception , (c) the sensitivity of hearing in early life and (d) the development of coherent perception for the important sounds of speech and music.

Are we equipped to hear at birth?

In many ways the auditory system is more mature in neuro-anatomical terms than the visual system at birth (there may be some 'stickiness' in the middle ear but that soon disappears). But does this imply coherent perception? For hearing, this means being able to distinguish between sounds (pitch and loudness) and also perceive similarities and patterns among sounds. Without these abilities, speech would be just a stream of gibberish and music would be noise. Is this how the world of sound is heard by babies? What methods have been used to answer this question?

The simplest procedure for testing infant audition involves observing whether a baby orients towards a sound source. Even neonates turn their eyes and head towards sounds that are sustained long enough and are relatively pleasant or interesting (e.g. rattles or voices). This reaction may be a reflex at first (i.e. not under control from higher brain centres) and by about three months of age may be more deliberately controlled (Muir and Clifton, 1985). In either case, it shows that the baby can hear the sound. Heart rate changes to sounds may also be measured (a small decline in heart rate is taken as a sign of attention). More complex abilities are measured with versions of the **high-amplitude** (HAS) or **non-nutritive** sucking procedure. In general this involves allowing babies to suck on a pacifier connected to equipment that controls the production of some sound (e.g. music). If the baby's sucking reaches a certain high rate (amplitude), the sound will come on. The baby may keep sucking at the elevated rate so as to continue to hear the sound, but eventually the rate may fall as the baby habituates to the sound. Then another sound is played to the baby. If the sucking rate resumes its high-amplitude level, then it is assumed the baby has perceived that sound as different from the old one. Variations on this method have been successfully used in many studies of early auditory perception, even with newborns (Nazzi, Floccia and Bertoncini, 1998). What do these studies reveal?

Can the foetus hear?

The auditory system seems to be functional by about 22 weeks after conception since this is the earliest that the foetus has been shown to react (by moving) to simple tones (Hepper, 1996). Certainly by the seventh month after conception, the auditory system is operational in some way since ultrasound studies show that a foetus about this age may move in response to sounds from outside the mother's abdomen and this includes speech sounds as well as music (De Casper and Fifer, 1980; Moon, Cooper and Fifer, 1993; Hepper, 1996; Wilkin, 1993). (See Chapter 2 for more detail.)

―――― CRUCIAL STUDIES ――――

Newborns show preference for their own mothers' voice over the voice of strangers (De Casper and Fifer, 1980; Moon, Cooper and Fifer, 1993) and for voices speaking their own mothers' native language. For example, French newborns have a preference for a woman's voice speaking French but not Russian, while non-French babies do not show this bias (Mehler et al., 1988). This does not mean that babies are born with a fixed ability to hear only the sounds of their own language (quite the contrary in fact: see below), but it suggests that the foetus may perceive basic aspects of speech sounds.

Moreover the foetus may even retain this auditory information as indicated by reactions to familiar in-utero sounds re-presented after birth.

An astonishing example of this is the finding of newborns' preferences for Dr. Seuss stories they had been 'read' while **in utero**. The babies distinguished between the regular Dr Seuss story and one with a slight change in content (**dog in the fog** instead of **cat in the hat**) (DeCasper and Spence, 1986). A similar finding was obtained for French babies who had been read a rhyme ('The chicken') in utero (DeCasper et al., 1994).

Moreover, the foetus responds to other types of sounds as well as speech, including music from television programmes which can be remembered even after birth (Hepper, 1996; Wilkin, 1993) (see Chapter 2 for more details).

Studies like these do not mean that the foetus should be enrolled in language, literature or music classes before birth, but they do give strong evidence that auditory perception is working and is capable of registering basic aspects of common sounds before a child is born.

How sensitive is early hearing?

Neonates and young babies are capable of hearing many sounds, but these also need to be louder than for older listeners – although more so for low-pitch (deep) sounds. For higher-pitch sounds, babies of six months are as sensitive as adults and sensitivity to these sounds peaks around four or five years of age, while for low sounds the peak is around 10 years of age (Trehub et al., 1988).

Is early audition coherent or just a lot of racket?

Coherent auditory perception requires that similarities and differences amongst sounds can be registered and that sounds can be conjoined into units that provide a basis for meaningful reactions.

Babies have a preference for complex sounds like speech and music, suggesting an ability to hear (a) the differences in sounds (e.g. '**b**at' as opposed to '**p**at') and (b) the similarities. These abilities are necessary for detecting the rhythm and melody patterns that set music apart from noise (*do-re-mi, do-re-mi*) and are essential to the perception of speech and the development of language.

Numerous studies have examined infant ability to hear differences in loudness and also in pitch. For example, one study showed that the heart rate of six-month-olds changed with only tiny changes in the loudness of sounds, suggesting good ability to distinguish loudness variations (Moffitt, 1973). HAS methods show even neonates can detect differences in the pitch of sounds (Nazzi et al., 1998).

These findings suggest that newborns hear these aspects of simple sounds in a coherent way. But what about more natural sounds? The studies of foetal audition discussed above suggest that even prior to birth there is some capacity for distinguishing particular musical sounds and also speech sounds. Moreover, more intensive studies of infant speech perception confirm that early auditory perception is essentially coherent.

Speech perception

The studies of neonatal reactions to stories and speech heard before birth (see above) have shown that some aspects of speech perception must be working *in utero*. Other research with babies of 1 month or more confirms that early speech perception is capable of detecting the basic types of sounds necessary for meaningful speech (phonemic differences or contrasts) across a wide range of languages (Jusczyk, 1995; 2002). The main method for testing this ability is the HAS procedures described above.

CRUCIAL STUDIES

A series of classic studies (Eimas et al., 1971) tested if babies could hear the difference between the sounds 'ba' and 'pa'. (Say these sounds for yourself and you'll hear that they are very similar, except that 'pa' is accompanied by a puff of breath.) The babies listened to a sequence of the same sound over and over again (e.g. *ba-ba-*) and then without a pause, the sound was switched to the other one (e.g. *ba-ba-pa-pa*). The babies showed increased sucking rate when the sounds changed, indicating that they detected the change.

Many sound differences (phonemic contrasts) have been tested in this way, with the same conclusion: young infants have a **better** ability to hear such sound differences for a wider variety of languages than is the case for adults. By the time a child is about 12–18 months old, the sounds of the native language environment will have taken over and the ability to hear other speech sound differences will be reduced.

This has been shown very clearly in a study of Japanese babies who appeared to hear the difference between 'l' and 'r' – a sound difference that does not appear in their native language and is very difficult for adult Japanese speakers to detect (Eimas, 1975).

Auditory perception is relatively mature very early in infancy. Even neonates can respond to sound and six-month-olds are as sensitive to high-pitch sounds as adults, with sensitivity to lower-pitched sounds peaking around 10 years of age. Infant auditory perception seems to provide a coherent impression of differences and similarities, as shown by the response to speech. However, experience can affect these early abilities as apparent by the loss of early speech discrimination ability with exposure to a particular language environment over childhood.

Quick test

1. Do neonates show coherent auditory perception? How do we know if this is the case?

2. What can infant studies tell us about the role of 'nature' and 'nurture' in regard to speech and music perception?

Section 5

The development of tactile-haptic perception

This section will consider if touch perception is coherent enough to provide infants and young children with a means for getting 'information' about the world.

Young children seem to have a strong urge to touch the things around them. Does this involve coherent perception or is it just aimless activity? There are several aspects to touch (tactile) perception, but perhaps the most important in early development is **haptic perception** – the use of the hands (and mouth) to explore the features of objects. Basic aspects of touch perception operate very early in development, since the foetus will move or react if the skin is stroked in utero and the newborn baby shows clear reflex reactions to different types of touch (see Chapter 2). However, these are fairly limited kinds of response to touch. Do babies use touch in the haptic way – to get information about the world? Many studies have shown this is the case.

Infant touch perception has been examined by either habituating or familiarising babies to a stimulus through touch alone, so testing is either done in the dark or babies may be fitted out with a bib that covers the view of the hands. Then the baby's preference for a different or novel item is measured in terms of time spent exploring it. As for visual studies, a preference for the new item is taken to mean that the baby can perceive the difference between the old and new items (or there would be no difference in the amount of exploration time for the two items). Babies as young as three months will show detection of the main tactile features of objects such as texture, shape, rigidity, and so on (Streri and Spelke, 1988) and even neonates show the capacity to detect object properties by touch. This was shown in a study in which newborns displayed habituation (decreased grasping) to an object placed in their hands with recovery of grasping to a novel object (Streri, Lhote and Dutilleul, 2000).

CRUCIAL CONCEPT

It seems that **tactile-haptic perception** is working in early life and is used by infants to gain a coherent impression of object features such as shape or texture.

Quick test

How do we know that young infants use touch to get information about the physical world?

Section 6

The development of taste and smell

This section will cover the development of taste and smell, with focus on early sensitivity and preferences in this regard. There will also be mention of changes in these systems in later life.

The last two perceptual systems, those of taste and smell (gustatory and olfactory perception, respectively), are perhaps most closely related to early physical survival since they are closely tied to nutritional needs.

These systems work well in newborn babies. Considering taste perception first, there have been numerous studies of the reaction of neonates to the four basic tastes (sweet, sour, salty, bitter) usually given in the form of solutions The reactions that are examined include facial expression, sucking rate, swallowing, and so on. It has been concluded that newborns have sensitive taste perception (in fact our taste perception gets weaker as we get older). Even more interesting is that newborns have strong taste preferences. Unfortunately for our waistlines but fortunately for candy companies, humans are born with a preference for sweet tastes and a dislike of bitter, sour and strong salty tastes

(Rosenstein and Oster, 1988). Neonates will 'savour' sweet solutions and drink more sweetened than unsweetened water (Harris, 1997).

Despite the apparently innate basis of taste preferences, taste is also affected by later learning. For example, by about four months of age, infants show a liking for moderately salty tastes around the time solid foods are introduced into their diets. Infants, like adults, can also develop learned reactions to foods that are connected with either pleasant or unpleasant experiences such as developing a dislike of foods eaten when ill (Harris, 1997).

Smell (olfactory) perception also makes an early appearance in life and may be important in helping young infants identify the familiar things and people in their world and to mark out objects that are safe to explore or approach.

Newborn smell perception is usually tested by putting cotton swabs or pads with certain odours under the baby's nose and observing if the baby turns towards or away from the smell. The sensitivity of early olfaction was confirmed in studies of neonatal response to the odour of breast milk. Newborns will orient to breast milk (Porter and Winberg, 1999) and show a preference for their own mother's milk by four to six days of life.

CRUCIAL STUDIES

Neonatal olfactory sensitivity has been shown in studies in which breast milk from the baby's mother was placed on one pad and milk from another mother on another pad. Babies turned towards their own mothers' milk by four to six days of life (Cernoch and Porter, 1985; MacFarlane, 1975). Newborn babies also show positive facial expression towards odours considered to be pleasant by adults (banana, vanilla, strawberry) and negative facial reaction to odours considered to be unpleasant or noxious (rotting fish and eggs) (Crook, 1987).

The development of odour perception does not stop in infancy. There may be another shift around puberty, as recent studies have shown that reproductive maturity in humans is associated with heightened sensitivity to pheromones in the bodily secretions. For example, one experiment (Russell, 1976) required university students to identify the sex of owners of t-shirts (including their own) on the basis of smell alone. People were not only able to find their own shirt, but could even identify the sex of the owners of the others. Females in particular were very adept at identifying the male items.

CRUCIAL CONCEPTS

Taste (gustatory) and **smell (olfactory)** perception function at a sensitive level in newborns providing a basis for coherent experience of the things that matter most to young babies – people and food.

Quick test

Is newborn smell perception sufficiently coherent to allow babies to distinguish different odours? Answer the same question regarding tastes.

Section 7

Getting it all together: inter-modal coordination

So far we have been talking about each of the different sensory-impressions as separate aspects. In this section we consider the combination of impressions across the senses.

Inter-modal perception

Adults expect different sensory impressions from the same object to be synchronous or coordinated. Anything that violates this expectation seems bizarre. For example, when you go to the movies and the sound-track is out of synch with the action, it is disturbing. But when does this inter-modal coordination develop? Do infants exist in a universe of disconnected sensations as proposed by James and Piaget? This issue has been examined in two types of situation.

CRUCIAL STUDIES

One approach is to measure the **transfer** from one sensory system to another. When six-month-old babies are habituated to an item by touch, this habituation carries over to vision as well, suggesting transfer of information between these modalities (Rose, Gottfried and Bridger,1981). Another approach is to examine whether babies have an **expectation** about the coordination of different sensory impressions from the same object or event. In one such study (Spelke, 1979), four-month-olds preferred to look at synchronised puppet displays (where the puppets were jumping in rhythm with a sound track) than those that were out of synch. This reaction has also been observed when babies look at the faces of people who are speaking. If there is a mismatch between lip movements and the voice of the speaker, then three-month-olds become distressed or look away (Broerse, Peltola and Crassini, 1983).

CRUCIAL CONCEPT

Many aspects of **inter-modal perception** appear to be working at birth or in the first few months of life. Further experience may enhance this coordination, but even in early infancy, inter-modal coordination and transfer occurs for many key aspects of the world (such as the sight and sound of someone speaking).

Quick test

What is the evidence for infant ability to coordinate impressions within and across sensory modalities?

Section 8

End of chapter assessment

How will you be assessed?

You could be asked to write essays about general issues such as the relative role of nature and nurture in sensory-perceptual abilities or about the patterns of early development in any of the sensory-perceptual systems (visual, auditory, tactile, olfactory and gustatory perception). You may also be asked to describe or appraise the methodologies used in infant perception research.

Question

What are the reasons for the contemporary rejection of the idea that the young infant's perceptual world is essentially a 'blooming, buzzing confusion'?

(This question relates to Learning Outcomes 1, 2 and 3 and if you can answer it in the manner suggested below, then you have grasped the main concepts, debates and research findings covered in this chapter.)

Answer

Your answer needs to begin with a brief explanation of the James-Piagetian position that the young infant is not capable of coherent perception and must therefore build perceptual competence through experience in the world. You would then go on to identify the main factor that forced the revision of this idea – namely the development of experimental procedures for assessing perception in young infants (especially: habituation, familiarisation, preferential responding, VEP, high-amplitude sucking methods). Your answer would then address the main findings for babies in the first months of life for each of the main sensory-perceptual systems in turn. Specifically, you would discuss :

- for vision: estimates of early visual acuity and findings regarding early shape, shape constancy and hue (colour) perception;

- for audition: the findings regarding early perception of speech, as well as those on sensitivity to loudness and pitch changes;

- for tactile-haptic perception: especially the results of the studies using habituation and familiarisation methods to test infant discrimination of texture, shape, etc.;

- for taste perception: the research dealing with neonatal differentiation of the four basic tastes and early preferences for sweet tastes;

- for olfactory perception: the studies showing neonatal bias to mother's milk and preferences for pleasant odours;

- the research findings on inter-modal coordination (especially visual-auditory and visual-haptic perception).

Finally, you should sum up the general impression from this research base that basic perceptual processes and structures depend at least in the first instance on innate mechanisms. However, you should also discuss the ways in which experience may impact on these abilities (referring here especially to the animal studies on early sensory deprivation) to indicate that even innate abilities may be influenced by environment. Your concluding paragraph should explain that the James and Piagetian viewpoints have been revised or rejected because the development of better methods for assessing early perceptual abilities has allowed a clearer understanding of early perceptual competencies. You should explain that the general pattern of results from research employing such methods indicates that at birth or soon after, the infant perceptual world is not 'confused'. On the contrary, it is structured and coherent – in regard to being able to register the differences as well as the unity amongst perceptual impressions – and these are the hallmarks of a coherent perceptual response to the world.

Where possible, your answer should describe the main aspects of relevant research studies (e.g. main method, approximate age of babies, basic results) and where the study is particularly significant, it is even better if you can indicate the researcher (e.g. MacFarlane's 1975 study of neonatal odour perception).

Section 9

Further reading

You should consult all the references for this chapter (list provided at the end of the book), but the following references may provide a useful starting point for further reading:

Slater, A. (1998). *Perceptual Development: Visual, Auditory and Speech Perception in Infancy*. Hove: Psychology Press.

Slater, A. and Lewis, M. (2002). *Introduction to Infant Development*. Oxford: Oxford University Press.

Chapter 5
Cognitive development: how the growing brain thinks

(Dianne Catherwood)

Chapter summary

The chapter will explain the main views on the development of cognition. In current terms, **cognition** is organised brain activity focused on information about the world and our experience of it. It is the extra processing of information beyond initial sensation or perception and it underlies all of our reactions to life. The most influential early theory about cognitive development was that of Piaget (1929, 1952, 1958) which will be described, but then more recent alternative interpretations of Piaget's findings will be considered. A contemporary account of cognitive development will then be provided, drawing on information-processing, neural network and knowledge-based concepts as well as recent research into the development of the brain.

Learning outcomes

After reading this chapter, you should be able to:

Outcome 1: Explain the main proposals and methods in Piagetian theory on cognitive development.
These include the theory that cognitive capacities develop in a series of four stages as a consequence of maturation as well as the child's action on the world.

Outcome 2: Appreciate the main critical points or alternative views regarding Piaget's major findings.
These include evidence from contemporary infant research as well as critical debate about Piagetian methods.

Outcome 3: Understand contemporary accounts of cognitive development.
These include information-processing, neural-network, knowledge-based and neurobiological accounts.

The questions at the end of this chapter test you on these learning outcomes.

Section 1

What is cognition?

In this section, a contemporary view of cognition will be provided, explaining the nature of cognitive content and processes.

Cognition was traditionally described as 'operations on mental structures' (Piaget,1952; 1958), the work of the mind as distinct from the body (Descartes, 1637). However, these ideas are not precise enough to describe how the living brain produces cognitive activity. Recent models of cognition are based more closely on actual brain structure, systems and function. Furthermore, they acknowledge the 'fuzzier' or messier quality of human cognition, with its tendency to rely on past knowledge and biases, as well as its links with emotional and motivational states (that involve both cognition and *bodily* arousal).

Current views on cognitive processes are based on **information processing** and **neural network** or **connectionist** approaches which essentially describe cognition as a set of processes for representing, storing and combining information within the neural systems of the brain. The information may be newly arrived from the senses or it may be older information stored previously in long-term memory and reactivated by some current stimulus – or it may be a mix of old and new.

Current approaches may involve analogies or models based on artificial neural networks (computers) but have been enriched by recent knowledge about the function of the brain during cognitive activity, especially from imaging studies (e.g. functional magnetic resonance imaging or fMRI), neuropsychological (brain damage) case data (Banich, 2003) and neurophysiological research with other animals (Pinel, 2000).

Cognition can be described in terms of **content** (information) as well as **processes** (the brain systems for dealing with the information), although in current views, cognitive content is closely tied to cognitive processes. A **thought** is an active state of the brain. The following commentary explains how this is the case.

The content of cognition

In current views, the contents of cognition are not static structures, but instead correspond to dynamic patterns of neural activity in one or more regions of the brain. A single thought may involve a tapestry of such neural activity, representing sensory-perceptual information, as well as more abstract-symbolic content (e.g. words) and may even include motor or emotional responses. Thoughts can involve new or old information or a mix of both.

For example, the cognition of a child on a roller-coaster ride may include a web of sensory-perceptual impressions (e.g. view of the ride, sounds of screaming passengers, etc.), symbolic information such as words (e.g. the name of the ride such as The Gut-Churner), emotions (such as stark terror) and activated motor knowledge (such as knowing how to grip the seat). As well as the new input, older memories about previous roller-coaster rides may be reawoken. All of this concurrent brain activity *is* the content of the child's thoughts about the roller-coaster ride.

CRUCIAL CONCEPT

In current views, the contents of cognition are not static 'structures', but correspond to patterns of neural activity in one or more regions or networks of the brain. A single 'thought' may involve a tapestry of such neural activity, representing sensory-perceptual as well as more abstract information such as language.

The processes of cognition

Current models of cognitive **processes** vary but most refer to the following types of brain mechanisms or systems.

CRUCIAL CONCEPTS

Basic cognitive processes involve : (a) selectively dealing with information (**attention**), (b) holding it in an active state in the brain (**working memory**), (c) storing it in a more enduring way in the brain (**long-term memory**) and later (d) reactivating it (retrieving it from long-term memory back into a working-memory state).

Memory is the underlying basis for **learning** (observable changes in behaviour) and depends on strengthening and growing the synaptic connections in particular neural pathways and networks within the brain (see Chapter 3).

As well as these basic cognitive processes, cognition involves additional treatment of information by the brain, especially associating or combining information (as in **reasoning**) whether this involves some goal (**problem-solving**) or not (**day-dreaming**). This activity can produce novel thought patterns (**creative thinking**) and these may not necessarily be tied to actual experiences (**fantasy** and **imagination**).

Serial or parallel processes?

Early **information-processing** models (Atkinson and Shiffrin, 1968) described cognition as an orderly series of processes moving from mechanisms for recording sensory impressions through to short-term memory and on to long-term memory. More recent views (Baddeley, 1990; Rummelhart et al., 1986), however, acknowledge the networking aspect of the brain which means that activation in one area may prompt activation in another because of the massive number of neural connections across the brain. This can lead to parallel processing. For example, while new information is being processed from the senses, all kinds of older information stored in long-term memory may be partially activated too, perhaps triggered by some similarity to the new input. In this way, prior knowledge can interact with new information in working memory and may affect our response to it, leading to biases and short-cuts (**heuristics**) in our cognition. Rather than approaching a problem using logical deduction, even adults may leap to the quickest and most familiar conclusion (e.g. Tversky and Kahneman, 1973).

Contemporary views also acknowledge that there is unconscious processing involved in cognitive processing (e.g. about one third of a second before we think we would like to get up from a chair, there is unconscious activity in relevant brain areas) (Libet, Wright, Feinstein and Pearl, 1979). Recent views ackowledge the links between cognition and emotion. For example, memory for moderately emotional experiences is better than that for more neutral ones (Christianson and Loftus, 1991). Some recent views even propose that emotional and motivational energy drives our cognition in the first place or we would be too listless to think about anything (Freeman, 1999).

Contemporary views of cognitive development essentially rest on these concepts and proposals about cognitive content and processes. These views will be considered in Section 3, but first an older model of cognitive growth will be discussed: the views of Jean Piaget.

Quick test

Briefly describe contemporary views of cognitive content and processes.

Section 2

Early views of cognitive development: Piaget's model

In this section the basic ideas in Piaget's theory of cognitive development will be described.

Piaget was one the first theorists to formulate a comprehensive theory of cognitive development (or, as he called it, the **growth of intelligence**) based on observation and tests of children's understanding of basic concepts about matter, space, time and causality (Piaget, 1929; 1952; 1958). Although his model of cognition and many of his proposals are no longer strictly accepted (especially in regard to cognitive capacities in early childhood), his work was seminal in indicating that infants and children actively engage with the world in order to understand how it operates. He proposed that children's understanding advances as a consequence of both maturation, as well as a desire to maintain an equilibrium between current knowledge and new information acquired through experience.

CRUCIAL CONCEPTS

Piaget proposed that cognition involved **operations** on mental **structures** built from the child's action on and exploration of the world and that cognitive development moved through four stages that he called: (a) **sensorimotor** (birth–2 years), (b) **preoperational** (2-6/7 years), (b) **concrete operational** (6/7-11/12 years) and (b) **formal operational** (11/12-19 years). This development involved **assimilation** of new information into older stuctures and **accommodation** or revision of older structures in the light of new information.

In this model, cognitive representation of an object or features separate from the child's own actions had to be built up in six sub-stages within the **sensorimotor stage** From this viewpoint, infants in the first 12 months or so of life do not have **object constancy** and cannot coordinate different sensory impressions of an object into a whole representation (e.g. they would perceive that they had multiple mothers). Moreover Piaget proposed they do not understand about **object permanence**, that an object exists independently of their actions and perceptions. Piaget drew this conclusion from tasks requiring searching for a hidden object (toy). Infants 8-12 months would search for the toy at one location (A) but not at a new location (B) and would return to the first hiding place (the A, not-B: $A\bar{B}$ error). Piaget's conclusion was that children of this age did not have a concept of a permanent object independent of their own actions.

In the next **preoperational stage**, it was proposed that children increasingly developed mental symbols to represent the world of objects and people, but that cognition was still limited as follows.

Piaget proposed that cognition during the preoperational stage was '**egocentric**' (limited to the child's own cognitive viewpoint), '**animistic**' (attributing life-like qualities to inanimate objects), '**centred**' (able to reflect only on one aspect of an object or event at one time) and '**irreversible**' (unable to mentally manipulate or reverse events). It was only when the child moved to the **concrete operational** stage that understanding about object identity emerged and true mental 'operations' (e.g. the ability to combine more than one aspect of an object) began to be used, although these were limited to concrete rather than hypothetical or abstract information. The transition from preoperational to concrete operational thought was assessed in a number of well-known tasks, including the **three mountains task** and the **conservation tests**.

CRUCIAL STUDY

The three mountains task required the child to observe a model of three mountains from one viewpoint. The child's appreciation of the viewpoint of another observer (e.g. toy doll) was then tested (e.g. by asking the child to select from different photographic views of the model). Children younger than six or seven tend to select their own or an incorrect view from the proffered options, being taken as evidence of egocentric cognition.

The conservation tasks assessed the child's understanding that despite changes in appearance, the identity of some object properties (principally: number, mass, quantity, weight and volume) remain unchanged or **invariant**.

─ CRUCIAL STUDIES ─

The **conservation of number** task involves presenting two rows with an equal number of items (beads, etc.), then spreading out one row and asking the child if this row now 'has the same as or more than the other one'. The **conservation of mass** task involves presenting two balls of clay of equal mass and appearance, then rolling one into an elongated sausage shape and asking the child if the objects are still the 'same' or if the longer one has 'more'. In the **conservation of continuous quantity** task, children are shown two identical beakers with the same amount of liquid and then the contents of one of the beakers are poured into a taller beaker and the child is asked if the beakers still have the 'same' or if one now has 'more'.

Concrete operational children can answer correctly in these tests, but preoperational children typically answer that the changed item 'has more' of the respective quality, with this error being explained by Piaget as the result of an inability to **decentre** away from the change in the object's appearance. Additionally in the conservation tasks, the child is said to be unable to combine the two changes of relevance (e.g. does not note that the change in length of the clay is compensated for by a change in its width).

Piaget proposed that the final **formal operations stage** was not achieved until adolescence. In this stage problem-solving was said to involve methodical and logical testing of possible solutions and was able to deal with abstract, hypothetical and symbolic information. To test this capacity Piaget developed such tasks as the **pendulum test** which required the calculation of the factor or factors affecting the speed at which a pendulum will swing. It required systematic testing of different factors (such as initial force) to identify the correct solution (length of the string).

Quick test

Briefly outline the main stages in cognitive development according to Piaget and describe some of the tasks used to assess transition from stage 2 to 3.

Section 3

Contemporary perspectives on cognitive development

This section provides an overview of the range of contemporary views on cognitive development, including neo-Piagetian, information-processing, neural network and connectionist approaches.

Most current viewpoints and research on cognitive development are based on information-processing and neural network approaches and recent findings on brain development, with a focus on the development of cognitive content (representation, knowledge domains, concepts) and the processes of attention, working memory, long-term memory, categorisation, reasoning and problem-solving. Some connectionist approaches also provide computer simulations of how the networks of the young brain may produce cognitive responses (Mareschal, 1998).

Piaget's perspective that cognitive development proceeds in stages is still a focus for research and debate and neo-Piagetians focus on how basic brain processes such as memory develop in stages (e.g. Case, 1992). However, prevailing opinion is that cognitive development does not occur in rigid stages but proceeds at a pace dictated by maturation

65

of the brain and body and by extent of knowledge or skill gained from experience. With increasing experience of particular domains, children's knowledge may become more explicit or available to deliberate use (Karmiloff-Smith, 1995). The broad course of development is essentially predictable from a logical standpoint (e.g. a child cannot read before acquiring language) but the patterns may vary considerably across children and cultural groups due to differing experience. Even for the one child, development may be uneven across different domains of knowledge depending on experience (Chi and Ceci, 1987).

Recent accounts of cognitive development agree that the content of cognition changes over childhood, with experience providing increasing knowledge of the world stored in long-term memory. This knowledge base grows in amount of information as well as the organisation or inter-connectedness of that information and its generality (the extent to which information relates to broad categories or concepts rather than only single items or events).

Opinions do differ however on the starting point for this development. Piaget (1929; 1952; 1958) proposed that the young infant brain was only capable of representing information related to reflexes and actions. However, more recent research has confirmed that even the foetus is capable of learning (Hepper, 1996) (see Chapters 2 and 4) and newborns can represent the features of objects, people and events (Slater and Johnson, 1999) (see Chapter 4). Some basic kinds of knowledge about objects may be built into the perceptual systems of the human brain (Baillargeon and DeVos, 1991; Spelke, 2000).

There is debate about whether this early knowledge is able to be used by infants in an explicit or intentional way (Haith, 1999), but in any case it is agreed that the acquisition of knowledge or cognitive content begins in earnest after birth.

There are differing views on the development of cognitive processes. Again Piagetian views (1929; 1952; 1958) were that true cognitive processes do not emerge until six or seven years of age and are not mature until the end of adolescence but evidence based on current models of cognitive processing indicates this view is inaccurate.

Research with neonates has established that the basic processes of attention and memory are functional at birth (Slater and Johnson, 1999) and perhaps even before (DeCasper and Spence, 1986). However, these processes are used more efficiently and strategically across childhood as children gain awareness of their capacity limitations (metacognition) and gain increasing knowledge and inhibitory control over their actions.

In regard to more complex cognitive processing as used in reasoning and problem-solving, traditional views are that young children have only limited capacities compared to those of adults. Recent studies, however, have indicated that even very young children can reason and problem-solve effectively (even using logical principles) provided the contexts are clear, familiar or meaningful and do not make heavy demands on working memory (see Section 6). In addition, research has confirmed that even adults may prefer reasoning and problem-solving approaches that rely on knowledge rather than logic and are not markedly different from those used by children (see Section 8).

CRUCIAL CONCEPT

The Piagetian viewpoint was that the content and processes of **cognition** were limited in early childhood. More recent information-processing and knowledge-based accounts as well as research with neonates has indicated that the basic processes of attention, representation and memory are operational from birth and are further enhanced by the effects of increased knowledge and awareness (**metacognition**).

Section 4

Alternative views on children's failure on Piagetian tasks

Are Piaget's findings and theories 'wrong' then? Yes and no. Piaget's findings can be repeated if the same tasks are used. However, contemporary views tend to differ with Piaget's interpretations about why young children fail these tasks. Examination of children's cognitive capacities in different tasks to those used by Piaget has led to the impression that Piaget's tests may be good indicators of children's cognitive limits but not of their cognitive possibilities. Why?

It is now considered that Piaget's theory vastly underestimates the cognitive capacities of infants (see Chapter 3 and next sections). Moreover, recent studies suggest that young children may fail many Piagetian tests because of (a) unfamiliarity with the task type, items or language which in turn may lead to (b) poor encoding and representation of the task aims and requirements with (c) failure to use or activate relevant knowledge and (d) overloading of working memory. In other words, young children may react to Piaget's tasks as if they were only capable of egocentric, animistic, centred, concrete cognition, but in other contexts may not respond this way.

--- CRUCIAL CONCEPTS ---

Piaget proposed that young children fail tests of **conservation** and **spatial reasoning** because they are egocentric, centred and limited to concrete and animistic thought. Recent views are that such failure may be due to unfamiliarity with task content or type, poor encoding and representation of the task aims, weak activation of prior knowledge and overloading of working memory.

Let us examine a sampling of studies which have tackled Piaget's claims about early cognition in alternative tasks or paradigms. If Piaget's ideas are correct then children's limits should be the same regardless of the task. Are they?

Is early cognition 'non-representational' and reflexive?

Piaget claimed that young infants are initially limited to reflexes and are unable to represent the features of objects separately from their own actions. However, a large body of research using habituation and familiarisation procedures (see Chapter 3) has established that even neonates can retain impressions of the features of objects such as colour or shape, regardless of whether there has been an 'action' on the object.

It is also clear that Piaget underestimated the capacity of young infants to respond to 'objects' as whole or unified entities. Infants are capable of processing features of objects in a joined or compound way necessary for perceiving objects in a 'whole' fashion (e.g. Catherwood, Skoien, Green and Holt, 1996). Moreover, neonates show both **size constancy** (knowing that the same object is involved despite apparent changes in size at different distances) and **shape constancy** (knowing that the same object is involved despite apparent changes in shape from different viewpoints) and in the first year of life, children show more appreciation of **object permanence** than revealed in Piaget's search task.

──────── CRUCIAL STUDIES ────────

Neonates were tested for **size constancy** by being habituated to ('bored with') a small cube-shaped item and then shown this old shape and a new larger copy (Slater, Mattock and Brown, 1990). (See Chapter 3 for an explanation of the habituation procedure.) The new larger shape was however shown further away than the old smaller shape, so that the images of the two shapes on the infant's retina were the same size. However, the infants were not fooled and showed more interest in the new shape, indicating that they had size constancy or could detect when an object had only changed in apparent as opposed to actual size. In a similar procedure, neonates also showed evidence of shape constancy (Slater and Morison, 1985).

Infant fixation has also been used to examine infant understanding of object permanence in **violation of expectation** procedures that observe the reactions of infants to 'impossible' events.

──────── CRUCIAL STUDY ────────

In one example (Baillargeon and De Vos, 1991), infants observed two 'carrots' moving behind a wall or screen with a window opening. One of the carrots was short and not visible at the window. The other one was tall and should have been visible, but was not: an impossible event. Infants of 3½ months showed more fixation for this event than the former.

Other variations of this approach have had mixed results (Cashon and Cohen, 2000) and there is ongoing debate about whether object permanence is innate knowledge (Karmiloff-Smith, 1999). However, some aspects of object permanence do seem to develop earlier than indicated by Piaget's object-hiding task.

──────── CRUCIAL CONCEPT ────────

Research with infants has overturned Piagetian notions that early cognition is limited to **non-representational**, **reflexive** or **sensorimotor** impressions.

Is early cognition necessarily 'egocentric'?

Children who fail Piaget's three mountains task are judged as **egocentric** but nonetheless can succeed on other tasks that measure the same skills.

──────── CRUCIAL STUDIES ────────

Three-year-old children were asked to watch a puppet (Grover from Sesame Street) drive around a model of a farm scene in a car. The children were seated in front of a duplicate model that they had to orient to the same view of the scenery that Grover had at various points (Borke, 1975). Children who failed the three mountains task could nevertheless succeed on this version. Similarly children who failed the three mountains task could answer in a correct (non-egocentric) way in a hide-and-seek task requiring the concealment of a toy child from toy policemen in spaces made from toy bricks (Donaldson,1978). Failure on Piaget's task does not mean that thought is necessarily egocentric in other contexts.

Other research has suggested that children may be egocentric in regard to inferring states of knowledge in other people and that they have **false beliefs** about others' ideas that are only corrected when they develop a **theory of mind** (i.e. can infer other people's understanding or state) (Flavell and Miller, 1998). When shown that a box of sweets contains an unexpected item (e.g. a pencil) and asked to guess what another person would think was inside, young children said 'pencil' rather than 'sweets' (Gopnik and Astington, 1988). However, such tasks may not necessarily reflect children's true understanding of others' views since even three-year-olds can play along to 'trick' adults with such items (Sullivan and Winner, 1993). Thus children's apparently egocentric behaviour does not always reflect their true understanding.

Is early cognition necessarily animistic?

Piaget's idea that children attribute lifelike or magical qualities to objects and events rested on children's answers to questions such as 'Is the wind alive?' However, other research has shown that children's incorrect answers in this context may stem from lack of skill in verbal expression and unfamiliarity with the actual object or event rather than from magical thought (Carey, 1985; Poulin-Dubois and Heroux, 1994). Even children as young as three years can appreciate physical causes for events (such as in a task in which a marble ball caused a Snoopy doll to appear: Bullock and Gelman, 1979) and four-year-olds have been shown to deny that magic can influence daily life, reserving magical explanations only for events for which they have no alternative explanation (Subbotsky, 1994).

Research by Susan Carey (1985) revealed that children had clear concepts that toy objects were not alive, but yet had not grasped the full meaning of the word 'alive'. For example, children replied that a toy monkey could not live/breathe/have babies (while a real monkey could), but nonetheless answered that the toy monkey 'was alive'.

Words and thought

How can there be such a gap between children's understanding and language? Cognitive and language development do not always develop at the same pace: children may have clear concepts but have yet to map the correct words to this knowledge. A criticism of Piaget's tasks is the reliance on verbal questions and responses, with doubts about whether young children have full understanding of some words in Piaget's tests (Siegal, 1997). For example, in the conservation tests, 'same' could be taken to mean 'identical in appearance' leading to replies that items changed in appearance were not the 'same'.

Crazy adults?

In fact, children may fail to grasp the aim of cognitive tests but still provide answers that they think the adult investigator wants (Siegal, 1997). Preoperational children have been shown to change a correct answer on conservation tasks after further questioning by the adult tester, possibly in deference to perceived adult disapproval of the first answer (Siegal, 1997). In one study of number conservation, preoperational children gave better performance if the adult tester was replaced by a 'naughty teddy' (Donaldson, 1978). Although these findings have not been consistently replicated, other evidence indicates children's test performance may sometimes be affected by deference to adults. For example, children will even attempt to answer adult questions that are nonsensical (e.g. 'Is red heavier than yellow?') (Hughes and Grieve, 1980) – possibly because children do not expect adult questions to make sense!

Is early cognition only limited to appearances or the concrete?

In current views all human cognition – even that of adults – operates more easily if it draws on prior knowledge and experience and has a 'concrete' aspect. However, Piaget's tests suggest that children are not able to go beyond concrete appearances and cannot deal with information not actually present in a situation. More recent studies suggest this conclusion is too extreme.

CRUCIAL STUDIES

Four-year-olds were taught about the different features of two animals (e.g. rhinoceros **vs.** dinosaur) and then asked to judge the properties of a third animal which looked like one of the former items but in fact was the same type as the other (e.g. a rhinoceros that looked like a dinosaur) (Gelman and Markman, 1986). The children were not deceived by appearances and answered correctly. Other research suggests differently that children are misled by appearances, such as assuming that a sponge painted to resemble a

69

rock really becomes a rock (the 'appearance-reality distinction': Flavell, Green and Flavell, 1986). However, recent research has shown that even three- to four-year-olds are aware of such deceptions and can play along with them to deceive adults (Rice, Koinis and Tager-Flusberg, 1997). Other studies show that children can reason correctly with fantasy content that may have links to concrete items but could not have been personally experienced. For example, four-year-olds who were told that 'Pogs wear blue boots' and 'Tom is a Pog', provided the correct deduction to the question, 'Does Tom wear blue boots?' in accord with logical syllogistic reasoning (Hawkins, Pea, Glick and Scribner, 1984).

CRUCIAL CONCEPT

Young children may fail Piaget's tests of conservation and other forms of reasoning and yet succeed on comparable tasks that may be more user-friendly or familiar in terms of content, language, aims and so on.

Quick test

Summarise the critical objections to Piaget's views on cognitive development and describe examples of research that provide alternative interpretations of children's failure on Piagetian tasks.

Section 5

Development of basic cognitive processes: attention

In the following sections of this chapter, an alternative view of cognitive development to that of Piaget will be provided, drawing generally on information-processing and neural network approaches and on research findings about the development of brain systems. The broad patterns of development in each of the basic cognitive processes of attention, memory, categorisation and reasoning will be reviewed. In this section a definition of attention and an overview of the development of attention will be provided.

CRUCIAL CONCEPTS

Attention is the selective or privileged processing of part of the information available to the brain at any point in time, involving engagement of processing **resources** (neural time and space).

It can be **covert**, but is usually **overt** or apparent in behavioural reactions, such as eye movements (saccades) and in physiological responses such as the slowing of heart rate or the P_{300} EEG wave 300 milliseconds after a stimulus has been encountered. Attention can involve sudden **orienting** to a stimulus in the external environment or a more sustained cognitive focus on either external or internal information, with these two aspects calling on different brain systems.

Two brains walking through a graveyard: orienting and sustained attention

To illustrate the brain processes in attention (see Chapter 3 for brain terms) let us accompany a man and woman walking through a graveyard at night. Suddenly a bat swoops down and hangs upside down on the railings of the fence in front of them. The woman shows an **orienting response** directed by **posterior attentional networks** in the parietal lobes and brainstem (Posner, 1992). These systems register the location of the bat and direct her eyes towards it. She then shows **sustained attention** to the bat, using more **anterior attentional** systems (in the temporal and frontal lobes of the brain) that allow her to dwell on the bat's features, ignoring everything else around her. In addition, her **limbic system** churns out the emotional-motivational energy to stay focused on the bat. In this state she does not even orient to a ghostly apparition emerging from one of the graves. Meanwhile her companion does not orient to either the bat or the ghost, since his attention is wholly directed to thoughts of a pizza he plans to buy in the restaurant across from the graveyard!

So, when do children develop such useful capacities for attending to bats and pizzas and ignoring ghosts?

Development of attention

Both orienting responses and sustained attention to the external environment are apparent at birth. Orienting responses such as eye movements and other physical reactions (e.g. decline in heart rate) to stimuli of moderate intensity are evident even in neonates (Graham and Clifton, 1966). More sustained attention as revealed in preferential or prolonged fixation to particular stimuli is also apparent in newborns (especially for human faces) (Slater and Johnson, 1999; Slater and Lewis, 2002).

However, it is also clear that there are developmental changes in attention (Ruff and Rothbart, 1996). There may be different rates of development for different aspects of attention (Ruff and Rothbart, 1996). The ability to attend or orient rapidly to objects in the external world may develop first due to early maturity in the so-called posterior attentional systems (in the dorsal parietal cortex and brainstem) (Posner and Rothbart, 1981; Johnson, 1993). Development of sustained attention may be due to increasing maturity in the ventral (underside) and frontal pathways of the brain, with the latter especially important in the ability to resist distraction.

At all ages, attention is influenced by knowledge about the world (e.g. children who are fans of a movie action hero will be more likely to notice pictures of that hero than children who are not fans). The acquisition of language and object names may also provide extra cues to direct children's attention to important aspects of the world.

CRUCIAL CONCEPT
Orienting responses and **sustained attentional responses** are evident in newborns but the former may develop sooner due to early maturity in the posterior attentional systems of the brain. At all ages, attention is affected by knowledge and motivational factors.

Quick test

What are the main patterns of development in regard to the capacity for attention?

Section 6

Development of memory

In this section an overview of the development of memory in childhood will be provided, with an explanation of the main factors thought to be responsible for improvement in children's recall ability.

Memory is the capacity to store and later retrieve information and is the basis for the observable changes in behaviour and capacities described as 'learning'. Memory is based on patterns of neural activity in the brain. It may be temporary as in **sensory memory** (the brief persistence of messages from the senses) and **working memory** (the maintenance of information in an active state) or it may be permanent as in **long-term memory** involving biochemical and structural changes in the neural or synaptic connections in the brain. Information can be retrieved from long-term memory by **recognition** (when the item is encountered again) or by **recall** (when the item is not actually present and it is necessary to search long-term memory).

CRUCIAL CONCEPTS

In general, **recognition** matures early and **recall** improves across childhood because of (a) the effects of increasingly organised knowledge about the world and (b) growing awareness of the limits of memory (meta-memory) leading to (c) the use of deliberate memory strategies. These strategies aid memory by increasing connections amongst items to be remembered. This increases the amount of information able to be held in working memory and improves retrieval from long-term memory.

Development of recognition memory

There is evidence of recognition memory in neonates from many studies using habituation and familiarisation methods.

CRUCIAL STUDY

One of the earliest demonstrations of recognition ability in newborns was that by Friedman (1972) who habituated newborns to checkerboard patterns (see Chapter 4 for details on this method) and then showed them a novel checkerboard pattern (with the new and old patterns being counterbalanced in the study to remove any biases due to preferences for one pattern or the other). If the babies had not retained any information about the habituation patterns then they should have shown equal interest in the new and old items (since without memory, there is no way to tell that one **was** old). The infants showed recovery of interest to the novel pattern, indicating that they had detected the old one and were essentially ignoring it: evidence of recognition memory.

Studies of this kind have been conducted for all types of sensory information (sights, sounds, etc.) indicating that recognition memory is well under way at birth. Indeed children's recognition memory often matches that of adults (Siegler, 1996), although recall skills are another matter.

Development of recall

It is more difficult to study recall in young children since it involves memory for items not actually present. However, some methods do give some idea about recall in infants.

CRUCIAL STUDY

A procedure called the **conjugate reinforcement method** (Rovee-Collier and Fagen, 1981) involves attaching one end of a ribbon to a baby's ankle and the other end to a mobile. The baby soon learns to kick furiously to make the mobile move, but if the mobile is now changed to a new one, the baby will not kick, suggesting recall of the features of the old mobile.

There is evidence of recall capacity in somewhat older children. For example, six-month-olds show recall of the way to operate a toy train after delays of two weeks and 12-month-olds after delays of two months (Rovee-Collier and Boller, 1995). Two-year-olds can easily find a hidden toy after delays of an hour (Deloache and Brown, 1983). It is clear then that recall starts early in life, but children seem to be able to recall more and at a faster rate as they mature. Four- to five-year-olds can typically recall about four numbers, 9–10-year-olds about six and adults about seven (Schneider and Pressley, 1997). This improvement relates to the more efficient use of working memory for several reasons.

One reason recall improves is the development of a more organised **knowledge base** in long-term memory and this helps the holding of information in working memory and the storage and retrieval of items in long-term memory: a bit like being able to put away and then find your socks in a tidy drawer, as opposed to a messy one. Studies of children who have particular interests such as dinosaurs (Chi and Koeske, 1983) show that better knowledge leads to better recall (and the same goes for adults).

CRUCIAL STUDIES

The effects of knowledge on memory were shown very clearly in studies of recall for arrangements of pieces on a chessboard (Chi, 1978; Schneider, Gruber, Gold and Opwis, 1993). Children who were competent chess players were tested against adults who were not. The children showed better recall than the adults for the chess placements (although not for digits in a digit span task).

The other reason that recall improves is children's increasing awareness that their memory has limits (metamemory) and that they may need to use deliberate strategies to support it (Schneider and Bjorklund, 1998). Three common strategies are:

- **rehearsal** (repeating the items over and over);
- **organising** the items to be recalled (e.g. *dog-bed-cow-chair* could be remembered in terms of animal and furniture categories: *{dog-cow}{bed-chair}*); and
- if no organisation is available then creating links within the information by **elaboration** (e.g. by creating imagery or a story to connect the items: such as linking *ghost-man-moon-pizza* in an image of a *ghost and man eating a pizza under a full moon*).

The reason why these strategies help recall is that they 'group' the items and this increases the amount that can be held in working memory (e.g. try recalling this number: 2512200301012004 and then see if it is easier to process it in an organised or grouped way as two dates: 25 December 2003 and New Year's Day 2004). Links also improve the chances of finding information again in long-term memory because the information is stored in a connected way in the brain. It is a bit like the handkerchiefs up a magician's sleeves: pulling one leads to the others because they are tied together.

Consistent strategy use emerges around six years of age. The first strategy is **rehearsal** although younger children may rehearse each item (e.g. *cat-cat-dog-dog-chair-chair-bed-bed*) rather than the whole set (*{cat-dog-chair-bed} {cat-dog-chair-bed}*), with the latter being more effective at making links amongst the items. The next strategy to be used is **organisation**, which improves with children's knowledge about categories of items. **Elaboration** is the final strategy to emerge possibly because it requires generating links amongst the items.

Quick test

Why does recall ability appear to improve with age?

Section 7

Development of conceptual knowledge

In this section the development of general knowledge will be described in regard to the growth of categories, concepts and scripts.

What are concepts and categories?

Children do not just store information about individual items, but store or acquire more general knowledge as well. This involves the growth of **concepts** (general ideas or representations) and **categories** (grouping or organisation of items based on similarity of items in regard to a concept). For example, instead of just storing information about their own cat Plato and their neighbour's cat Socrates, children may also store knowledge about cats in general. This may involve a concept (e.g. a cognitive impression or memory of 'cats' as things with four legs and whiskers, etc.) and a category or grouping based on that concept (e.g. a grouping of Plato and Socrates as similar and belonging to the category of 'cats' as distinct from 'dogs' or anything else). Categorisation is a critical aspect of cognitive development. It enables children to organise the mass of information they acquire in daily life and to apply it more effectively in reasoning and solving problems about the world.

Categorisation can be based on similarity in appearance or perceptual features (colour, shape, movement, etc.) or on more abstract features (Rosch, 1978). There are **super-ordinate** or 'global' categories in which the items are not necessarily similar in appearance (e.g. 'living things' includes bacteria as well as plants and humans: not exactly look-alikes). At the other extreme are **subordinate** categories in which the items are very similar to each other and are based on fine details (e.g. the category of Siamese cats *vs.* that of Persian cats). Somewhere in between these extremes are **basic** categories in which there is moderate similarity in the appearance of the items (e.g. the category of 'cats' or that of 'dogs').

Category boundaries are sometimes fuzzy or are not rigidly fixed or agreed on by everyone (e.g. as in ad-hoc categories such as 'things to save in a fire': Barsalou, 1983). However, for common categories, there is agreement that some items are better examples than others (Rosch, 1978). For example, a robin is a better example than a penguin for the category of 'birds'.

How does categorisation develop?

New categories are formed throughout life whenever similarities amongst items are detected. This can lead to either (a) the storage of the **best examples** as the basis or frame of reference for the category or (b) the formation of a **prototype**, an abstraction of main qualities of the examples. When new items are then experienced, any overlap with the examples or prototype leads to inclusion in the category and any dissimilarity to exclusion. This may require some fine-tuning for some categories (e.g. knowing that 'horses' and 'ponies' can be categorised separately) and it may take time for children to correctly name categories. For example even infants can distinguish basic categories of hue (colour) (Teller and Bornstein, 1987), but it can take a number of years before children attach correct labels to colours.

It was once considered that children developed basic categories first (e.g. 'cats' or 'dogs') before superordinate (e.g. 'animals') or subordinate (e.g. 'Siamese cats'), because basic categories can be most easily detected from appearances (the items in the category have moderate similarity to each other and the distinction between different basic categories can be easily detected for the same reason). However, more recent evidence has shown that this is not necessarily the case and some superordinate categories may develop before some basic categories (Quinn and Eimas, 1998).

For example, new studies have shown that young children may categorise some 'animals' together before distinguishing the more basic sub-categories such as 'cats' and 'dogs' (Quinn and Eimas, 2002). In any case, the process of categorisation begins very early in infancy although the extent and type of categorisation depends on experience or input to the system. A child whose parents breed different types of cats may develop subordinate categories of 'cats' (Siamese, etc.) earlier than a child who has little contact with cats.

A number of different methods have shown that the process of categorisation begins in infancy. One method involves **habituating** or **familiarising** infants to items from one category (e.g. different pictures of cats) and then showing them two new items: one from the familiar category (e.g. a new cat) and one from a new category (e.g. a dog). Greater fixation to or interest in the new-category item is taken to mean that the children had detected the category in the habituation items and being 'bored' with that, were more interested in the change of category. This method has been used to show that infants in the first months of life are sensitive to categories of hues, shapes and natural things such as cats and dogs (Quinn, 2002). Other methods involve observing older children playing with toys from different categories. Children will often show **sequential touching** of items from the same category suggesting they are reacting to the category similarities (e.g. Mandler, Bauer and McDonough, 1991).

CRUCIAL CONCEPTS

Concepts are general ideas or representations and **categories** are the grouping or organisation of items based on similarity of items in regard to a concept. These begin at birth and improve the efficiency of cognition. Experience may lead to the storage of the **best example** or **prototype** (an abstraction of main qualities of the examples) as the frame of reference for the category. Even infants can detect basic level categories (e.g. cat or dog) from perceptual input but some broader **superordinate** categories such as animals may be used before more basic distinctions such as cat or dog.

Section 8

Development of reasoning and problem-solving

In this section the capacity of children to reason and solve problems will be reviewed.

Reasoning is the capacity for cognitively combining or reorganising information to produce additional information : a 'conclusion' or solution. When reasoning is used to reach a particular desired output, it is called **problem-solving**.

Reasoning can be conducted according to logical principles which show how information can be systematically combined to reach an inevitable or necessary conclusion, provided the initial information is true (although it is not concerned with establishing if the latter is the case). However, even adults can find this approach challenging and will often opt for 'short-cut' ways of reasoning based on prior experience or knowledge rather than logic as such (Tversky and Kahneman, 1973). Even adults reason better with familiar information, they often rely on **analogy** (seeing some similarity between a current problem and a past one) or will reason by **heuristic** or **rule-of-thumb** means that worked in the past, spring most easily to mind or fit their biases and beliefs (Manktelow, 1999).

CRUCIAL CONCEPT

Reasoning can be performed in accord with the principles of logic although even adults will often rely on other **heuristic** (rule-of-thumb) modes of reasoning, based on prior knowledge, biases and beliefs.

Can children reason?

The short answer to this question is 'yes' and 'no'. Even in early infancy, the rudiments of reasoning and problem-solving are apparent in babies' exploration of their environment. Just like adults, even young children are adept at using past knowledge in analogical and heuristic ways to solve problems. They may even be able to solve problems in a logical way if (a) there is a link to past knowledge, (b) the problem is clearly understood and (c) does not overload working memory. As discussed in Section 4 (above), Piagetian tasks may test children's limits in this regard and thus produce poor performance in children who can reason effectively about the same essential types of problems in other contexts. (See Figure 5.1.)

CRUCIAL STUDIES

The use of past knowledge to reason and solve problems in an **analogical** way has been demonstrated in a study in which children as young as 10 months had to retrieve a toy from behind one barrier and then repeat the task with different toys and barriers. The infants showed increasing efficiency with each successful retrieval reflecting analogical-type problem-solving (Chen, Sanchez and Campbell, 1997). In another study (Holyoak, Junn and Billman, 1984), two- to three-year-olds were also able to use **analogy** based on more **abstract** information. They were told stories about a genie who needed to retrieve a precious jar without leaving his lamp and used his magic staff to rein in the jar. The children were then presented with analogous problems such as reaching a jar of sweets on the other side of the table without moving from their chair. Those children who had heard the genie story solved their problem by analogy, using similar tools (e.g. using a staff that was on the table to retrieve the sweets).

Are young children limited then to such knowledge-based approaches to reasoning? As shown in Section 4 this is not necessarily the case and even four-year-olds have been shown to reason via formal logical principles in some cases, even when the information is not directly based on experience (e.g. see the 'Pogs' example in Section 4) or is actually contradictory to experience (as in example below).

CRUCIAL STUDY

In one study of logical reasoning, even two-year-olds were able to correctly answer logical syllogisms such as 'All sheep ride bicycles. Bill is a sheep. Does Bill walk or ride a bicycle?' as long as they were encouraged to imagine the contexts. This is despite the fact that the syllogisms involved hypothetical information counterfactual to real life (Richards and Sanderson, 1999) (see Figure 5.1).

Does this mean that there are no differences between adults' and children's reasoning?

No, children's reasoning is often weaker than that of adults. One main reason for this is that in general, the younger the child, the poorer knowledge or information about the problem or the problem domain. In particular domains where children do have expertise (e.g. 'dinosaur experts': Chi and Koeske, 1978) it is clear that knowledge has positive benefits to reasoning and lack of knowledge has drawbacks. Why?

Figure 5.1 Piagetian conservation tasks indicate weaker reasoning abilities in children compared to the tasks of Richards and Sanderson (1999) which attempted to engage children's knowledge and imagination

Increased knowledge is a key factor in the development of problem-solving. If activated from long-term memory during problem-solving, it helps to focus attention on relevant aspects of a problem and may free up capacity in working memory. The latter can occur because familiar information can be detected as such, processed speedily ('automatically') and organised into manageable chunks, easing the load on working memory (Case, 1992). Reducing the load on working memory means that all the relevant information about the problem can be held in an active state at one time, improving the chances of combining it to provide an effective solution. Moreover, prior knowledge stored in long-term memory may even provide a rapid analogical or heuristic solution with little extra processing required. It may also be that children's knowledge becomes more 'explicit' or available to use with increasing exposure to particular domains of experience (Karmiloff-Smith, 1995).

CRUCIAL CONCEPT

Children's reasoning or problem-solving develops partly as a result of an increased and better-organised knowledge base. This enhances attention to, and memory for, information that is relevant to the problem to be solved and may provide analogical or heuristic (rule-of-thumb) solutions based on prior experience.

The effects of knowledge on children's reasoning or problem-solving has been shown in studies of 'street maths' with Brazilian children (6–15 years) who sell sweets and fruit on the street and can perform accurate calculations about the cost of these items with actual money, better than the same calculations in an abstract numerical form (Saxe, 1988).

There are also indications that children become more aware of their own limitations in problem-solving and develop a **metacognitive** awareness of their own thinking. This may improve problem-solving by making children think more strategically and methodically (Siegler, 1996). This awareness and control may stem from better knowledge or from development of frontal lobe brain function that allows better control of attention and information-processing (Johnson and Morton, 1991) – or both factors may play a role.

CRUCIAL CONCEPTS

Piaget proposed that children develop their **reasoning capacities** in four stages from early infancy to adulthood. Information-processing, neural network and knowledge-based models of cognition indicate instead that children may reason effectively provided that prior knowledge is engaged, working memory is not overloaded and the aims of the problem are clear.

Under user-friendly conditions, even young children may display capacities for logical reasoning although as for adults, children are more adept at reasoning and solving problems on the basis of prior knowledge and experience through such means as **analogy** or **heuristic** approaches.

Quick test

How is knowledge important to the development of reasoning and problem-solving abilities in children?

Section 9

End of chapter assessment

How will you be assessed?

You may be asked to write an essay outlining the main ideas in Piaget's theory of cognitive development and possibly to explain the critical objections to, or alternative explanations of, his research findings. You could also be asked to describe cognitive development from more contemporary perspectives, explaining the main patterns of change in attention, memory, categorisation and reasoning and problem-solving capacities. This could also require a comparison with Piaget's theory, especially on the issue of whether cognition develops in stages. The following examples may illustrate the kinds of questions you could encounter.

Questions

1. Explain the main proposals about cognitive development from a Piagetian viewpoint and discuss alternative interpretations and research findings regarding these proposals. (This question relates to Learning Outcomes 1 and 2 for this chapter.)

2. Discuss cognitive development from contemporary information-processing, neural network, and neurobiological perspectives. (This question relates to Learning Outcome 3.)

Answers

1. Your answer should begin with a description of the concept of 'mental structures and operations' as the Piagetian notion about knowledge and cognitive processes. Next, explain that Piaget proposed that children build mental structures following actions on the world that lead to 'accommodation and assimilation' of knowledge. Then you should give a summary of the Piagetian proposal that mental operations develop in four stages as a result of experience and maturation: sensorimotor (cognition based on reflexes and action), preoperational (animistic, egocentric, centred thought), concrete operational (cognitive operations but only for concrete items), formal operational (true logical abstract-symbolic thought) (see Section 2). The next section of the answer should

identify the main critical objections or alternative explanations for Piaget's findings (see Sections 3 and 4) including:

- an account of current (information-processing/neural-network/neurobiological) models or concepts regarding cognitive content and processes, explaining how these ideas of dynamic and fuzzy cognition differ from Piaget's ideas about more static structures and logical operations;

- explanation of the views that Piaget's tasks may be especially challenging for children because of (a) unfamiliarity of task type, instructions, language, (b) leading to poor encoding and representation of the task aims and requirements and (c) failure to use or activate relevant knowledge from long-term memory and (d) overloading of working memory;

- more recent research suggesting that children's cognition is not necessarily ego-centric, animistic, or limited to appearances (see Section 4: include the studies on infant size and shape constancy, infant object permanence, alternatives to the three mountains task, alternative accounts of 'false belief' and 'theory of mind' tasks, understanding about living things, social deference issues with adult testers, logical reasoning research with four-year-olds).

This essay should be fully referenced where necessary using examples provided in Sections 2, 3 and 4.

2. Your answer should essentially be a summary of the main points in Sections 3, 5, 6, 7 and 8. You should begin with a brief summary of contemporary views or concepts about cognition (see Sections 1 and 3) as a set of processes for representing, storing, and combining information within the neural networks and systems of the brain. Explain that the content of cognition involves active neural patterns corresponding to new input from the senses or old material reactivated from long-term memory, with information held in active working memory during reasoning and problem-solving. Explain also that children acquire a store of knowledge in long-term memory and this has a critical effect on development of cognitive competence. You then need to work systematically through the development of each basic set of cognitive processes.

- attention (explaining that the 'posterior attentional networks' for rapid orienting may develop earlier than the networks for more sustained attention, but both are in action after birth);

- memory (explaining that recognition memory is apparent in newborns and recall is evident in infants too, but develops further in childhood due to the effects of increased and more organised knowledge about the world and the use of deliberate strategies of rehearsal, organisation and elaboration);

- conceptual knowledge and categorisation (explain that these processes begin in infancy but that experience can dictate the direction of development);

- reasoning and problem-solving (explain that even young children can use logical forms of reasoning but as for adults, are more adept when past knowledge can be involved).

All of this discussion should be fully referenced to appropriate research examples provided in this chapter.

Section 10

Further reading

You should consult the full list of references for this chapter in the list at the end of the book. However, the following references will help to start your extra reading on cognitive development.

Borke, H. (1975). Piaget's mountains revisited: changes in the egocentric landscape. *Developmental Psychology,* 11: 240–243.

Cashon, C. H. and Cohen, L. B. (2000). Eight-month-old infants' perception of possible and impossible events. *Infancy,* 1: 429–446.

Chi, M. T. H. (1978). Knowledge structures and memory development. In R. S. Siegler (ed.), *Children's Thinking: What Develops?,* 73–96. Hillsdale, NJ: Erlbaum.

Donaldson, M. (1978). *Children's Minds.* Glasgow: Fontana.

Holyoak, K. J., Junn, E. N. and Billman, D. O. (1984). Development of analogical problem-solving skill. *Child Development,* 55: 2042–2055.

Hawkins, J., Pea, R. D., Glick, J. and Scribner, S. (1984). 'Merds that laugh don't like mushrooms': Evidence for deductive reasoning by preschoolers. *Developmental Psychology,* 20: 584–594.

Karmiloff-Smith, A. (1999). The connectionist infant: Would Piaget turn in his grave? In A. Slater & D. Muir (eds.), *The Blackwell Reader in Developmental Psychology,* 43–52. Oxford: Blackwell.

Piaget, J. (1952). *The Origins of Intelligence in Children.* New York: International Universities Press.

Quinn, P. C. and Eimas, P. D. (1998). Evidence for global category representaiton for humans by young infants. *Journal of Experimental Child Psychology,* 69: 151–174.

Richards, C. A., and Sanderson, J. A. (1999). The role of imagination in facilitating deductive reasoning in 2-, 3- and 4-year-olds. *Cognition,* 72: B1–B9.

Siegal, M. (1997). *Knowing Children: Experiments in Conversation and Cognition.* Hillsdale, NJ: Erlbaum.

Slater, A. and Johnson, S. P. (1999). Visual sensory and perceptual abilities of the newborn: Beyond the blooming, buzzing confusion. In A. Slater and S. P. Johnson (eds.), *The Development of Sensory, Motor and Cognitive Capacities,* 121–141. Hove: Sussex Press.

Chapter 6
Early attachment
(Rachel Gillibrand)

Chapter summary

Theorists have argued that the strongest emotional bond exists between an infant and his or her mother. This chapter discusses the formation of strong emotional bonds between the infant and parent, a bond that is called attachment. It has often been believed that the formation of a strong attachment in infancy predicts the development of strong attachments and better social development in later life. This chapter looks at the main theories underpinning our understanding of the role of attachments, with the notion of a critical period following birth for forming attachments and the importance of this for both infant and mother. This chapter will introduce you to key stages in the formation of attachments and to different types of attachment between infant and mother.

Learning outcomes

After reading this chapter, you should be able to:

Outcome 1: Understand the development of social relationships.
You will be able to describe the importance of synchrony and the formation of attachment and bonding between the parent and child.

Outcome 2: Define the fundamental concepts surrounding the main theories of social development.
You will be able to describe, evaluate and contrast the main theories of social development.

Outcome 3: Understand the key stages and styles of attachment.
You will be able to relate the findings of key studies to our understanding of key stages and styles of attachment.

The question at the end of the chapter tests you on these learning outcomes.

Section 1

Synchrony and attachment and their relation to social development

We will begin with some basic definitions of synchrony and attachment and explain why it is important to know about the development of these capacities. This chapter will then focus mainly on attachment. First we will briefly describe early views on attachment and then explain how more recent research has had an impact on our understanding of the formation and importance of social relationships.

What are synchrony and attachment?

The development of social relationships is an important part of human life. We all have the need to feel an emotional connection to other people and as an infant this need is very much geared towards the adults closest to us, our parents. Although smiling at any adult by the age of two to three months, babies will often smile best and most for their parents, they will look in the direction of their parents' voice and smile when their parent approaches. Generally, given the choice of a smiling adult or a smiling parent, the infant will turn to their parent and smile and kick their legs in excitement. In turn the mother or father often reports a much stronger feeling of affection for their infant at this stage and may be seen engaging them with much more eye contact and smiles, tickling and playing than previously.

During this phase, the infant is unable to communicate verbally whether she or he needs nourishment or warmth, security or comfort and it is up to the parent to decipher the infant's facial expressions and sounds to determine what it is the infant needs. By spending time watching and playing with their baby, parents can often develop an understanding of their baby's moods and needs and in time learn to respond to their baby effectively. During this period of watching and playing with the baby the parent and infant are engaged in developing synchrony.

CRUCIAL CONCEPT

Synchrony is the coordinated activity where the parent and infant watch, copy and respond to each other.

During moments of synchrony the infant may for instance watch the parent display a comic facial expression. The parent will watch the child to see if they respond, for instance by smiling, trying to copy the facial expression or by showing pleasure. If the child responds, the parent then reacts to the child by perhaps smiling back, making encouraging noises or by copying the face the child has made. By watching and copying each other the parent and child are engaged in something called synchronous play. Bremner (1988) argued that by engaging in synchronous play the child learns to 'take turns' with the parent and by doing so the child begins to learn the basic skills of social interaction.

Synchrony is usually only used to describe the playful interactions between parent and child that occur during the first year of life and mostly before the child is able to talk. As the child gets older, the relationships that occur between the parent and child are called attachments.

CRUCIAL CONCEPT

Attachment: 'An enduring emotional connection between people that produces a desire for continual contact as well as feelings of distress during separation' (Berger, 2001).

Attachments are characterised by the parents' need to be near to and touch the infant and conversely by the infant's need to be near to and touch his or her parent. This need to be near to the person for whom you have an attachment is demonstrated by **proximity-seeking behaviours**. For example, a parent who is showing proximity-seeking behaviour keeps the infant within reach at all times and spends time cuddling and stroking the child. When the parent puts their child into their carry-cot or push-chair, the child will often reach up and cling to the parent and may fuss or cry. The **contact-maintaining behaviours** that the child is demonstrating here are geared towards regaining proximity to the parent. This constant interplay of seeking to touch and be touched between parent and child is considered an important aspect of developing a good attachment relationship.

Note here that we are talking about basic attachment behaviours. Later on in the chapter we will learn about different types of attachment and stages of attachment formation.

What are the main viewpoints on attachment?

Why is it that we form attachments so early in our lives? On a simple level engaging in synchronous play does not seem to achieve anything in particular. The parent and child are learning to copy each other and gain a great deal of pleasure from it, but what use is there to be gained from this kind of interaction? Synchrony seems to develop in us a sense of emotional connection with our parents and our children, but what do we gain by forming an emotional connection with our parents or our infants?

Early theories emphasised the idea that a child is born with the ability to form attachments. This process was considered automatic and to have survival value to the infant.

CRUCIAL CONCEPT

Survival value: any activity or provision that provides us with warmth, food, air, water and security is said to have survival value – it encourages the survival of an individual or group.

The formation of attachments was originally thought not to be influenced by the child, but was considered very much the responsibility of the parent. Later theories emphasised the idea that both the parent and child were actively involved in the development of the child-to-parent bond. The responsibility was not so much with the parent in forming a good attachment but could be influenced very much by the child's response during the period of relationship formation. The main differences between early and more recent viewpoints on attachment are the change in focus from attachment being considered an innate process (an ability the child is born with) that is necessary for the survival of the child to more recent theorists suggesting that both the parent and the child are active participants in the attachment process.

What did the early theorists believe about the development of attachment?

Psychoanalytic theory

Sigmund Freud (1856-1939)

Sigmund Freud first published his works detailing the **psyche** and his understanding of the development of the personality in 1935. His work suggests that the psyche consists of three parts: the **id**, the **superego** and the **ego**. These parts of our psyche are governed very strongly by the need for sexual gratification. The id is the part of us which represents our biological needs and which drives our behaviour to satisfy our needs, for instance to eat, to drink, to keep warm and to have sex. Our drive to have sexual satisfaction Freud called the libido. It has been described as the part of us that seeks pleasure. Freud argued that, during infancy, all our behaviours are aimed at gaining pleasure and avoiding pain. This he called the pleasure principle.

CRUCIAL CONCEPT

Pleasure principle: our need to feel pleasure means that we will do anything to feel pleasure and to avoid any feeling of pain.

For instance, when you see a baby crying you will notice that the parent tries to pacify the baby by offering him or her something. In this example, that something could be food or a blanket, a change of nappy or the parent may pick the baby up. The baby may not yet understand why he or she cries but knows that the attention of the parent usually makes them feel better. Freud considered the first few years of life to be critical in the development of personality and the formation of social relationships was seen to be key to this.

The **superego** is the part of us that understands our social responsibilities and boundaries, for instance our laws and restrictions which allow us to live in a large social group which aim to reduce conflict or encourage justice. The superego is described as our sense of morality and of guilt at breaking these laws or restrictions. The ego is the part of our consciousness that tries to keep the id and the superego happy, for instance if we are hungry, our need for survival drives our behaviour to eat. Should we as infants see a packet of biscuits on the table, the superego will make us aware that we cannot just take whatever food is available as we have a moral responsibility not to steal. The ego will placate both the id's need for survival with the superego's need for moral satisfaction by making us aware of the possibility of asking for food. This allows food to be consumed (thus satisfying the id) and in a morally satisfying way (thus satisfying the superego). The superego is engaged in a constant battle between satisfying the pleasure-seeking id within the boundaries set by the superego.

How does this affect our development of attachments? Freud argued that attachments developed as they satisfied the pleasure seeking needs of the id within the limits set by society. From birth onwards we have our biological needs that can be satisfied by feeding, clothing and protection but as we get older these needs cannot be satisfied as easily. Our needs develop in complexity and as they do so, we become more aware of the limits society places upon us. Our parents start to restrict us and tell us when our behaviour is inappropriate. If we choose to behave within the laws and moral norms our family expects of us then we begin to limit our pleasure-seeking behaviour. This process Freud called the reality principle.

> ──────────── CRUCIAL CONCEPT ────────────
>
> **Reality principle:** our need for pleasure is curbed by our awareness of the boundaries that society sets for us.

Freud argued that infants who are able to satisfactorily integrate this sense of reality into their psyche will form good close relationships with the people around them – in this case, their family members. If the infant is not able to do this then Freud suggested that they will be unlikely to form a good relationship with their family. In particular, Freud considered the mother-child relationship to be the most influential in determining future relationships the child may have with others. His argument for this was that the mother spent the most time with the child in the first few years of life and was the person who gave the child everything they needed during infancy – food, warmth, security. Indeed, so strongly did Freud feel about the mother's role in childhood that he called her:

> unique, without parallel, established unalterably for a whole lifetime as the first and strongest love-object and as the prototype of all later love relations. (Freud, 1964)

So how does the child–mother relationship affect the development of attachments? Freud suggested that the pleasure needs of the id developed over a number of so-called **psychosexual** stages. The first is the oral stage.

> ──────────── CRUCIAL CONCEPT ────────────
>
> **Oral stage:** a stage of life where we get sexual pleasure from oral stimulation, e.g. eating and sucking.

The oral stage occurs from birth to age two years. Freud suggested that the infant gains sexual pleasure via the mouth, for instance by sucking and eating. So when the infant demands feeding, the parent (usually the mother at this stage) feeds the infant, the infant feels pleasure and the id is satisfied. If the mother progresses from breast feeding her child to weaning them onto other foods at the developmentally 'right time', the child will have no problem adjusting and will grow up quite happily. However, if the mother stops breast feeding before the infant is ready to move onto other forms of feeding Freud suggested that the child will become traumatised. The id's sexual demands are not being satisfied. It will not be able to develop fully and the child will become depressed and anxious. Freud argued that if the child feels depressed and anxious during the oral stage then this feeling will affect the child's attachment to his or her mother.

A second important stage in the development of attachment in infants is the anal stage.

CRUCIAL CONCEPT

Anal stage: a stage of life where we get pleasure from anal stimulation, e.g. bowel movements.

During this stage the infant develops an interest in the sensations related to bowel movements and seeks sexual pleasure from toilet activities. During this stage, the id is satisfied by sensory pleasure through bowel movements. Freud argued that the mother's response to her child's interest in potty-training is vital to the child's id development. If the mother is very strict about potty-training and begins to wean the infant from nappies to the potty too early, Freud suggested that the child will resist by becoming argumentative and anxious. The distress the child feels will again affect his or her attachment to the mother.

The **phallic stage** of development occurs after toilet training and was considered by Freud to be even more important in the formation of successful attachments.

CRUCIAL CONCEPT

Phallic stage: a stage when we become preoccupied with our genitals and develop a sexual attraction for our opposite-gender parent.

The **phallic stage** of development is characterised by either the **Oedipus complex** if you are a boy or by the **Electra complex** if you are a girl. The Oedipus complex suggests that as boys develop a fascination for their genitals, they become sexually attracted to their mothers. However, their drive to become the sexual partner of their mother is thwarted by the presence of their father. Boys see their father as a love-rival to the mother and engage in aggressive behaviour towards them. Eventually, the boys realise that the only way they are going to become the sexual partner of the mother is to emulate the behaviour of their father. Thus, boys create a role model for masculine behaviour from their father and in turn earn the attention of their mother. The Electra complex works in just the same way. Freud suggested that girls develop a sexual attraction to their father. The mother becomes the love-rival and aggressive behaviour towards her results. The girl then realises that the best way to get the father's attention is to emulate the mother. She then creates a role model in her mother and gains the attention of the father. In this way, boys and girls associate same-gender parent as the role model. They develop their attachment to include mannerisms and behaviour of the same-gender parent. Freud suggests that copying the same-gender parent induces love and attention from the opposite-gender parent and thus develops the attachment.

Successful completion of the oral, anal and phallic stage results in a child who has formed a strong attachment to both their mother and father. The child forms strong attachments to other people they meet as they get older and will form healthy, strong attachments in adult life. However, not everyone completes each stage successfully. As we know, difficulties in resolving the issues of each stage result in trauma, anxiety or depression. What can also happen is a fixation at each stage.

— CRUCIAL CONCEPT —

Fixation: the child unsuccessfully resolves the conflict at any of the psychosexual stages of development and cannot progress to the next stage as a result.

Children who fixate on the oral stage might show incorporative traits such as dependency, gullibility or jealousy or sadistic traits such as sarcasm and verbal aggression. Children who fixate on the anal stage might be expulsive and messy, cruel or destructive. Or they might be retentive and be obstinate, neat or stingy. Boys who fixate at the phallic stage might show macho aggressive sexuality, an excessive striving for career potency or sexual and occupational impotence. Girls who fixate at this stage might show flirtatious, seductive behaviour that does not result in sexual interaction. Although these traits might be present during a happy childhood, it is when you are placed under stress and cannot cope that these traits really emerge. Freud argued that under stress a person reveals many defence mechanisms for dealing with that stress, one of which is called regression.

— CRUCIAL CONCEPT —

Regression: when stress gets too much you revert to behaviours exhibited at the psychosexual stage at which you became fixated.

Therefore, if you were fixated at the oral stage, under stress you might regress to using cigarettes, alcohol or food to resolve the anxiety you are feeling. Thus you assume behaviours that satisfy your perceived oral conflict. If you were fixated at the anal stage you might experience irritable bowel syndrome, constipation or diarrhoea under stress. If you were fixated at the phallic stage you might experience sexual aggression, impotence or lack of sexual desire.

Evaluation

The key principle to Freud's views on the development of mother-infant attachment is whether the overall pattern of maternal behaviour is characterised by warmth and empathy or by coldness and control. Infants raised in a family characterised by warmth and empathy are much more likely to develop good attachments to both family members and to others in later life. If you fixate at a certain stage, then you will regress to this stage at periods of stress. However, many people find it difficult to believe in Freud's theory. Perhaps we do not remember feeling orally, anally or genitally fixated. Perhaps we do not remember idolising our mothers and resenting our fathers. The most difficult part of the theory for most people to accept is the notion of infants having sexual drives. As a society we completely de-sexualise our children and are outraged when we hear of sexual activity in children. Does this mean though that Freud is wrong? Theorists have argued that there is no biological evidence for the existence of the id, superego and ego structures within the psyche and further that there seems to be no evidence that a child experiences the psychosexual stages during development to adulthood. Indeed there appears to be no evidence that resolution or otherwise of oral, anal or phallic conflicts predict adult personality (Crews, 1996). If you think, however, of people around you, can you identify certain personality traits that could be related to the oral, anal or phallic conflicts? Freudian theory is as difficult to disprove as it is to prove. It could be that we do not yet have the tools to offer an undisputable view on Freud.

Erik Erikson (1902–1994)

Erik Erikson was a committed follower of Sigmund Freud but he had his own views on psychoanalytic theory. He also described a number of stages that an infant would progress through in their pursuit of social relationships, but Erikson's theories expanded very much more from childhood right into old age. When considering how an infant forms attachment Erikson also argued the importance of the first few years of life. Again, the mother's relationship with the child was considered to predict the child's ability to form relationships in later life.

Erikson suggested that during the first year of life the infant is engaged in a struggle called **trust** *vs.* **mistrust**. The baby has needs – again these are mainly food, warmth and security – and the baby has to learn who will provide what they need.

CRUCIAL CONCEPT

Trust *vs.* **mistrust**: the baby has to learn who to trust and who not to trust.

During the trust *vs.* mistrust stage the baby has to learn who will care for them and give them what they need. For example, a baby feels hungry and cries to alert the mother to his or her needs. When adults approach the cot the baby must decide which of those adults is going to provide food. The baby will calm when he or she sees the mother (the baby has learnt to trust the mother to provide food) but the baby will become more distressed when he or she sees a stranger (the baby has not learned to trust the stranger). Learning who to trust allows the infant to develop a sense of security. Erikson argued that children with a strong sense of trust and security develop the confidence to engage with and explore the world.

Once the infant has learned who to trust and who not to trust the next stage of development Erikson proposed is the autonomy *vs.* shame and doubt stage.

CRUCIAL CONCEPT

Autonomy *vs.* **shame and doubt** – during this stage the child learns to carry out tasks without the mother's help and learns to doubt their abilities.

During the autonomy *vs.* shame and doubt stage, the child learns to eat, walk, use the toilet and talk without their mother's help. The child also starts to doubt their ability to carry out a task that is new and will often need encouragement to tackle it successfully. As the child develops they start to explore and parents have to set boundaries for what is considered acceptable behaviour. A child who is starting to feed themselves will make a complete mess of it in the beginning, often getting more food on their face and hands than in their mouth! However, with firm supportive guidance, the parent can soon help the child develop the skills needed to eat less messily. If this is achieved, then the child develops a stronger sense of autonomy. If, however, the parent subjects the child to ridicule and shame whilst they are learning, the child develops a strong sense of shame and doubt. By developing autonomy, Erikson argued that the child develops self-confidence and an ability to meet the challenges of growing up. Without autonomy the child may grow up suspicious and pessimistic or feel shame that they have not achieved their full potential.

Evaluation

Erikson agreed with Freud's notion of the mother being important in the development of attachment but suggested that rather than the child purely wanting satisfaction via the mouth or anus, the child actually had many and varied needs. During the trust *vs.* mistrust stage, when the parent correctly identified the needs of a child and managed to satisfy them, the child learned to trust the parent. When the child trusted the parent, the child developed a good attachment to the parent (Erikson, 1963). During the autonomy *vs.* shame and doubt stage, when the parent helped the child to develop the ability to carry out tasks for themselves, the child developed a sense of confidence which is reflected in their future attachments. As with Freud's theory of psychosocial development, Erikson's theory cannot be proven, and the same arguments apply. Is the theory too vague to be testable or have the necessary tools to test the theory not yet been invented? However you feel about Erikson's theory, like Freud his work was important in being one of the most influential theories of developmental psychology in the twentieth century. Indeed, their work can be seen to underpin many commonly held notions of the importance of childhood. Both Freud and Erikson believe that we progress through a series of stages in infancy, which must be successfully completed for the development of a psychologically health personality. The theories explain why we exhibit certain behaviours under stress (Freud's notion of regression) and consider that the early family experiences of a child predict their future social and psychological outcome.

Learning theories

The psychoanalytic approach to the development of attachment is based very much on the ability of the mother to respond to her child's needs. What is key to the psychoanalytic approach is that these needs are grounded in the psyche and exist as unconscious states. A different view on how attachment develops comes from the **learning theory** approach. Again, attachment develops based on the satisfaction of the child's needs but learning theorists differ in that they believe that the unconscious state of the child is not the main focus. Learning theories suggest that the needs of the child are very much biological needs. By satisfying the biological needs of the child, the child becomes attached to the parent. The contribution of learning theory to our understanding of attachment is demonstrated here in the works of Harry Harlow.

Harlow's primary drive theory

Harlow (1958) used the term **cupboard love** based on his primary observation that a child learns to love his/her mother because she satisfies the basic needs of hunger and thirst. A mother's main priority when caring for her baby is to feed him or her. However, when you see a mother with her baby you will notice that she does more than this. Harlow suggests that mothers also provide comfort and warmth. A mother is not just a provider of food but also offers comfort and warmth by wrapping the baby in blankets, holding the baby tight and keeping the baby safe from harm. To test this theory. Harlow conducted a series of studies involving infant Rhesus monkeys.

CRUCIAL STUDY

Harlow's studies on the role of the mother. (Harlow, 1986)

The infant monkey was given the choice of a wire 'mother' that could dispense milk and a cloth 'mother' that could not dispense milk (see Figure 6.1). Since the infant monkey clings to the mother it had to choose between a mother providing nourishment (milk) and a mother providing comfort (cloth).

Figure 6.1 Harlow's infant monkeys suckled from the wire 'mother' but sought comfort from the cloth 'mother'

When given the choice, the monkey would cling to the cloth 'mother', go to the wire 'mother' to feed and then return to the cloth 'mother'. Harlow suggested that the infant monkey wanted comfort most of the time, but when hungry the monkey would feed regardless of the comfort (or lack of) provided by the 'mother'. When Harlow provided a heated wire 'mother' that would dispense milk (a mother that was warm and provided nourishment), the monkey chose the heated wire 'mother' all the time instead of clinging to the cloth 'mother' (providing comfort) then feeding from the wire 'mother' when hungry. Therefore, the infant monkey chose the 'mother' that provided warmth as well as food.

Harlow then provided the monkey with two cloth 'mothers', one that dispensed milk and one that did not. The monkey made the choice to cling to the 'mother' that could dispense milk. Therefore, the infant monkey chose a 'mother' that provided comfort and nourishment. Harlow reasoned that the infant monkey needed warmth and comfort over and above their desire for feeding (as shown by their preference to cling to the cloth 'mother'), but ultimately the monkey preferred a 'mother' that provided warmth and comfort as well as nourishment.

Evaluation

Harlow's research changed advice given to parents dramatically. Rather than advising mothers that caring for the child revolves purely around feeding the infant, new mothers were encouraged to pick up and cuddle their babies when they cried. Harlow's theory suggests that infants have many survival-related needs – warmth and comfort are just as necessary as nourishment. Harlow's studies show us that mothering is not just about feeding but about providing warmth and security. Harlow argues for a hierarchy of needs that is demonstrated by the choices made by the monkeys – specifically that a mother providing warmth, comfort and nourishment is better than one who provides just nourishment.

So do we form social relationships and attachments to others purely because we have biological needs? If we do, does that suggest that we are born with the ability to form attachments and have thus inherited this ability because it has evolutionary or survival value? The scientists who subscribe to ethological theories would suggest that our ability to form attachments has evolutionary or survival value. The next section describes these theories and relates them to the notion of a critical period.

Quick test

1. Define synchrony and attachment.

2. How is synchrony different to attachment?

3. Describe and contrast early theorists' views on the development of attachment.

4. Why is Harlow's work important in helping us to understand the complex needs of the infant?

Section 2

Ethological theories of attachment and the critical period

Remember this crucial concept? **Survival value**: any activity or provision that provides us with warmth, food, air, water and security is said to have survival value – it encourages the survival of an individual or group.

Ethological theories

Konrad Lorenz (1903–1989)

Konrad Lorenz could be described as the founder of applying ethological theories to the development of attachments. Lorenz observed a number of species in their natural habitat and noticed that young goslings would follow almost any moving object – their mothers, a duck or even a human being (see Figure 6.2). Lorenz considered this behaviour to be an innate or instinctual form of learning which he called **imprinting**. Imprinting has survival value.

CRUCIAL CONCEPT

Imprinting is a form of learning in which the young of certain species, in this case the young goslings, follow and become attached to moving objects.

Figure 6.2 Goslings imprinted on Konrad Lorenz

Lorenz argued that imprinting had three main characteristics:

- It was **automatic**. The following behaviour did not need to be learnt, it appeared to be instinctual.
- It occurred within a very short time after birth or hatching, a time Lorenz called a **critical period**. During this critical period the young of certain species will follow anything that moves.
- The attachment that developed was **irreversible**. Once the goslings had chosen to follow something, they would always follow that something whether it was an adult goose, a duck or a human. Once the goslings had become attached to this figure that attachment could not be broken.

Lorenz considered that imprinting was an adaptive response.

CRUCIAL CONCEPT

An **adaptive response** is something that is beneficial to the survival of the species.

The goslings had an instinctual sense to follow anything that moves because usually that figure is the mother and by following the mother the young will be led to safety, food and warmth. Thus the goslings are engaged in behaviour that has survival value.

How does Lorenz's view of attachment in goslings and certain other species relate to our understanding of attachment in humans?

Human infants do not imprint like some animals do, but what Lorenz noticed was that human infants seem to have inherited certain physical characteristics that encourage contact with other humans and encourage other humans to provide care. These characteristics are large rounded head, large forehead, large eyes and soft rounded body features. Infants have what Lorenz described as the **kewpie doll** appearance (see Figure 6.3) and this seems to encourage caring behaviours from other humans. These features are soon grown out of and the child loses this kewpie doll appearance after a couple of years. Lorenz argued that there may exist a critical period in humans too when attachments are made between a mother and her child. Lorenz argues that the physical appearance of the infant triggers caring behaviours from adults which in turn encourages attachment between the mother and her child.

Figure 6.3 Infant with 'kewpie doll' appearance

Evaluation

Lorenz's view of attachment is very much based in his observations of certain species and the behaviour they exhibit in the critical period following birth. However, as Lorenz himself pointed out, human infants do not show imprinting. Human infants take much longer to attach to humans. Lorenz's view on human attachments related to the role endearing physical aspects of the infant play in encouraging caring behaviours from adults. The infant then develops an attachment to the adult if the adult provides safety, food and warmth – three important factors of survival of the species. What is important in Lorenz's view is that once formed, an attachment cannot be broken. Therefore, once an infant has developed an attachment for their mother, the infant will always have a strong emotional relationship with their mother. However, if this notion is true, then so must the reverse be true. If a mother and child do not form an emotional bond in the critical period following birth, then Lorenz would argue that an attachment cannot be made. This is an important concept particularly so for mothers whose children are placed in intensive care following birth or who have adopted their children. Can these mothers now form an emotional bond with their children? This extremely emotive notion triggered a number of important studies.

CRUCIAL STUDIES

Crucial studies suggesting a critical period following birth for the development of strong bonds between mother and baby.

Klaus and Kennell (1976, 1982) were inspired by the theory of attachment to investigate the role of early contact and separation in mothers and babies. The mothers selected to participate in the study were split at random into two groups. Mothers in group 1 were encouraged to restrict the physical contact with their newborn baby to essential duties of care during the first three days after birth. Mothers in group 2 were encouraged to hold and carry their baby almost continuously and thus have an additional 16 hours of contact during the first three days following birth. Klaus and Kennell then kept in contact with the mothers and babies of each group for the next five years. They kept records of observations of the mother and baby at play and carried out interviews with the mother. The researchers found that those mothers who had extra contact with their babies in the first three days after birth exhibited warmer, more caring and more sensitive maternal behaviour towards their children. Klaus and Kennell claimed that these results suggest that extra mother–child contact in the very first few days of the baby's life can influence the long-term mother–child relationship.

Therefore, there is a critical period during which it is necessary for the mother to have close contact with her new-born baby. Klaus and Kennell argued that if there is no close contact between the mother and baby in this critical period then there will be problems forming an attachment between the mother and her child. The authors argue that if there are problems then the mother's ability to provide effective parenting of the child will be affected. These conclusions have major implications for mothers and their babies who have been born prematurely and needed special care at birth, babies born by caesarean section, mothers who have experienced post-natal depression, mothers who have adopted their babies and babies who have autism. In all these cases there have been obstacles placed between the mother and baby. The obstacles are physical in the case of babies born needing special care, the mother is recovering from a caesarean section or the baby is adopted. The obstacles are psychological if the mother has post-natal depression or the baby has autism.

Thus the study presented here argues for the notion that there is a critical period of time for forming a bond between mother and baby. This study also argues that attachment is related to the amount of time available for mother–baby contact. However, anecdotal evidence would suggest that babies who have had limited contact with their mothers for any reason are capable of forming attachments. Certainly children who are adopted will often demonstrate attachment for their adoptive mothers and fathers, so does this critical period truly exist?

John Bowlby (1907–1990)

Bowlby applied some of Lorenz's ideas on attachment to develop his theories of human emotional development. Bowlby was very interested in understanding the emotional attachments that humans make. He argued that in early infancy the child has a powerful, instinctual desire to attach to the primary carer (usually the mother). Initially this attachment is related to survival needs such as safety, food and warmth. However, he also recognised that the child later develops many complex emotional ties with other adults, siblings, peers and so on. The child often forms an attachment to the father, sister and brother, aunts, uncles and grandparents. Bowlby's theory of emotional development therefore criticises the notion of a critical period for forming attachments.

Bowlby called these strong ties that we feel for the special people in our lives **emotional attachments**. People who have strong emotional attachments with others sense a great deal of pleasure in their everyday dealings with these people. They also gain strength and comfort in stressful situations from being in the presence of these important others. Bowlby argued that these emotional attachments developed first with the mother and then as the needs of the infant change and become less 'mother-focused', for instance, the infant progresses from breast-feeding to eating of solids, the infant slowly develops attachments to siblings and father. Then as the infant becomes acquainted with others the infant becomes attached to other members of the extended family (aunts, uncles, cousins etc.), then to neighbours, school friends and so on.

Bowlby believed the strength of these emotional attachments was related to the strength of the child-to-mother attachment. He suggested that parent–child relationships are reciprocal. The infant becomes attached to the parent and the parents develop strong bonds to the child. The infant encourages the strong bond with the parents by sucking, clinging and cuddling, looking at the parent and trying to elicit eye contact with the parent, smiling and crying. All these behaviours are believed to be instinctual for the infant and geared towards encouraging a bond between parent and child.

In addition the parent engages in behaviours which foster attachment in the child. Bowlby noted that mothers and children who exhibited strong attachments demonstrated **synchronised routines**. The mother would play with the child when he or she was awake and alert but would recognise sleepiness and tiredness in the child and change from play to peaceful or quiet time. The mother responds to the waking and sleeping state of the child and changes her behaviour accordingly. Mothers and children who showed synchronised routines also showed signs of strong emotional attachment.

Evaluation

Bowlby's theory of emotional attachment takes into account both the role of the child in forming emotional attachments and illuminates the importance of the role of the parent in fostering these attachments. In agreement with the previously mentioned theorists, he suggests a strong instinctual predisposition for infants to develop an attachment to their primary carer (usually the mother) but considers the reciprocal nature of the parent-child relationship vital in the development of further emotional attachments. Bowlby does *not* rely on a critical period following birth for the development of attachment. By suggesting that the relationship between the infant and others is reciprocal, he is suggesting that attachment can develop over a longer period of time and with many people.

CRUCIAL STUDIES

Crucial studies suggesting **no** critical period following birth for the development of strong bonds between mother and baby.

A study conducted by Carlsson, Fagerberg, Horneman, Hwang et al. (1978) in Sweden investigated the effect of close mother-baby contact in two groups of mothers. The first group of mothers held the naked infant in her bed for one hour after delivery, there was extra contact encouraged between feeds, the mothers received extra support from nursing staff and the mothers were encouraged to breast-feed. The second group of mothers held their babies for only five minutes after birth, the mothers had limited early contact with their babies and the baby was kept in a separate crib by the mother's bed. Carlsson et al. made observations of the mother-baby interactions during the first four days in hospital and again at a six-week follow-up at home. The authors found significant differences in the mother–baby relationship between the two groups during the first four days but at six weeks following birth these differences had disappeared.

A study conducted by Svejda, Campos and Emde (1980) randomly assigned 30 lower middle class mothers to either a 'routine care' group or an 'extra contact' group during the babies' first 36 hours of life. Those mothers in the 'routine care' group were allowed a maximum of five minutes contact with the baby after delivery. The contact allowed during feeds was limited to 30 minutes. The mothers in the 'extra care' group were allowed to hold their babies skin-to-skin for 15 minutes after birth and a little later for 45 minutes. During feeding, the mothers were allowed contact with their babies for an hour and a half. Thirty-six hours after birth an interaction session and a feeding session were videotaped. Each session was scored for 28 different response measures indicating mothers' affectionate, proximity-maintaining and care-giving behaviour patterns. Svejda, Campos and Emde found that none of the response measures differed between the two groups.

Thus the studies presented here argue *against* the notion that there is a critical period for forming a bond between mother and baby. The studies also argue against attachment being related to the amount of time available for mother-baby contact following birth. These studies offer support to the anecdotal evidence that children form strong attachments to their adoptive parents even though the parents were not present during the first few months or even years of the child's life.

If we argue against the notion of a critical period for developing attachments, when then are attachments formed? Freud and Erikson argued for a development through stages where the unconscious part of the psyche, the id, was a key player. The satisfaction of the needs of the id determined whether or not you developed a good emotional relationship to your mother. Lorenz, however, considered these needs to be biological and to have survival value. The development of attachments was driven by your mother's ability to satisfy your biological needs. Harlow disputed this by showing us that infant monkeys demand warmth and comfort from their mothers as well as food. An attachment could not be made purely on the basis of satisfying your biological, survival needs. Bowlby's work showing us that we form a number of attachments through life further supported the notion that we do not form attachments based purely on biological needs. Bowlby suggested that we have the capacity to form many emotional relationships in life. How do we go about forming so many attachments? The next section of the chapter will help you understand.

Quick test

1. What is your opinion on the presence or otherwise of a critical period following birth for the formation of attachments?

2. What are the implications of a critical period for parents who adopt their children?

Section 3

Different types of attachment and how they develop

This section will show how attachments may develop and give an idea of the different types of attachment shown by infants. Schaffer and Emerson (1964) conducted a series of studies investigating how attachments may develop in the first few years of life and published their findings as a series of stages.

Stage 1: the asocial phase. The asocial phase occurs within the first six weeks of life. During this phase the infant shows no preference to parent or stranger, human or inanimate object. The baby will smile for anyone and anything, but by the end of the six weeks, the baby is smiling best and most for humans.

Stage 2: the phase of indiscriminate attachments. This phase generally occurs from approximately six weeks to six or seven months of age. During this phase the infant enjoys human company and will smile more at people. The baby shows no preference for family members and will quite happily be cuddled by anyone. Towards the end of this phase (at approximately three to six months) the infant will smile most and best for familiar people, for example the mother, father, siblings, possibly grandparents and so on.

Stage 3: the specific attachments phase. Phase 3 generally occurs when the infant is seven to nine months of age. During this phase the infant no longer cries when put down and only protests when separated from the mother. The child is demonstrating separation anxiety.

CRUCIAL CONCEPT

Separation anxiety: the infant makes fearful responses, for instance crying or clinging when the caregiver (usually the mother) attempts to leave the infant.

During this phase, the baby will try to follow the mother everywhere and not allow her out of sight. The baby has developed a mistrust of strangers and will only explore if the mother is near by. You will often see children who will peep at a stranger while holding on to and standing behind their mother. The child is demonstrating stranger anxiety.

CRUCIAL CONCEPT

Stranger anxiety: the infant makes fearful responses, for instance crying or clinging, when in the presence of strangers.

During this phase, if the mother leaves the room, the infant may become distressed and cry but when she returns the baby will smile and stop crying.

Stage 4: the phase of multiple attachments. It is during this phase that the infant may develop attachments to other people including father, siblings, grandparents and play friends and by the age of 18 months the infant may have developed attachments to five or more people.

Schaffer and Emerson's theory of stages of attachment development allows us to understand how we progress from becoming attached to our mothers to forming attachments to our fathers, brothers and sisters, family friends and grandparents. What it does not allow for is our different styles of relationship with each of these people. It took Mary Ainsworth's work published in 1978 to decipher the different relationships we have with others as an infant or child. In particular, Ainsworth's work looked at the different relationships children have with their mothers.

Security theory

Mary Ainsworth (1913–1999)

Mary Ainsworth's main contribution to our understanding of attachment and its role in the development of social relationships is **security theory**. Essentially this suggests that the infant must develop a strong attachment to his or her parents before the infant is able to feel confident in his or her ability to cope with an unfamiliar situation on their own. For example, the first day of school is often a daunting experience for a child yet some children are quite happy once they are at school and others seem very tearful.

Ainsworth suggested that if the child had developed strong attachments, the child will feel secure that their parent will return for them at the end of the day and that the child will approach school confidently. This child is said to show secure attachment.

CRUCIAL CONCEPT

Secure attachment: infants who show secure attachment will often use their mothers as a base for exploring a new environment. The infant will explore their immediate environment but always keeping the mother in sight or knowing where the mother is. The infant will venture out but will return to the mother periodically.

If the child had developed weak attachments then the child is likely to be distressed and anxious. The child is not certain whether their parent will be there for them and collect them after a period of separation. The child will feel anxious about going to school because they do not trust that the parent will be there at the end to take them home. The child will show it by becoming upset and fearful of the school environment. On the parent's return to collect the child from school the child may show an emotional reunion with the parent based on their mistrust and possibly blame the parent for deserting them. This child is demonstrating resistant attachment.

CRUCIAL CONCEPT

Resistant attachment: infants who show resistant attachment show mixed reactions to their mothers and may either approach them or push them away in an unfamiliar situation.

CRUCIAL STUDY

To test this theory, Ainsworth developed a series of studies investigating this **strange situation**. The **Baltimore study** (1969) is a series of observations investigating the reaction of infants to parent absence and return. The mother and child were asked to play in the room then the mother was asked to leave the room for a brief period of time. Sometimes a 'stranger' (an experimenter) walked into the room, stayed for a little while, then left. The parent then returned to the room and reunited with the child. The room was set up with a two-way mirror to allow observation by Ainsworth of the child's reaction to the absence and reunion with his or her mother. Ainsworth noted that when the mother was present the child investigated the playroom and toys much more than when the mother was absent or when the stranger was in the room. Ainsworth interpreted this suggesting that the presence of the mother had a reassuring effect on the child.

Although not specifically being investigated, Ainsworth noticed an interesting aspect related to this series of studies – that the children often displayed quite different reunion behaviours with the mother. Ainsworth expanded the series of studies to investigate this phenomenon further and concluded that the way a child reunited with their mother reflected the type of attachment *style* the child had with his or her mother. Ainsworth's attachment styles are indicated by the infant's reaction to mother's absence and subsequent reunion.

Secure: Some children showed signs of missing the mother when she left; when she returned, the child made efforts to reunite with the mother. Satisfied that the mother was back to stay, the child returned to playing with the toys. Mary Ainsworth called this behaviour a sign of **secure attachment**. Secure attachment is associated with **synchrony**. The mother and child had learnt to interact through **synchronous activity**.

Insecure-avoidant: If the infant shows few or no signs of missing the parent and actively ignores and avoids her upon reunion, the infant is said to show **insecure-avoidant attachment**, which is associated with poor synchrony. The mother and child have not learnt to interact through synchronous activities. Indeed, the infant who is said to show insecure-avoidant attachment is specifically rejecting behaviours that the parent uses to foster attachment such as looking and smiling.

Insecure-ambivalent: If the infant becomes distressed when the mother leaves but cannot be settled by the parent on reunion, the infant is said to show **insecure-ambivalent attachment**. The infant is expressing anger at the mother because she left. The infant is also unlikely to return to play. Insecure-ambivalent attachment is often seen when the mother is insensitive to the needs of the child and may therefore respond to the child's needs in a way that is unpredictable and unsatisfactory to the child.

Insecure-disorganised/disoriented: These infants were considered unclassifiable as they seemed to show reunion behaviours that could not be included in the other categories. The infant may react by stopping all movement in the parent's presence or changing their behaviour completely when the parent is present or absent. It is suggested that infants demonstrating this style of attachment may be fearful of their parents and either change their behaviour or stop all movement until the infant has gauged the parent's mood.

Evaluation

Ainsworth's theories of attachment and studies into styles of attachment have been ground-breaking in furthering our understanding of the development of social relation-ships. Ainsworth has employed rigid experimental techniques in the study of attachment behaviour which has allowed her to hypothesise the existence of different styles of attachment. Previous theorists have relied mainly on the observation of attachment behaviour whereas Ainsworth has scientifically tested her theories in a controlled laboratory setting. It is important to consider that a laboratory setting is not a real-life setting and one might argue that Ainsworth's findings may not reflect the experience of infants at home. However, Ainsworth's studies have been replicated in the home environment and the results remain the same, thus lending support to her work on attachment.

Quick test

1. Write down the key stages of the development of attachment.

2. What are the different styles of attachment?

Section 4

End of chapter assessment

How will you be assessed?

You will be expected to understand the importance of infant–parent synchrony and attachment in the formation of social relationships and you will need to be able to refer to the key stages in the development of attachment. You will need to be able to discuss the relative contributions of attachment theories explaining the development of social relationships and in particular you may be asked to refer specifically to one or more of the main theorists.

Question

Discuss the importance of bonding and attachment in the formation of social relationships. Will the mother–child relationship be affected if there is no physical contact during the critical period following birth?

This question relates to all three learning outcomes and tests your grasp of the main concepts, debates and research findings reported in this chapter.

Answer

This is a question in two parts, first to discuss the importance of attachments and bonds and how these develop. Second is to discuss the notion of a critical period following birth during which mother–child contact is considered essential if the mother and child are to bond and attach. Tackle the first part of the question first. To begin you will want to discuss the terms 'bonding' and 'attachment' and offer a brief description of how they differ. You will need to demonstrate the importance that attachment has in our understanding of the formation of social relationships. Here you will need to discuss the stages of attachment as described by Schaffer and Emerson (1964), how the stages act as a 'progression' from being an 'asocial' being to a social being with 'multiple attachments'.

You will then need to discuss different theorists' views on how attachment develops and what it is that triggers the infant's need for attachment. You might want to discuss this in relation to the biological/survival-need type theories such as those espoused by Freud, Harlow and Lorenz, who see attachment as performing a function (such as obtaining warmth, food, safety). Then you might want to move on to discuss the contribution of theorists such as Bowlby and Ainsworth who see the mother–baby relationship as reciprocal and satisfying a need to both attach (child-to-mother relationship) and to bond (mother-to-child relationship). You will need to be very clear and demonstrate a good understanding of the key differences between these types of theories and be able to discuss the theorists' relative contribution to our understanding of the formation of social relationships.

For the second part of your answer, you will need to demonstrate your understanding of the notion of a critical period following birth and the importance of physical contact between the mother and child. The studies reported in this chapter will help you formulate your answer to this, but you will not get marks for simply reporting studies arguing for and against this notion. To get a good mark you must critically discuss the evidence presented for both sides of the argument and formulate an opinion based on this evidence.

When you are presenting the studies as evidence for both sides of the argument you will need to make sure the reader has enough information to grasp the main points of the study. These are: participant details (numbers of, age, class etc.), methodology used (random allocation to groups, observations or interviews, period of time involved and so on), summary of main findings and then provide a brief statement of the authors' interpretation of the findings.

When you have presented the evidence for and against the statement and are ready to present your opinion, all that remains is for you to summarise the main points of the essay and present your answer to the question. This last paragraph is important and it is worth putting some thought into its structure. Go back to the question and answer each point in turn. For this example, state how important bonding and attachment are in the formation of social relationships, state what this critical period **is** following birth, briefly summarise the main findings of the studies presented to investigate this point and finally present your opinion on the validity or otherwise of mother–child physical contact during this critical period following birth on the future mother–child relationship.

Section 5

Further reading

There are a number of useful texts covering research into attachment and bonding and the role of these in the successful formulation of social relationships. Suggested texts are:

Bee, H. (1995). *The Developing Child* (7th edn.). London: Harper Collins. Chapter 11.

If you would like to read Bowlby's original work, try:

Bowlby, J. (1969). *Attachment*. London: Penguin. (This has been reprinted several times.)
Holmes, J. (1993). *John Bowlby and Attachment Theory*. New York: Routledge. Chapter 4.
Meins, E. (1997). *Security of Attachment and the Social Development of Cognition*. Hove: Psychology Press. Chapters 1 and 2.

Chapter 7
Early social development
(Rachel Gillibrand)

Chapter summary

In this chapter we are going to expand our study of social relationships. We are going to look at how we develop a sense of 'self' and 'others'. We will then focus on relationships beyond the parent-child, to include sibling relationships and friend relationships. By the end of this chapter you will know how we develop a sense of 'self'. You will know the main theories of forming social relationships with siblings and friends. You will see the contribution of work by Piaget (1952), Sullivan (1953) and Bandura and Walters (1963) to our understanding of social relationship development. You will understand the importance of play and the development of different play types. You will also be introduced to an important theory, the theory of mind (Baron-Cohen, 1995) and see how it helps us to understand why children play as they do at different ages.

Learning outcomes

After reading this chapter, you should be able to:

Outcome 1: Understand the development of self and others.
You will be able to describe how we develop a self-concept and how we learn self-recognition.

Outcome 2: Understand the importance of sibling and friend social relationships.
You will be able to describe the importance of early developments in social relationships and in particular, the role of play in this process.

Outcome 3: Understand how the key theorists' work allows us to better understand the formation of sibling and friend social relationships.
You will be able to describe, evaluate and contrast the main theories of sibling and friend social development.

Outcome 4: Understand the key types of play and the importance of these in forming social relationships with siblings and friends.
You will be able to relate the findings of key researchers to our understanding of the development of play and different play types.

The question at the end of the chapter tests you on these learning outcomes.

Section 1

The self and how it develops

We begin with a discussion of the notion of 'self' and 'self-concept'. We will look at the work of key theorists who have formulated ideas on the development of self, and look at why this notion of self is so important. This will be discussed within a developmental context.

Theories of the self and self-concept

CRUCIAL CONCEPTS

Self: the unique physical and psychological aspects of a person.
Self-concept: your own perception of your unique physical and psychological aspects.
Self-recognition: the ability to recognise yourself in a mirror, a photograph or on film.

The two key theorists in the study of the self are Charles Cooley (1902) and George Herbert Mead (1934). Both were sociologists with an interest in understanding how we go about differentiating ourselves from the mass of sensory experience that is the world we live in. Cooley and Mead argue that your self-concept comes from the social interactions you have. This self-concept develops and changes over time as your social interactions become more numerous and more complex. Cooley's notion of the self was called the **looking-glass self**. Cooley argued that a person's understanding of their self is a reflection of how other people react to him or her. The social group is therefore the 'mirror' that shows your self reflected.

Both Cooley and Mead considered the self and social development to be inextricably intertwined. Both the notion of self and your social development occur alongside each other and neither will evolve without the other. Cooley and Mead thought that infants see people and events as single parts of a continuous stream of sensory experiences. The infants as yet do not see any connection between people and events, they merely exist as part of a chaotic, noisy environment. Until the infant can distinguish him or herself from the surrounding sensory material, he or she has no sense of self. Cooley and Mead argued that without the ability to separate your thoughts and actions from those thoughts and actions of others, you have no idea that you exist as a separate entity.

Cooley and Mead suggest that when the infant develops the idea that they are separate from others the child then learns about having **interactions** with others. Thus, the people and events happening around you are not just random occurrences. These are people you need to interact with and events you can become an active player in. Following on from this, infants soon learn that certain interactions between them and other people are predictable. As an infant you learn that if you cry, you get attention and if you smile, people smile back. By learning the 'cause and effect' nature of interactions, an infant soon develops the idea that the way he or she behaves will elicit a specific response. The infant has learnt that he or she is part of a social group and has begun to develop the notion of the 'social self'.

So when does a child start to differentiate his or her self from the total sensory experience? Samuels (1986) believes that we learn the physical limits of our bodies during the first two months. Infants of this age play with their fingers and toes and demonstrate a growing awareness of the size and location of their bodies. The next logical development of this is to learn to recognise yourself and to see yourself as different to other infants.

CRUCIAL STUDY

Lewis and Brooks-Gunn (1979) asked mothers of infants aged 9–24 months to daub a little red make-up on their infants' faces before placing them in front of a mirror. Lewis and Brooks-Gunn proposed that if the infants can recognise themselves in the mirror, then they should see that there is an anomaly – the red make-up – and reach to touch it or even wipe it off. The results were interesting. The 9–14-month-old infants did not reach to touch their faces or try to wipe the make-up off. The 15–17-month-old infants showed some recognition of their faces but did not try to touch the red mark or try to wipe it off. The 18–24-month-old infants readily recognised their faces in the mirror and immediately went to touch the red mark of make-up and tried to wipe it off. The authors concluded that the infants aged 9–14 months had no self-recognition. The infants aged 15-17 months were developing self-recognition and the infants aged 18–24 months had a clear, well-developed sense of self-recognition.

As a toddler, your sense of self-recognition and the notion of the social self develop quite rapidly. As Cooley and Mead suggest, the notion of self and social development occur concurrently and as the toddler develops their sense of social self so they begin to engage in more complex interactions. Subsequently, as the child engages in more complex interactions, so they develop a more complex view of their self than their social self. Ask any child the question 'Who are you?' and their answers will be very specific about their physical and basic psychological attributes. Their answers might be 'I am a good boy' or 'I am a big girl now'. By the age of two to three years, the child is developing a sense of the 'categorical self' (Stipek, Gralinski and Kopp, 1990). The child's view of his or her self is based on age, gender and evaluations based on their physical or psychological attributes. All are considered important information to impart when asked the question 'Who are you?'. As the child gets older, the statements might become quite evaluative, e.g. 'I am bigger than my brother'. These statements are more complex considerations by the child of who he or she thinks they are and stem from a much more complex appreciation of social interaction with other children and adults.

By the time the child is three to five years of age they will be much more likely to answer the 'Who are you?' question in terms of physical and material characteristics. A four-year-old might answer, 'I have dark hair and I have a red ball'. The answer tells you what the child looks like and what toy they have. There is rarely given an answer which mentions any complex psychological attributes (Damon and Hart, 1988). Indeed, researchers used to think that children were incapable of thinking 'psychologically' about themselves for quite a long time. However, research conducted by Rebecca Eder (1989; 1990, cited in Shaffer, 1999) demonstrated that children will talk about psychological characteristics of themselves if they are asked quite specifically about them. Eder's work included asking children to make a choice between two statements. The children had to pick which statement was 'most like them'. For instance, the statements might be, 'I like to play by myself' and 'I like to play with my friends'. Eder discovered that the children were very good at choosing the statements which most reflected themselves. Eder argued that although children of this age were unlikely to make any spontaneous statement of their psychological attributes, when pressed they did seem to have a simplistic view of their psyche. The children were not able to make complex judgements of themselves (such as 'I am sociable') but could say whether they preferred to play alone or with others.

As we can see, Cooley and Mead's belief that the development of self and social development occur at the same time is supported. The evidence we have reviewed shows that the development of self and social development are complexly intertwined, that one cannot exist without the other. Section 2 of this chapter will introduce you to the development of social relationships and play. The role of these in social development will be explained. Section 3 will show you how social development and the notion of self and 'others' is connected.

Quick test

1. Describe the concept of the looking-glass self; what does this mean?

2. At what age does self-recognition seem to occur?

3. If asked the question 'Who are you?', what are the likely replies of children aged, say, from two years to five years?

Section 2

Theories of social development and the function of social relationships with siblings and friends

Theories of early social development

Sullivan's work (1953) emphasised the role of friendships in child's development. Sullivan suggested that there was a special function to these friendships. When children are born they are initially not aware of other children. The important relationship at this age is with the mother or carer. The chapter on attachments demonstrated that for the first two years of life, the child–carer bond was crucial for survival. The child learned to communicate with the parent that food, warmth and care were needed. In response, the parent learned to provide the food, warmth and care that the child required. The relationship is reciprocal. During the attachment phase, the parent and child are strongly bonded together which increases the chance of survival of the child. Thus, child-to-child relationships are not necessary, certainly at birth and for the first few months afterwards. However, once the child develops a sensitivity to or an awareness of his or her peers, the child often forms deep, long-lasting and complex relationships with other children. Sullivan argued that these early relationships with siblings and other friends start to shape the type of adult relationships the child will have in the future.

Think back to Chapter 5 when Piaget's theory of cognitive development was discussed. At different stages in childhood, the child developed a capacity for different styles of thought and other cognitive tasks. Piaget's discussion of the development of social relationships considered the role and characteristics of child-to-child relationships in contrast with the role and characteristics of the parent-to-child relationship. Piaget (1952) argued that children's relationships with adults are very different to children's relationships with other children. He suggested that the child-adult relationship was one which existed in a 'vertical dimension'. That is, the adult is an older, wiser and usually more powerful member of the relationship. The child is younger, naïve and usually a less powerful member of the relationship. As a result of this vertical dimension, Piaget argued that the main characteristics of this relationship are power assertion and dominance. The adult dominates the relationship by setting boundaries of acceptable behaviour, for example. The adult ensures that the child obeys by engaging in manipulation of their status. This could be by enforcing a system of punishments and rewards, by cajoling or commanding. Piaget suggested that the child–child relationship on the other hand exists in a 'horizontal dimension'. The children are equal to each other in terms of age, experience and power. The child-child relationship, Piaget argued, was one characterised by egalitarian practice and balance. Thus, no power struggle can be enforced by one member of the relationship, as each child has equal say. The main advantage of this type of relationship is that it creates a safe haven to allow the children to explore conflicting ideas. Hopefully, if the arguments are not too fierce, the children will learn the skills of compromise and negotiation. They will learn important skills required in the adult world.

Bandura and Walters (1963) hold a strong **social learning theory** view of the role of sibling and friend social relationships. They suggest that children learn about their social world and social norms through their interactions with peers. Thus, through engaging in play and other social activities, children interact with each other and 'pick up' on rules, boundaries and norms of behaviour whilst doing so. Bandura and Walters noticed that children learn both directly and indirectly. **Direct learning** occurs when a child is taught by another child how to play with a new toy or how to play a new group game, for example. **Indirect learning** occurs when the child observes the other children playing or engaging in other social behaviour. For instance, a child may watch a complex outdoor game in the playground and learn the rules of play. Another instance might be if a child is putting together a jigsaw, and another child or children may watch how it is done. They are learning how the pieces are put together to make a picture. Although Piaget indicated that child–child relationships are egalitarian and balanced, Bandura and Walters noticed that children can exert a tremendous amount of power in a play situation. Children will quite often reinforce or punish behaviours that they consider to be appropriate or inappropriate. By setting and abiding by the boundaries within the sphere of play, children are learning an important lesson for adulthood. They are learning to set and abide by perhaps legal, moral and social rules and norms.

The ethologists would argue that the formation of this child–child relationship by engaging in play activity is not just about preparing the child for the adult world but indeed has both a biological and evolutionary basis.

CRUCIAL CONCEPT

Ethological theory: All behaviours are limited by the biological constraints related to their adaptive evolutionary function (Rubin et al., 1998).

Thus, every behaviour that we exhibit has an evolutionary adaptive significance. So what does play have to do with evolution and subsequent successful adaptation to the modern world? By learning social boundaries and norms, children are learning how to function efficiently in a social group. A group works best in survival terms if all members are aware of the rules of behaviour governing that group. If the group splits into factions under pressure, then its effectiveness is reduced. Also, when children are at play they are forming strong friendships. With these friendships comes a sense of loyalty and of commitment. These principles are essential to encourage group cohesiveness, again strengthening the coherence of the social group.

Evaluation

The three theorists presented explaining the function of play are all quite different. Piaget extols the virtues of play based on equality of players, fairness and the lack of power struggle. He views children as all having equal status to each other. No child carries greater favour within the group at play and no child is excluded from play on the grounds of unpopularity. However, one glance at a playground or your own recollection of playground behaviour demonstrates that some children are more popular than others and some are more likely to take the lead role in a game. Children can be very competitive and equality of members of a play group is rare. Bandura and Walters recognised this and observed that the stronger members of a play group were in charge of the choice of game played. The stronger members would know the rules of that game and would ensure that the other children adhered to these rules. Piaget and Bandura and Walters shared a common assumption though, that play prepares a child for adult social life.

The ethologists, however, see play as performing an important function for social group living at any age. They value the importance of membership of a social group as a child as much as when an adult. They see groups as providing safety and protection as well as power and persuasiveness: all important concepts to ensure the survival of the species. To fully understand the role of play in childhood we need to know more about the types of play a child engages in. The next section will help you with this.

Quick test

1. What are the key differences in parent-child relationships versus child-child relationships according to Piaget?
2. What is the function of play according to social learning theorists?
3. What is the function of play according to ethologists?

Section 3

Early social development and types of play

In Chapter 6 we learnt about attachment and in Chapter 8 we will look at the development of language. Both attachment and language use were based on the parent-child relationship. As the child grows older, the number of attachments increase to include siblings, aunts and uncles, and friends. Similarly, as the child grows older, their linguistic capability develops from the use of a few sounds to the use of a few words, to using complex language. Child social development works in exactly the same way. First the child engages in simple relationships (usually mother-child). As the child grows older, these relationships develop both in complexity and in number.

During the first year of life children go from seemingly being not aware of other children to acknowledging them and making efforts to communicate with them. From birth to the age of six months the child starts to become aware of other children. They may encounter these children at home as siblings, or at a day-care unit. Towards the age of six months the child starts to take an interest in the other children and may babble and smile at them. By six months of age, the child is also starting to make sounds and is making an effort to communicate with others. From the age of six months to one year, the child starts to show a clear awareness of other children. They start to make contact with them. This might be by 'making faces' at their siblings or other children. These 'faces' communicate what the child is feeling to the others. If they are feeling sad, they will show a 'sad face' to the other children. If they are feeling happy, they will show a 'happy face' to the other children. The child at this age too will enjoy imitating the other children and can spend many an hour copying the sibling's expressions. By the age of 12 months, the child is learning to communicate emotion and has learnt the basics of being able to 'read' a basic social situation.

From the age of 12 months the child starts to engage in much more complex activities. The child might begin to engage in something called parallel play. This is where they sit with other children and play games alongside them. Their social interactions become longer and more complex. The child's social interactions start to involve verbal communication. As you remember from the chapter on language, at this stage the child is using a few simple words. The child is also developing an understanding of the notion of self. Items become 'mine' not 'yours' and parents are asked to read a story to 'me'. The child also develops an understanding of the rules of social exchange. If they say 'please' they will get what they ask for. If they take a toy from another child, they have to give it back. During this time, the child engages in a number of different play types. Play is a complex behaviour and, as with other behaviours, develops in complexity as the child grows older.

Play types

From the age of 12 months onwards the child begins to operate in much more complex interactions with his or her peers and siblings and begins to engage in play with them. Parten (1932) described six different types of play. There is parallel play, cooperative play, associative play, onlooker style, unoccupied play and solitary play. Each of these play types occurs at certain periods in a child's life and can be seen to parallel the changing cognitive abilities of the child. Parten's observations are based on the level of social interaction during play. This is different to Piaget's observations which are based on the cognitive complexity of play.

CRUCIAL CONCEPTS

In **parallel play** the children play beside each other but not with each other. They might use the same toys but the children do not interact with each other. For instance, children might sit next to each other colouring or doing simple jigsaws. They are completing the same task but not working together to achieve a goal. This form of play is very simple and is common in two-year-olds.

In **cooperative play**, the children engage in formal games. The children play together rather than side-by-side and the games have rules and boundaries. They may involve role-playing social roles (such as playing 'mummies' and daddies' or 'doctor and patient') and can develop into quite complex games. Another type of cooperative play is called constructive play. This is when children play with plastic or wooden bricks, sand or water for instance and work together to build something. Children engaged in this kind of play may be involved in anything from making sandcastles to building houses and cars out of interlocking plastic bricks. This type of play is more complex than parallel play as it involves effective communication and cooperation. It is rarely seen before the child is three years of age.

In **associative play** the children may talk to one another whilst they are playing. They may share the same materials. However, they do not take on different roles within the play or work towards completing a joint project, e.g. building a bridge. Associative play is seen when the children sit at the same table in front of a box of wooden bricks. They will be chattering to each other about what they are making, but each child will be making something unique. None of the children is making anything collaboratively. They are being social and enjoying the task but are not working together with a goal in mind. This form of play is common in four-year-olds.

The other forms of play are much less about social interaction with other children. These are play types that the child carries out on their own. One form of this type of play is 'onlooker' play.

CRUCIAL CONCEPT

Onlooker play is where the child observes other children playing but does not join in. This is commonly seen in children who are being introduced to a new game or have been introduced to a new group of children. The child does not engage with the other children until ready to take part in the game. This is different from 'unoccupied play' where the child watches the game but does not do so to learn the rules before taking part in the game. This child seems happy watching the game and is a keen observer of other children's play. The third type of sole-child play is that of solitary play where the child plays happily by themselves and is engaged in a completely different game to that of the children around them.

These are all important lessons to learn to set the child up for wider social interactions that they will encounter at school and eventually, at work. Play and social development is very much connected to the developing notion of the self. Part of this learning is demonstrated in the ability of children to feel sympathy. Our child who sees another one fall over in the playground may go up to the other child and offer them comfort. The child knows that if they fall over, they will hurt, but more interestingly, the child has also learnt that if other children fall over, they will also hurt.

The child is developing at this time a sense of the **private self** and the **public self**. The private self denotes how we feel inside and the public self denotes how we display our notion of self to others. By learning the distinction between a person having a private self and a public self the child is gaining an important understanding of the adult world. It is more complicated for the child to understand that a person may act happy on the outside but inside they might be unhappy, although they will eventually learn to do so. However, initially the child is learning that if another person is acting happy on the outside, they are also happy on the inside. This ability to read feelings by the physical expression of them is important if the child is going to be able to empathise with others. The ability of children to empathise with others is discussed in Simon Baron-Cohen's work on the theory of mind (1995).

CRUCIAL CONCEPT

Theory of mind suggests that we interpret actions in terms of beliefs, desires, intentions and emotions.

An example of theory of mind in action would be this. If you show a child a picture of an event, say a girl on a bicycle and a boy on the pavement crying and ask the child what is happening, they might say that the girl is riding a bicycle and the boy is crying because he wants a go and she will not let him on it. Alternative explanations might be that the boy is crying because it is his bike and she has stolen it from him and so on. The child infers emotions, desires, and intentions from this simple vignette in order to explain the picture. Thus, the child has learnt to infer a mental state from a visual image which allows them to explain why the behaviour occurs. This is an important ability to acquire for a child. If we were not able to infer a series of events based on key amounts of information, we would not be able to read a social situation. As we know, if we read a social situation incorrectly, we might display inappropriate behaviour. By behaving inappropriately we might be putting ourselves at risk – physically or, more likely, socially. None of us wants to feel uncomfortable at a party because we were unable to read the situational cues and see that the party was no longer fancy dress!

The child aged between 12 and 24 months is developing important social skills which correspond to the **desire stage** of theory of mind. The desire stage suggests that we understand that people have internal states or emotions which correspond to desire. The boy was crying because he wanted to ride the bicycle and could not. We can predict what people want from their internal state/emotions. So, the boy was crying because he was upset at not being able to ride the bicycle. We also understand that people will act to satisfy their desires. In our example, the boy's crying might attract the girl's attention. If she sees that he is upset that she is riding the bicycle, she may pass it over to him, for him to ride. Thus, by crying, the boy has communicated that he is not happy that the girl is riding the bicycle. He has communicated by this that he wants to ride the bicycle (otherwise he would not be upset) and his action of crying has brought about the action he wants, for the girl to hand over the bicycle and let him ride it.

By the age of three years the child has developed a much more sophisticated level of social interaction. The child's language is improving rapidly and they are learning 10 to 20 words a week. The child is engaging in cooperative play and has started to allocate a hierarchy to their friendships. Children of this age start to have 'best' friends – a status that may change from day to day. This hierarchy is an important part of childhood as it demonstrates the child is able to allocate greater importance to certain people and lesser importance to others. The child's ability to sympathise with other children's feelings expands to an ability to **empathise** with other children. The child can understand what the other child is thinking and act accordingly. An important part of this learning is that the child is also beginning to understand deception. The child might, for instance, be able to keep a birthday party a secret from a younger sibling, knowing that part of the act of surprise is that the recipient does not know that the event is about to happen.

The child's understanding of events can again be explained by theory of mind. At age three, the child enters the **belief–desire stage**. In this stage the child understands that a person has beliefs as well as desires. Thus using our example above, the boy might have a desire to ride the bicycle and may also have the belief that he is allowed to ride the bicycle. If the beliefs match the desires then the subsequent action will be aimed at resolving those desires. However, what children of this age are also beginning to understand is that someone may have a desire for something but has a conflicting belief. In our example, the boy might have the desire to ride the bicycle but has the belief that he is not allowed to ride it, perhaps as he is too small or too young to do so. As a result, the child might interpret the vignette as 'the boy, although upset because he wants to ride the bicycle, does not do so as he knows he is not allowed to ride the bicycle'. Children at age three are beginning to understand that you might not act on your desire if it goes against your beliefs. However, they do not understand yet that the beliefs may be false. In our example, the child interprets the picture as 'the boy does not ride the bicycle because he believes he is not allowed to'. However, it may be that he is not allowed to ride the bicycle on the road which is dangerous, yet the situation is occurring in the relatively safe garden. The child cannot yet make the judgement that the belief might be false.

At age four years the child engages in associative play and as a result starts to encounter conflict in his or her peer relationships. Associative play does not need cooperation between children. As long as there are sufficient play materials the children will happily work alongside each other. At age four the child is considered to be at the **representational stage** of theory of mind. The child has learnt that beliefs may be false and that someone might misrepresent a situation because of these false beliefs. In a 'pencils and sweets' test, the experimenter shows a tube of sweets to the four-year-old and asks them what is in the tube. The four-year-olds always reply 'sweets'. The experimenter then opens the tube and shows the child that what is in the tube is actually pencils. The experimenter then asks the child what they think the another child would think is in the tube. The child will always answer 'sweets'. The four-year-old knows that pencils are in the tube but can understand that another child does not know this and will assume the tube contains sweets. Compare this to the response of a three-year-old. The three-year-old will expect there to be sweets in the tube as did the four-year-old. However, the difference occurs when the experimenter asks the three-year-old what the next child will think is in the tube. The child will invariably say 'pencils'. Because the three-year-old knows there are pencils in the tube, they assume everyone knows there are pencils in the tube. The four-year-old knows that the task is about deception. They understand that we may act on our own representation of reality – which may be false – not on reality itself.

By the time the child reaches the age of six years there is a sharp increase in the amount of time they spend with their peers. Their peer groups increase in number and their peer interactions occur in a number of different situations. The child's friendships are based on shared interests and involve coordinated play. Theory of mind suggests that children at this age are engaged in **second order states**. The children understand that people may want to evoke an emotion in another person. That we might say something to make someone feel good or bad. For example, Fred wants Bill to think he has a present waiting for him at home. Fred has a desire to make Bill believe he is being rewarded. Alternatively, Susan tells Mary that no one wants to play with her. Susan has a desire to make Mary believe she is unpopular. Children of this age also develop an understanding that people sometimes say things that mean the opposite of what they want to convey. They are starting to understand sarcasm. Children of age six will understand when for instance the following story is told to them. 'Fred won the lottery, passed all his exams and got lots of presents. Fred said 'I had a really bad day.'' The child needs to be able to infer the likely belief of Fred in order to be able to appreciate the sarcasm.

From the age of seven to nine years the goal of social interaction is peer acceptance.

CRUCIAL STUDY

A study conducted by Coie, Dodge and Cappotelli, (1982) asked classrooms of children to nominate their three best friends from the class. Their findings indicated that if a child was labelled 'popular', then that child would be one who was most liked, good at starting new friendships and good at maintaining friendships. If a child was labelled 'controversial' then that child would be both one of the most liked and also one of the least liked by their peers. If a child was labelled 'neglected', that child would have been a low scorer as both least liked and most liked by their peers. 'Neglected' children were not disliked by their peers, just not rated popular by them. The authors also found that some children could be labelled 'average' which meant that they fell between the categories of 'neglected' and 'popular'. The last category a child might be considered as fulfilling the criteria for was that of 'rejected'. It is these 'rejected' children that are of most concern in a social setting. They are low scorers on the 'most liked' scale and high scorers on the 'least liked' scale. Within this group of 'rejected' children were two subcategories called 'aggressive' and 'non-aggressive'. If a child was labelled 'aggressive' he or she would be more likely to have a high incidence of behaviour problems. If a child was labelled 'non-aggressive' he or she would be more likely to be socially unskilled, withdrawn and socially anxious.

What does this mean for children within this 'rejected' category? Children who have low peer status often experience academic difficulties, truancy and, ultimately, drop out of academia altogether. Children in this category are often the target of hostility. They are rejected by their peers and both their peers and their teachers rate them as weak students. 'Rejected aggressive' children are often described by their teachers as noncompliant, troublesome and disruptive. 'Rejected' children often suffer loneliness and social dissatisfaction. However, the presence of even one quality friendship can act as an effective buffer to these negative experiences and a 'rejected' child can make a sizeable adjustment to school life.

By early adolescence, friendships are based much more on intimacy and self-disclosure. Our child, who is now a young person, may start to organise his peer groups into cliques and crowds. He may no longer view the whole school as an homogenous mass of possible friendships. Young people start to become very particular as to who is a suitable person to join their clique or crowd.

CRUCIAL CONCEPTS

Clique is a close-knit group of friends. It usually consists of three to nine members of the same sex.

Crowd is usually a larger group of friends. Membership is determined by having similar beliefs and attitudes. Members could be stereotyped by others.

Both cliques and crowds serve a function. They are safe havens of similarly-minded people where personal expression can occur but within safe boundaries and usually for the purpose of gaining the approval of your friends. Cliques tend to be smaller than crowds and soon dissolve as the members pair off into romantic or dating relationships. Crowds, with the basis in shared attitudes and reputations, are less cohesive than cliques. Although other young people may readily stereotype members of a certain crowd, membership of that crowd can be less certain than in a clique. Belonging to a crowd could allow a young person to experience a wide range of behaviours. As the crowd has many members, there are plenty of opportunities to try something new. Within the crowd, members may feel influenced to do something they do not feel happy with just to gain respect and status in that group. Any group, especially of young people, will have some level of hierarchy of members and completing certain tasks may be necessary to improve your standing within the group. However, there is also the strong likelihood that a member could meet a person with similar attitudes and beliefs with whom a romantic relationship could occur. Whereas romantic relationships tend to break up cliques, the commonality of beliefs in members of the crowd actually foster these emotionally intimate relationships. During adolescence, whichever social grouping the young person chooses, clique or crowd, the friendships they form provide an enormous amount of emotional and social support.

You have by now learnt about the role of social relationship and how we develop from having a simple attachment relationship to our parents to complex, emotionally supportive relationships with our peers.

Quick test

1. Describe Parton's view of different types of play.

2. What is theory of mind?

3. How does theory of mind explain how children make sense of social relationships?

Section 4

End of chapter assessment

How will you be assessed?

You will be expected to understand the importance of key theories in the development of the notion of self. You need to understand the importance of sibling and friend social relationships and you will need to be able to refer to the key types of play and social behaviour. You will need to be able to discuss the relative contributions of key theories in explaining the development of sibling and friend social relationships and in particular you may be asked to refer specifically to one or more of the main theorists.

Question

How does a child develop a sense of self? Relate to theories of social development.

Answer

This question is in two parts. First you are being asked to discuss what the self is and what it means to be able to distinguish self from 'others'. Secondly you are being asked to locate this discussion within the theoretical framework of social development. This will include social interactions, social relationships and social behaviour. As this chapter has focused mainly on play as an example of social behaviour, you will want to focus on play in your answer.

First, you will need to define 'self'. What does it mean to us when we think of our self? Your definition should include both the physical and psychological characteristics that make up 'you'. Then discuss why it is important that we are aware of the self. Why do we need to differentiate between our 'selves' and 'others'? What practical purpose does this distinction serve? Then use examples of where it is useful to know the difference between self and 'others'; base these on play and this will help the rest of the essay to flow logically.

Now you have set the scene with a definition and explanation of why this question is important to answer, move onto discussing self in much more detail. Begin with a discussion of Cooley and Mead's significant work on understanding the self. Why did they think it was important that we differentiate self? Think about being at the centre of a mass of sensory information and not being able to distinguish which related to us and which related to other people. What is meant by the 'looking-glass self'? We determine who we are by the way people react to us. Societal reactions act as our 'mirror' reflecting our 'selves'. Use a couple of examples to illustrate this concept. Would the counter-argument to this theory be that perhaps we are born with a sense of self? Evidence against this counter-argument would be Samuels' study (1986) about infants learning their physical boundaries at around age two months. A key study to mention would be Lewis and Brooks-Gunn's (1979) experiment where the mothers daub make-up on the infants' faces and set them in front of a mirror. Lewis and Brooks-Gunn's studies reveal a development basis to self-recognition. This again is evidence for the developmental argument for self.

With the argument geared towards a developmental basis for the self, you can move on to show how at different ages children begin to identify themselves. At age 24 months the child begins to identify themselves by their physical or psychological characteristics. Report Stipek, Gralinski and Kopp's (1990) work on the development of the self-concept in the toddler. Children describe themselves as 'I am a good boy'. They are identifying their gender and the psychological concept of being 'good'. There is very little detail in the children's statements, their identities are based on age, gender and evaluations based on their physical or psychological attributes. The children are engaged with the categorical self. Once the children enter the pre-school years (age three to five years) their descriptions of self become more complex. They evaluate themselves in physical as well as material terms. Thus, 'I have dark hair and a red ball' is typical of the type of statement you might get from a child this age. Again, little is mentioned of psychological attributes. You will want to introduce the argument here of whether children at this age are aware of their psychological attributes or not. Use Rebecca Eder's work (1989; 1990) as evidence for children being aware of their psychological traits, e.g. 'I prefer to play alone'.

With the ever-increasing complexity of the child's notion of self, you might want to return to Cooley and Mead's suggestion that self and social development go hand in hand. Now you have to turn the essay to the link between self and social development. Use the theories of Piaget, Sullivan, Bandura and Walters to support the notion that children learn a lot about themselves and about the world they live in through social interaction with siblings and peers. This supports Cooley and Mead's notion of social development being intertwined with the development of the notion of the self. Mention briefly that theory of mind allows you to explain how a child develops their ability to distinguish self and others. It also allows you to demonstrate that the ability to function in different social situations is reliant on a child's notion of self and 'others'. Then pull this paragraph together by setting the scene for the remainder of the essay. You are going to talk about social development and relate to theory of mind to demonstrate how social development is interlinked with the child's notion of self.

First, when thinking about the theorists, think about what the argument could be. Is the child–peer relationship essential for social development or does it have an evolutionary bias? Ethological theory would suggest that these relationships have an evolutionary significance. Piaget, Sullivan, Bandura and Walters would argue for the social development angle. With Piaget's theory in mind, talk about the notion of child-sibling/peer relationships as existing on a horizontal dimension rather than a vertical dimension. This allows the child freedom to explore boundaries that they might not experience with the child–adult relationship. Then discuss Sullivan's theory that children's friendships are important in shaping future adult relationships. Sullivan believed that children's friendships had a very special function. Move on next to Bandura and Walters' work suggesting that children learn directly from other children as well as indirectly. What is the importance of this ability to learn from other children? Children learn about their social world and social norms through their interactions with their peers.

At this point you might want to bring in examples of child social development from birth to say school age. What can children do at significant points in their infancy and childhood? Break the years down into significant milestones and use the child's achievements to illuminate your discussion. Talk about the role of play in these milestones. From birth to 12 months, children go from being indifferent to other children to starting to notice them. From 12 months to 24 months they start to engage with other children and become involved in social interactions. Their sense of self becomes more complex and can begin to be vocalised. From the age of three years you might want to bring in stages of theory of mind to illustrate how children's cognitive abilities are reflected in their play and also in their notion of self and of others. You will need to mention desire theory, beliefs–desire theory, representational stage and second order states. These stages of theory of mind all indicate social development and appear at quite specific age points. The essay will now be quite long and I would suggest that unless you are specifically asked, you only present a brief view of what happens from age six years. If you want to stop your discussion of social development at age six years, then tell the reader you are going to do so in your introductory paragraph.

You now need to tie this essay together. There are a few things to keep in mind. First, always relate back to the question asked. Start your concluding paragraph with a statement to the effect of you were asked to discuss the development of the notion of self and to relate this to theories of social development. Reiterate perhaps Cooley and Mead's supposition that the development of self and social development occur concurrently and cannot function in isolation. Briefly summarise the importance of knowing the self from others and make a conclusion on whether the main theorists were able to inform the development of self within the context of social development. Briefly mention that you have provided evidence that the notion of self and social development do exist in parallel. Conclude with reference to theory of mind that the two seem to be interlinked. Complete the essay with a statement reflecting your beliefs on the development of the notion of self and its connection with social development.

Section 5

Further reading

There are many books on developmental psychology which will have material covering the development of the notion of self and others and social development. Of particular interest might be:

Cicirelli, V. G. (1995). *Sibling Relationships Across the Life Span*. New York: Plenum Press.

Forrester, M. A. (1995). *Development of Young Children's Social-cognitive Skills*. Hove: L. Erlbaum.

Gauvain, M. and Cole, M. (1997). *Readings on the Development of Children* (2nd edn.). New York: W. H. Freeman.

Kleiber, D. A. (1999). *Leisure Experience and Human Development: A Dialectical Interpretation*. New York: Basic Books.

Miller, P. H. (1993). *Theories of Developmental Psychology* (3rd edn.). New York: W. H. Freeman.

Wood, D. (1998). *How Children Think and Learn* (2nd edn.). Oxford: Blackwell Publishers.

Chapter 8
Language development
(Rachel Gillibrand)

Chapter summary

One of the key stages of development is gaining the ability to form words and sentences. Communication is fundamental as it allows us to convey our wants and needs, our moods and feelings to others. This can be in a verbal form, called 'language' and in a non-verbal form. This chapter discusses the development of language and shows how our ability to talk with others has evolved into an extremely sophisticated form of communication. By the end of this chapter you will know the main theories underpinning our understanding of the acquisition and development of language. You will also be aware of the notion of a critical period following birth for language acquisition and the importance of this. This chapter will introduce you to key stages in the development of language and to the development of different styles of language including the use of metaphor and sarcasm.

Learning outcomes

After reading this chapter, you should be able to:

Outcome 1: Understand the acquisition of language.
You will be able to describe the importance of early socialisation and, in particular, the role of parents in the formation of language.

Outcome 2: Understand the key stages in the development of language and changing styles of language.
You will be able to relate the findings of key studies to our understanding of the development of language and different language styles.

Outcome 3: Define the fundamental concepts surrounding the main theories of language development.
You will be able to describe, evaluate and contrast the main theories of language development.

The question at the end of the chapter tests you on these learning outcomes.

Section 1

Language and communication and why it is important to study these

We will begin with some basic definitions of language and communication and explain why it is important to know about the development of these capacities. This chapter will then focus mainly on language. First we will briefly describe early views on language development and then explain how more recent research has had an impact on our understanding of the development of language.

What are language and communication?

Language and communication could be considered to be one and the same. However, much of our communication with others can be verbal (both written or spoken) or it can be non-verbal (for instance, body language). This chapter will focus on verbal communication or language. To clarify exactly what we mean by language, two definitions are provided here, one for communication and one for language.

CRUCIAL CONCEPTS

Communication is the process by which one organism transmits information to and influences another. (Shaffer, 1999).

Language is a small number of individually meaningless symbols (sounds, letters, gestures) that can be combined according to agreed-on rules to produce an infinite number of messages. (Shaffer, 1999).

The way we communicate verbally with other human beings can be described in four dimensions. These are:

- the creation of sounds that make up words;
- learning the understanding of those words;
- learning how to put those words together to follow an appropriate grammatical format that others understand;
- and finally, how to use those words to effectively communicate with others.

Psychologists who study language acquisition and language development use specific terms to identify these dimensions. The specific terms they use are phonology, semantics, syntax and pragmatics.

CRUCIAL CONCEPTS

Phonology is the study of how we produce meaningful sounds.
Semantics is our knowledge of word meanings and how we acquire a vocabulary.
Syntax is the grammar of our language. This is the study of how we learn the rules for combining words into meaningful sentences.
Pragmatics is the term used to describe how we use language to achieve our communicative goals. This might be for example how we use language when we want to be polite, when we want to be sarcastic and when we want to be humorous.

Psychologists who study language development might be interested in just one of these four aspects of language use or they might be interested in language as a whole. Whichever aspect of language psychologists are interested in, they will generally adopt one of the three main theoretical approaches. These are: the behaviourist approach, the nativist approach and the interactionist approach. The next section will tell you about these and demonstrate how they are applied to the learning of language.

Quick test

1. Describe the difference between communication and language.

2. What are the four key components of verbal language?

Section 2

Language development

This section will tell you how language develops from a very simple but effective method of communication to a complex, colourful communication tool.

─────────────── CRUCIAL CONCEPT ───────────────

There are five stages of language development. They are:
• Preverbal communication.
• Phonological development.
• Semantic development.
• Syntax and grammar development.
• Pragmatics development.

First you develop an ability to create sound (phonology) and later start to understand that the sounds have meaning (semantic development). Following on from this you start to put the sounds together to form small sentences (syntax and grammar development). Then much later on you begin to understand that words can be used to different effect, to be humorous or sarcastic, for example (pragmatics development).

The first stage in language development is called **preverbal** communication. At this stage the infant begins to make sounds. The infant begins to make movements when people draw near (Adamson, 1995) and starts to form different facial expressions such as joy and sadness. At 12 months, the infant responds to others by making most of the sounds and movements and begins to control the length of interaction (Schaffer, 1971). If you refer back to the chapter on early social development you will see that we talk about **synchronous activity** between infants and others. The infant holds their gaze with the parent until they break it. The infant is very much in control of the interaction. The infant at this stage mimics others and also tries to touch and point at objects (Bates, O'Connell and Shore,1987). They might point at objects they like and see if the other person seems interested (**protodeclarative** pointing) or they might point at something they want that is out of reach (**protoimperative** pointing). At this stage, the infant is learning to communicate with others but is not ready to engage in verbal behaviour. The infant's use of sounds and facial expressions demonstrates that they are beginning to learn the basics of forming language. However, their main outlet for communication is the use of facial expressions to reveal emotions and reaching and pointing at objects that are of interest to them.

The next stage of language development is that of **phonological** development. This stage occurs alongside the stage of preverbal communication from birth but extends up to the fourth year of life. During phonological development, the child has to separate out the sounds it hears and learn to recite them and to allocate them meaning. Thus when you speak to a child, first the child simply hears a babble of sound. But as the child develops, they acquire the ability to locate certain words within that babble – usually meaningful words related to 'mummy' or 'daddy' or 'lunch' or 'sleep'. It does however take a long time to distinguish sounds from within free-flowing speech. Indeed, it appears that infants do not learn to separate words within free-flowing sentences until they are 24 months of age (DeVilliers and DeVilliers, 1979). However, Jusczyk et al. (1993) think this happens earlier. Jusczyk and colleagues argue that at age 12 months infants can identify rhythm of speech in terms of intonation and pauses etc.

Although there may be some dispute about when infants can distinguish whole words from sentences of babble, before the child starts to identify individual words they begin to make a few sounds. It seems fairly certain that in their first year infants start to make sounds themselves (Ingram, 1989). In their first month the infant will nearly always make the sounds 'd' and 'n', possibly repeating them such as 'd-d-d-d-d' or 'n-n-n-n-n'. In their second month, infants begin to make the sounds 'a' and 'i'. Hoff-Ginsburg (1997) suggests that infants learn by **categorical speech perception**. This means that infants learn the sound of consonants or vowels in a categorical way – the sound either is or is not an 'n' or a 'd'. At age six months infants start to babble. They start to string together vowels and consonants sounds into what we would consider gibberish. This babble though can sound very much like a real language. Certainly by the age of 12 months, the babble that infants are making starts to resemble patterned speech – a string of vowels and consonants that sound like real words. By the time the infant has entered their second year of age they are starting to make more meaningful sounds. The words are structured very similarly and follow the order of consonant-vowel. For example, the most commonly spoken words at this time are 'bye-bye' 'ma-ma' and 'da-da'. Note that in most languages the first sounds a child can make are used as words identifying the parents. Words are nearly always based on the sounds 'ma-ma', used to indicate mother, and 'da-da' to indicate father. Whilst the child is learning to create sounds and to identify words from free-flowing sentences, the child is also developing something called **phonological awareness**. Phonological awareness is the ability to be aware of and to analyse speech sounds. At this stage, children are quite good at beginning to identify sounds that rhyme with others. Their developing phonological awareness means that if, for example, you asked a child 'What rhymes with "ma-ma"?' they will quickly respond.

Now that the child is learning to identify words from strings of sounds and are starting to make their own sounds, they need to learn the meaning of those sounds. This stage of language acquisition is called **semantic development**. Children learn their first words at about the age of 10-13 months. Generally, these words refer to important people in their lives, to familiar actions and to familiar objects (Nelson, 1973). Examples are 'ma-ma', 'da-da', 'drink', 'eat', 'cat', 'dog'. The pronunciation of these words may not be entirely accurate, but the child will use similar sounds to indicate each of these things. At the age of 12–18 months, children are learning about three new words a month (Reznick and Goldfield, 1992). By the age of 18 months, infants know about 22 words but then suddenly a 'naming explosion' occurs and infants start to acquire 10-20 words per week (Reznick and Goldfield, 1992). By the time children are six years old their vocabulary has expanded to an enormous 10,000 words and children are learning language at a rate of five new words a day (Anglin, 1993).

So how do children learn words so quickly? There are two main theories to explain semantic development: **fast-mapping** (Taylor and Gelman, 1988) and **syntactical boot-strapping** (Gleitman, 1990). First, we will look at a process called fast-mapping.

CRUCIAL CONCEPT

Fast-mapping: the process whereby a child learns the meaning of a word after only hearing it once or twice.

Children learn the meaning of some words very quickly, in a process called fast-mapping, and it seems they only have to hear a word a few times before they are competently speaking and using that word. However, if you observe a child closely, you will see that they make many mistakes. The child has often not learnt all the meanings of the word, but has allocated a very narrow meaning to it. For instance, children often exhibit something called **whole-object constraint**. When an adult points at a dog, for example, and says 'look at his tail', the child may assume that 'tail' refers to the whole animal, not just the part the parent is referring to. In some textbooks you will see errors made by whole-object constraint being referred to as overextension. Overextension refers to exactly the same process as whole-object constraint. Another error a child may make is called taxonomic constraint. When an adult, to use the same example, points at a dog and says 'look at the dog' the child may assume that the new word applies to everything smallish, furry and with four legs. A common mistake children make is to call all animals by the one name they have learnt – cats, rabbits, sheep, even horses could all be called 'dog'! The child is using a word they have learnt to apply to everything which vaguely fits the description. In some textbooks, this process is also referred to as underextension. Again, underextension refers to exactly the same process as taxonomic constraint.

CRUCIAL CONCEPTS

Whole-object constraint or **overextension**: when an adult points to something and names it, the child assumes the word applies to the whole object, not just part of it.

Taxonomic constraint or **underextension**: the new word applies for the whole range of things, e.g. 'dog' applies to all things hairy with four legs.

Children are also very good at **inferring** the meaning of a word, as shown by giving a child two objects, one of which they know the word for and one of which they do not. Ask them for the object they know, for example, 'book', and they will give it to you. Ask them for the 'microscope' and they will always give you the object that they have no name for. This strategy is called mutual-exclusivity constraint. The child knows some words for objects, but when given a new word, will identify the object for which they have no name.

CRUCIAL CONCEPT

Mutual-exclusivity constraint: the child knows some words for objects, but when given a new word, will identify the object for which they have no name.

All these three strategies show us how children learn the meaning of words for objects or nouns, but it does not account for how children learn verbs. This is where Gleitman's theory of syntactic boot-strapping (1990) comes into effect.

CRUCIAL CONCEPT

Syntactic boot-strapping: this refers to the notion that children gain information about a word by how it is used in a sentence.

For example, the verb 'to see' is used a lot with children. It is a simple verb to learn as it needs only one other noun phrase to make a complete sentence, e.g. 'see the cat'. However, if we look at the verb 'to give', we can see that its use is a lot more complicated. To use 'to give' correctly, you need to have both a noun phrase and an understanding of the notion that a receiver is necessary, e.g. 'give the cat its food'. Gleitman argued that children learn the meaning of verbs by being observers of the use of language and being encouraged to see the link between the words and an action.

Thus by using strategies such as fast-mapping and syntactic boot-strapping, children learn the meaning of words very quickly indeed. From about the age of five years, semantic development occurs very rapidly, and by the time we reach adolescence we know the meaning of approximately 30,000 words. It seems that children have a fascination with the meaning of words. By the time they enter school and are taught how to use a dictionary, children will often spend time just reading words and committing them and their meaning to memory. A large part of primary school education revolves around learning words and being tested on their spelling and meaning – a task that children are generally very adept at.

As children develop their proficiency in language use they start to use word-related humour. When children go to school they learn language use through puns and jokes. Their jokes become more sophisticated and rely on knowledge that words can sound the same and have different meanings. An example of a child's joke might be based on a pun of the word 'willy'. A popular cartoon series features a character called 'Groundskeeper Willy'. Once a child has learnt that the word 'willy' can refer to a person's name (an abbreviation of William) or to a boy's penis, they will find this connection hilarious – often to the utter distraction of the parents!

On entering adolescence, children learn the idea of metaphor. Metaphor refers to the notion that not all language use is literal. During this stage of adolescent development schools use the study of poetry and Shakespeare to encourage the development of this skill. Adolescents start to understand that a phrase such as 'Juliet is the sun' does not mean that Juliet literally *is* the sun, but that she is *like* the sun. She is radiant like the sun. At this time, adolescents develop a much greater understanding of literature and music and often develop quite a sophisticated interpretation of novels and songs.

Now we have a greater understanding of how we learn words and their meanings, we will move on to see how we learn to put those words together to form comprehensible sentences. We will now look at syntax and grammar development.

Generally, our first sentences are spoken when we are between the ages of 18 and 27 months. The sentences convey meaning but have sparse grammatical structure. For example, a child might say 'Daddy read' rather than 'Daddy, will you read to me?'. This abbreviated form of speech is known as 'telegraphic speech' (Reich, 1986).

CRUCIAL CONCEPT

Telegraphic speech has many characteristics. First, there is no past, present or future tense. Second, there is no special syntax to identify questions. Third, the sentence usually includes pronouns such as 'me' or 'you'. Fourth, possessive adjectives such as 'mine' or 'yours' are commonly spoken as well as demonstrative pronouns such as 'this' or 'that'. Lastly, the sentence uses verb particles such as 'put down' or 'take off'.

Telegraphic speech, although limited, allows children to communicate quite effectively. By uttering very simple phrases such as 'put down', the child and parent know that what is required is for Daddy to perhaps take the child from his shoulders and put her on the floor. Two simple words convey a lot of meaning.

At the age of about 27–36 months, there is a rapid expansion in the use of grammar in speech (DeVilliers and DeVilliers, 1992). Sentences become three words long and thus more sophisticated. The child starts to use modal verbs, for example, 'I will do it' and negotiations such as 'I won't do it'. Use of tenses become more prominent, for example 'I went to the party'. Children are learning to apply grammatical morphemes to sentences (Brown, 1973) and are thus learning to change the meaning of their sentences.

At 30–48 months of age the sentences are becoming much more complex and are combined in much more free-flowing speech. Certainly by the time the child enters the school years they are learning more and more about using grammar to convey messages and are learning that sentences can be constructed in different ways to offer the same meaning. One important grammatical lesson that children learn is that of the passive voice. Use of passive sentences is complicated and demonstrates a sophisticated grasp of your language. Children learn quite simple phrases initially such as 'the boy kicked the ball'. As they develop their competency, they develop the skills necessary to be able to convert the phrase into the passive voice whilst conveying exactly the same meaning. In this case, 'the ball was kicked by the boy'. The construction of the sentence is now object-verb-subject rather than in the active voice – subject-verb-object. Passive sentences are usually expressed at around age six and older.

The child is now using language very effectively. He or she has developed some understanding of words and their meanings. The child has learnt that some words sound the same but have different meanings and can use this to humorous effect. The child has also learnt how to put words together to form an active voice sentence as well as a passive voice sentence. The final skill the child needs to learn is that of reading the social situation. In English, some social situations demand the use of one certain style of language whilst in other social situations a different style of language is appropriate. For example, the language style you use to address your manager at work would be very different to the language style you might use with your friends. The ability to gauge situations for language style comes through the process of pragmatics development

———————————— CRUCIAL CONCEPT ————————————

Pragmatics refers to the ability to identify a social situation and to use the language style considered appropriate in that situation.

Before you can identify the language style appropriate for a situation you need to be able to communicate effectively first. A skill that toddlers have to learn is that of conversation. This is the first skill necessary to function well in social groups. By the age of two years, you understand that it is important to make sure the listener understands your message before continuing. By pre-school (ages two-and-a-half to five years) children will adjust their tone and rate of speech in accordance with the age of the listeners. They will exaggerate and simplify their speech when talking to younger siblings (Dunn, 1988). Pre-school children are also much better at conversing one-to-one rather than in groups. They often display a need to interrupt when lots of people are present.

Once the child has entered the school years a sense of 'say-mean distinction' develops. The child develops an understanding of the difference between what a person may say and what they may mean in their speech (Olson, Forsberg and Wise, 1994). Schoolchildren develop quite an extraordinary capability for using sarcasm. Certainly, older siblings will say something to a younger sibling in a sarcastic manner leaving the younger child confused. As the younger child has not developed an understanding of sarcasm as a communication style, they will often take what the older sibling has said quite literally. An example of this would be the older sibling saying to the younger 'Mmmm ... more sprouts for *me* John ... I just *love* them ...'. When the younger child, John, hands him the bowl of sprouts, the older sibling will often laugh and say something like 'I didn't really want them. I hate sprouts'. Not being able to pick up on the sarcastic emphasis in the sentence has placed the younger sibling at a disadvantage. However, with the 'coaching' of older siblings, the younger ones soon catch up with this type of communication style.

Communication with others is a vital part of our survival. A lot of communication concerns actions that have occurred in the past or behaviour that is about to occur in the future. Indeed, some theorists believe that language is a form of action. Speech act theory (Austin, 1962; Searle, 1969) sees language as social and cooperative. In this sense, it is important to consider the beliefs and intentions of the speaker and listener whilst communicating. Speech act theory discusses the locutionary act, the illocutionary force and the perlocutionary effect.

———————————— CRUCIAL CONCEPTS ————————————

The **locutionary act** is the act of saying something.
The **illocutionary force** is the way in which something is said.
The **perlocutionary effect** is the effect what was said has on the audience.

Both Austin (1962) and Searle (1969) argue that speech acts can be promises, assertions, denials and warnings, for example. It focuses very much on the function of language and is considered useful for understanding the development of effective communication. Grice

(2001) expanded this theory further into his notion of **conversational implicature**. Grice suggested that people use contextual information to understand what the speaker really means. So, in conversation we try to cooperate with our conversational partners. How we do this is guided by four maxims. First, there is **quantity**. The purpose of conversation is to make your contribution as informative (but not more informative) as is required for the current purpose of the conversation. Second, there is **quality**. You try to make your contribution to the conversation, one that is true. It should not be false or be something that you have no evidence for. Third there is **relevancy**: you try to make your contribution relevant to the communication exchange that is occurring. And fourth there is **manner**. This is where you try to avoid obscurity and ambiguity in your manner.

People, Grice argues, also use **non-literal** language. This is **indirect** speech. For example, if you to say to a friend 'Is that window open?', the purpose of the exchange is to get them to either close the window or to offer to turn the heating up. The listener has to infer what the speaker intends to communicate through indirect means. Grice also suggested that people use **idiomatic** speech. The English language is rich with idioms. If you had told someone's secret to another, you might be accused at a later date of 'spilling the beans'. You have not literally spilled the beans, but an idiom we use for conveying the notion that secret information has spread quickly is to liken it to spilling a sackful of beans. Again, Grice also touched on an advanced communication style, that of sarcasm. Sarcasm as we have noted before is that non-literal speech where the speaker does not say what they mean. The ability to communicate in this way develops around age six but it is not until around age 12 that most children fully understand this form of communication. Indeed some people may never fully get to grips with this form of communication.

You have by now learnt about our ability to acquire language and how we develop our language skill from using very simple words to using commands and sophisticated communication styles.

Quick test

1. What are the five stages of language development?

2. What theories are given to explain the speed at which children learn words?

3. What are the strategies 'fast-mapping' and 'syntactic boot-strapping'?

Section 3

Language acquisition

Now you understand how language develops, we shall look at three main theories of language acquisition. The three main approaches to understanding how we acquire language are the **behaviourist** view, the **nativist** view and the **interactionist** view.

--- CRUCIAL CONCEPTS ---

The **behaviourist** view is related to B. F. Skinner's and Albert Bandura's early work investigating the role of classical and operant conditioning on **learning** behaviour.

The **nativist** view is championed by Noam Chomsky and considers there to be a part of us **biologically** that is responsible for language development.

Note: Chomsky's approach does acknowledge environmental influences on the acquisition of language and could therefore be considered more an interactionist approach, by discussing the biological aspect which works in partnership with environmental stimulus.

The behaviourist view of language acquisition

The behaviourist approach to language acquisition depends very much on B.F. Skinner's work on operant conditioning (1957). Language, according to this viewpoint, is learnt as the parents selectively reinforce 'appropriate' linguistic behaviours. For example, if a child utters 'ball' when presented with a ball, the parents will reinforce that statement by encouragement, for instance they might say 'yes, that's right! A ball.' If the child does not say anything, the parents will say 'ball' and repeat the word over and again until the child has a go themself. When the child eventually says 'ball' the parents will then reinforce that statement by encouragement again – 'yes, that's right! A ball.' By positively reinforcing the child's utterances, the parents are using operant conditioning techniques to help the child acquire language.

CRUCIAL CONCEPT

Operant conditioning: a form of learning in which behaviour becomes more or less likely depending on whether it is rewarded or punished.

Albert Bandura expanded on the theory of operant conditioning enabling language acquisition to focus on observational learning. Observational learning is the process whereby you learn from watching others and copying them. Bandura suggested that children observe others (usually older siblings and parents) talking to each other and try to copy them. By watching people speak quite lengthy and complex phrases, children can observe what are quite complicated rules of discourse. If the child copies the adults and says something that is quite similar to what the adults are saying, then the parents will often reinforce the child's efforts. Again, this reinforcement could be in the form of verbal encouragement or praise. Bandura argued that by reinforcing this observational learning, the parents encourage the child to learn to copy the adult's spoken language. The child might also repeat this newly learnt material in a different setting. For instance, the child has learnt to say 'thank you for having me' after visiting a friend. When the child visits the doctor, they might repeat the same phrase. Depending on the parents' or doctor's response, the child will learn whether that phrase was the right one to use in that situation. The child is trying to apply their newly learnt language skills to a new situation but will not know how appropriate it is until they receive feedback from the others around them.

Evaluation

How useful is this approach in understanding the acquisition of language? Critics of the learning approach to language argue that learning anything in this way is time-consuming. If a child has to learn every word or phrase from his or her siblings or parents, then the child must have to hear every word or phrase. This process would take decades for the child to develop any satisfactory competence yet language acquisition and development itself actually occurs over a relatively brief period of time. Brown and Hanlon (1970) argue that parents do not just reinforce grammatically correct statements, but will also reinforce children if their utterances convey the appropriate meaning. For example, if a child was to say 'daddy read me', the parent would likely say 'would you like daddy to read to you?' or 'of course daddy will read to you.' The parent is not correcting the grammar but is saying to the child, I understand what it is you want me to do. The parent reinforces the child's language attempt by acting upon their request – reading a story to them. Both responses by the parent are very simple sentences. In Noam Chomsky's critique of Bandura's work he argued that the behaviourist approach does not account for the development of complex language. Children are generally exposed to grammatically simple language such as 'do you like this?' or 'would you like to play with the ball?'. Chomsky argued that children could not learn complex language if they were only exposed to simple language. So how do we acquire the ability to formulate complex sentences?

The nativist view of language acquisition

The nativist view of language acquisition is based on three key shared assumptions. The first is that all languages appear to have a similar structure. Although the precise word order of a sentence may vary between people speaking French, German and English, for example, there are similarities between sentence composition in all languages. Sentences, however simple or complex they might be, are composed of nouns, verbs and adjectives the world over; because of this, Chomsky argued that the ability to generate language may therefore be innate.

CRUCIAL CONCEPT

Innate: a behaviour or pattern of behaviour that is present from birth and does not need to be learned.

To follow up the notion that language may be innate, Chomsky proposed the second key assumption that children have a biological predisposition to acquire language. This suggests that all children when born have part of the brain already allocated to the ability to acquire and develop language skills. If there is such an area of the brain, then Chomsky further argued that this part of the brain could actually hold perhaps key sounds or grammar that he called the 'building blocks' of language. This notion that we are born with the building blocks of language development allowed Chomsky to theorise on the ability of children to formulate new and complex statements – regardless of whether they had heard them before. This is the third key assumption of Chomsky's theory. The learning theorists have difficulty in explaining the ability of children and adults to do this.

The part of the brain that is devoted to holding basic language structure is called the **language acquisition device**. The language acquisition device or LAD allows the child to acquire both more and complex grammatical principles for their own language, but also allows for other languages to be acquired. If, as Chomsky argues, most languages have a similar grammatical structure, then the presence of the LAD will allow the child to apply these innate grammatical principles to learning a language different to that of the mother tongue. The set of common principles held within the LAD that the child can use with other languages are called **universal grammar**. As new grammatical principles are learned, these are added to the LAD and can be applied to novel situations. Knowing these grammatical principles of language is effectively about knowing the parameters or rules of your language. Without these parameters, we could not understand each other's communications. We need to know that a sentence is constructed in a certain way to convey a certain meaning otherwise we would live in a very ambiguous world. Take the following example: if a friend came up to you and said 'Frank hit Alan', you would understand that your friend was telling you who had hit whom. The first person acts upon the second person. If, however, your friend had said 'Frank Alan hit', the sentence does not comply with your language parameters and you would not understand who had done what to whom. Language parameters enable us to make sense of the world and of each other's verbal communication.

Evaluation

What evidence is there that a language acquisition device exists in the brain? Studies of the brain involving people with damage to parts of the brain and people with no damage suggest that there is a language centre in the left cerebral hemisphere. If you have damage to the left cerebrum in one of the language areas then you tend to experience a form of aphasia.

CRUCIAL CONCEPT

Aphasia: the loss of one or more language functions.

Depending on the area affected, you might experience different language problems. For instance, damage to Broca's area (in the frontal lobe of the left hemisphere of the cerebral cortex) would affect your ability to speak rather than your ability to understand speech (Slobin, 1979), whilst damage to Wernicke's area (an area in the temporal lobe of the left hemisphere of the cerebral cortex) would affect your understanding of speech rather than your ability to speak (Shaffer, 1999). Critics of Chomsky disagree that there truly is a universal grammar common to all languages. The critics argue that the number of similarities is much lower than the number of differences between different languages. If there really is a universal grammar for all languages, then it must be very small. Thus, not only are there very few similarities between languages but the rules of language need to be learned as well. Therefore the acquisition of language cannot be purely biological. Chomsky's theory of language acquisition is, although predominantly nativist, in fact interactionist in nature. Nature works alongside environmental influences. Children have to learn grammar, they are not born with it. If Chomsky's assertion that the existence of the LAD predisposes us to acquire language rapidly, why then does it take quite so long for children to learn all the rules of their mother tongue? Children often make grammatical mistakes up until they reach the age of seven years and beyond. Thus the LAD cannot operate in isolation. Children still have to learn to speak, and a system of core capability existing at birth, which is then combined with a learning environment, seems to be more realistic. In fact, this appears to be the case. There are a number of studies that show there is a **critical period** for language acquisition, beyond which language is rarely learnt to proficiency.

CRUCIAL STUDY

Curtiss (1977) reported a case where a young girl called Genie was discovered at the age of nearly 14 years locked away in a back room of her parents' house. She had been locked away as an infant and had not been permitted to make any sounds nor been spoken to by her parents. Once rescued, Genie was given a lot of assistance to try to teach her language but even though she learnt a few words and could put them together into meaningful sentences, by no means did it come naturally to her. She had to be taught intensively to acquire proficiency in her mother tongue.

This study provides evidence for the existence of a **critical or sensitive period** for own-language acquisition, but what of learning a second language? A study reported by Johnson and Newport (1989) monitored the mastery of American English by Chinese and Korean nationals. Johnson and Newport discovered that if the Chinese or Korean nationals were of up to 10 years of age when they arrived in the USA then they soon acquired a level of proficiency in American English similar to their peers born in America. Those Chinese or Korean nationals who were aged between 11 and 39 years when they arrived in the USA showed a much worse command of American English lending support to the notion not only of a sensitive period for own language acquisition, but also for second language acquisition.

So far we have discussed the contribution of nativist (if not in actuality, pure nativist in practice) and learning approaches to our understanding of language acquisition. Each approach has its strengths and weaknesses. The biological view of language acquisition seems to need some input from the learning approach to explain the pace at which language is learnt, whilst the learning approach does not have an explanation for why we all demonstrate a tendency to express ourselves verbally. A popular third approach of psychologists interested in the development of language is the interactionist approach.

The interactionist view of language acquisition

---CRUCIAL CONCEPT---

The **interactionist** view of language acquisition suggests that there is a link between the environmental and biological factors in the process of acquiring language.

The **interactionists** stress the importance of parents as providers of social support for language acquisition in children as well as the social contexts language acquisition occurs in. A key interactionist theorist, Bruner (1983), defined this support as a language acquisition support system (LASS) and is a collection of strategies that parents use to encourage language acquisition. One technique that parents might use is scaffolding. This is where the parent pitches their language use at a level slightly higher than currently used by the child in order that the child develops a more sophisticated command of their language. An example of this would be where a child says 'Daddy read me' the parent might say 'would you like Daddy to read to you?', thus providing a more complex and more accurate version of what the child is saying. By scaffolding the child's use of English the parent is encouraging them to develop their proficiency in their language use. This way, the child learns a more accurate and more complex way of communicating with others.

Parents also introduce names for things during play. For example, a mother might pick up a toy car and say to the child 'Would you like to play with the car?'. The child sees that the object the mother has in her hand has a name, 'car'. During play, the mother will monitor the child's use of the word 'car' and correct the usage or reward appropriate usage throughout the game.

---CRUCIAL STUDY---

During play and in other interactions between parent and child, the parent might use something called **infant directed speech** also known as 'motherese' (Fernald, 1989). Parent–child verbal interactions are often characterised by the parent speaking to the infant more slowly and in a higher pitch than to older children or adults, stressing important words in the sentence. Parents using this strategy will often repeat the important words to the child and encourage them to say the word themselves.

A further strategy that parents employ to encourage language acquisition is called **expansion and recast** (Bohannon and Stanowicz, 1988). This strategy involves the parent taking the child's simplistic statement and expanding the complexity of it. For example, if a child said 'Felix eated' then the parent would say 'yes, that's right. Felix ate his dinner'. The parent using the expansion and recast strategy is adding complexity to the child's statement whilst also correcting the grammar.

Evaluation

All these strategies work towards developing the child's linguistic proficiency. Each strategy targets a key stage of language development – from naming objects to forming more complex, grammatically accurate statements. With parental involvement in this stage of a child's development, effective communication between child and parent soon becomes possible. However, there are criticisms of the interactionist approach, in particular the notion of the language acquisition support system. DeVilliers and DeVilliers (1992) argue that in real life it is rare to see a parent giving a child direct feedback on the appropriateness of their language use, and these strategies cannot be considered an essential element of the LASS. Parents do not usually have just the one child but often have several children. DeVilliers and DeVilliers suggest that if the LASS depends so highly on parental involvement in language acquisition, then surely the verbal abilities of a child in a household of say three or more children would be less than the verbal abilities of an only child. A child may receive help from older brothers and sisters, but these children may be passing on inaccurate information on the use of the language. Another critic is Hoff-Ginsberg (1997). He argues that language acquisition appears to occur at the same rate across all cultures not just those who use techniques present in LASS. Thus in some cultures there is minimal use of language acquisition strategies between parent and child whereas in others it appears to be a main focus of attention. Yet, according to Hoff-Ginsberg, all children seem to acquire the ability to communicate effectively at much the same age. So where do we go from here? Each of the theoretical approaches has strengths and weaknesses. There is evidence to back up each approach and critics who can find fault with each. Think about the different approaches and weigh up the pros and cons of each. Is there a strong biological connection? Can the biological exist without the social? This is one area of developmental psychology where a strong nature *vs.* nurture debate exists. Formulate an argument in which you advocate the use of one approach and convince the reader that you have chosen the theory that answers the question best.

Quick test

1. What are the key differences between the behaviourist view of language acquisition and the nativist view of language acquisition?

2. What evidence exists for the existence of a language acquisition device located in the brain?

3. What are the main language acquisition strategies a parent might use according to the interactionists'?

Section 4

End of chapter assessment

How will you be assessed?

You will be expected to understand the importance of both the biological argument as well as the social psychological argument in the development of language and you will need to be able to refer to the key stages in the development of language. You will need to be able to discuss the relative contributions of key theories in explaining the development of language and in particular you may be asked to refer specifically to one or more of the main theorists.

Question

Critically discuss theories of language acquisition and development.

Answer

To answer this question you first need to set the scene. How do we communicate with others and how much of that communication is verbal? You might want to talk about the purpose of language. Why is it that we talk to each other anyway and how do we go about creating a conversation? Speech act theory (Austin, 1962; Searle, 1969) will provide you with a theoretical reason for why we talk to each other. Think about what speech act theory tells us: language is a form of action and language is social and cooperative. The speaker needs to be aware of the beliefs and intentions both of him or herself and of the listeners. Speech act theory also segments conversation into three parts: the locutionary act; the illocutionary force and the perlocutionary effect. Describe these parts to the reader so they are clear on their meaning. Consider too Grice's work (2001) describing how contextual information helps the listener to understand what message the speaker is putting across. Think of the four maxims of conversational implicature: quantity; quality; relevance and manner.

Then focus the essay on verbal communication and describe the four key dimensions of language: phonetics, semantics, syntax or grammar and pragmatics. Describe what each dimension is and provide a brief simple example of each. Briefly discuss the difference between language acquisition and language development and set the plan of the essay for the reader.

You should then start to introduce theories of language acquisition. For this you need to think of behaviourist theories and nativist theories. Look at the behaviourist view of language development. Think about the focus on operant conditioning – Skinner's work (1957) and Bandura's work (1989) are a good place to start. Think about the positive aspects of each theory and also critically discuss the limitations of each theory. Do not dwell too much on language development, but you will need to consider that as a limitation of the theories.

Next move on to Chomsky's nativist view of language acquisition (1957). Talk about the language acquisition device or LAD and the notion of a universal grammar. Think about cross-cultural evidence for a universal grammar. Consider too the supposition that there is a critical period for language acquisition – think of an example to act as evidence for this. You will also want to consider Bruner's work (1983) which defines a language acquisition support system or LASS. Give examples of LASS strategies such as scaffolding or infant-directed speech as evidence for this. Again, as with the behaviourist theories, critique the nativist theories. What are the strengths and weaknesses of each? Summarise the section on language acquisition with a statement of which theory you believe is most convincing or state that the theories have equal strength, whichever your position is here.

To tackle the part of the essay on language development you need to take a similar approach. First define the different stages of language development: preverbal communication; phonological development; semantic development; syntax and grammar development; and pragmatics development. Take each stage in turn and discuss what each stage is about and talk about the key theorists in each stage. For instance, Hoff-Ginsburg (1997) has published a lot of material on phonological development, so use him here. Gleitman (1990) published on the notion of syntactic bootstrapping so talk about Gleitman's work in moderate detail. Each stage needs tackling in turn and illustrating with good examples and references to key researchers. Do not forget to include different styles of communication – the use of puns, sarcasm, metaphor and so on. These are important stages in the development of language proficiency and need to be considered in full.

Once you have considered each stage of language development, tie up the essay with an overview of the key points you have addressed. Think critically about the evidence you have provided as support for your arguments – have you persuaded the reader? Consider the implications for our future understanding of the development of language and give pointers to where future research might take us. Finally, complete the essay with a suitable conclusion.

Section 5

Further reading

The following texts might be of interest to you. They offer an insight into the field of language development in more detail than is possible in this context.

Bloom, P. (1993). *Language Acquisition: Core Readings*. New York: Harvester Wheatsheaf.

Chomsky, N. (1968). *Language and Mind*. San Diego, CA: Harcourt Brace Jovanovich.

DeVilliers, P. A. and DeVilliers, J. G. (1992). Language development. In M. H. Bornstein and M. E. Lamb (eds.), *Developmental Psychology: An Advanced Textbook* (3rd edn.). Hillsdale, NJ: Erlbaum.

Hoff-Ginsberg, E. (1997). *Language Development*. Pacific Grove, CA: Brooks/Cole.

Shaffer, D. R. (1999). *Developmental Psychology: Childhood and Adolescence*. Pacific Grove, CA: Brooks/Cole. Particularly Chapter 10.

Chapter 9
Adolescence
(Rachel Gillibrand)

Chapter summary

Everything we have covered in this book has described the psychology of child development from birth to late childhood. In this chapter we are going to move on from childhood to discuss the particular time of our lives called 'adolescence'. Adolescence is a term for a period of our lives that has only really existed from the early 1900s. Prior to that we would have simply progressed from childhood to adulthood, a transition that would have been marked by the end of schooling and the beginning of paid work. By the end of this chapter you will understand how the notion of adolescence and the adolescent has developed and been incorporated by society into a distinct developmental phase. We will look at the unique characteristics of adolescence. We will describe both the physical development and psychological development of the young person and briefly touch on important issues of adolescence such as sexuality, common psychological disorders and changing social relationships.

Learning outcomes

After reading this chapter, you should be able to:

Outcome 1: Understand the development of the period of adolescence and the adolescent.
You will be able to describe how we as a society have encouraged the development of a distinct period of adolescence and how we have created the adolescent.

Outcome 2: Understand the physical and psychological development of the young person during adolescence.
You will be able to describe the physical and psychological developmental changes in the young person during adolescence.

Outcome 3: Understand some key issues of adolescence: sexuality, common psychological disorders and changing social relationships.
You will be able to describe and evaluate some key issues of adolescence and appraise them within a developmental psychological perspective.

The question at the end of the chapter tests you on these learning outcomes.

Section 1

What is an adolescent and how has the notion of adolescence developed?

We will begin with a discussion of the notion of adolescence and the adolescent. We will look at how changes in society, in particular the industrialisation of nations, have encouraged the development of a period of adolescence. We will then look at how the adolescent has become a person with their own social and cultural values. This will be discussed within a developmental context.

Theories of adolescence and the adolescent

CRUCIAL CONCEPT

Adolescence: period of physical and psychological transition from childhood to adulthood.

Adolescence is a fairly modern construct. The term was coined by G. S. Hall in 1904 who studied the effects the changing nature of society was having on the perception of childhood and young adulthood as separate and distinct periods of human development. The most important influence of society over the last 150 years or so has been the increasing industrialisation of the way we live. No longer are people engaged in the 'cottage industry', a way of working located within the home to produce bread, wool, cloth and other commodities to sell or market. As the steam engine and other important feats of engineering began to influence the way products were made, so people changed from working from home to working within specialised manufacturing units, mills and factories. Alongside this change in manufacturing style came increasing efficiency and availability of long distance travel. People were no longer restricted to working within a few miles of their home, they could realistically travel between counties and even between countries to search for work. Both the industrialisation of manufacture and the availability of a travelling, perhaps immigrant, workforce combined to create the most important change to the structure of society in centuries. Children and young adults were no longer needed as cheap, readily available labour and the increasingly complex nature of the work demanded a highly educated workforce. In the late nineteenth century laws were passed to restrict child labour and schooling was made compulsory (Kett, 1977). As a result, young people began spending time together and developed their own 'youth culture'.

Following the Second World War there were changes in the way society viewed young people. Periods of prosperity in the 1950s presented more opportunities for young people, and society condoned an extended period of adolescence by demanding a more educationally specialised workforce (Elder, Liker and Cross, 1984). Many young people began to extend the period of time engaged in education rather than simply leaving school for work or marriage. As manufacturing and business needs have become more and more complex, so the average age at leaving school has risen. Whereas young people commonly left school at approximately 14 years of age before the Second World War, now, with the government's commitment to education, a substantial number of young people are currently staying in education to university degree level. In fact, the average age for young people to engage in adult 'real life' (such as joining the workplace and getting married) has risen to approximately 25 years of age (Hartung and Sweeney, 1991).

CRUCIAL CONCEPT

The **adolescent**: the young person engaged in the period of adolescence who is usually also experiencing puberty or sexual maturation.

Who is the adolescent? Essentially, the adolescent is partly a socio-cultural construct. The adolescent is a person engaged in the period of adolescence, and this period of adolescence is the transition time between childhood and adulthood. In the USA and Europe, adolescence is a time based on the physical changes of puberty: the transition to sexual maturity. For girls, this usually occurs in the period of time between 11 years of age to 15/16 years of age. For boys, this usually occurs from 11 years of age to 17/18 years of age. During puberty, a number of physical changes occur to bring the body from its previously child-like status to one of adult sexual maturity. Following successful completion of puberty the young person is fertile and able to procreate. For this to happen, the body increases in height, weight and overall proportions. Changes in fat/muscle composition occur. The girls' bodies start to increase the amount of fat present whilst the boys' bodies build more muscle weight. The gonads start to mature. In girls, the ovaries develop and begin to release eggs or ova and menstruation begins. In boys, the testes develop and release sperm. As this process occurs the secondary sexual characteristics develop. For girls this means the development of breasts, the broadening of the hips and the growth of pubic hair. For the boys this means the development of facial, body and pubic hair and penis growth (Tanner, 1990).

Quick test

1. How has the period of adolescence evolved in society?
2. What physical changes characterise adolescence?

Section 2

Adolescent physical and psychological development

There are two main hormones responsible for the development of a sexually mature adult. These are testosterone (a form of androgen) and oestradiol (a form of oestrogen). As with other hormones present in the body, testosterone and oestradiol have both an organising effect and an activating effect. The organising effects of testosterone and oestradiol are responsible for the growth of the body and the sexual organs. In boys testosterone manages the growth of the body and the penis. In girls oestradiol manages the growth of breasts and release of mature ova and menstruation. The activating effect of these hormones, and in particular testosterone, is primarily one of sexual arousal in both males and females. Sexual arousal is a complicated function and involves the influence of testosterone first on the cortex. Peters et al. (1988) noted that testosterone increases the activity of neurons at specific sites within the cortex. Sensory, perceptual, cognitive and emotional processing are all influenced by increasing levels of testosterone. Testosterone also acts via the hypothalamus to facilitate physical arousal. Testosterone encourages increased blood flow to the genitals resulting in penile erection for the young men and vasocongestion in the vagina for the young women. For both sexes there is increased sensitivity of the pudendal nerve which, if stimulated, induces a feeling of heightened sexual arousal and orgasm. In both men and women, their sexual interest is greatest when their levels of testosterone are highest. For men this occurs generally between the ages of 14 and 24 years. For women this can occur during puberty and following menopause.

Without testosterone, men and women experience a much reduced or non-existent sexual interest (Bancroft et al., 1983).

Interestingly, the age at which young girls reach menarche or experience their first menstruation has changed a lot over the last 150 years. In 1850, the average age at menarche was 17 years. In 1900 this had reduced to an average age at first menarche of 14½–15 years. Following the Second World War, average age at menarche in 1950 was 13½–14 years. Currently, the average age at menarche is now 12–13 years (Tanner, 1990). But why is this? If puberty is determined by an increase in hormones responsible for sexual maturation, why should puberty be occurring earlier and earlier? This trend for earlier menarche has been demonstrated in all industrialised societies over the past 150 years whilst non-industrialised societies have shown a much more stable pubertal age. However, non-industrialised societies that are becoming more prosperous are also starting to show this trend towards earlier menarche.

A number of theories have been put forward to explain this trend, most notable is that of increasing quality of nutrition and better medical care (Tanner, 1990). There is evidence that taller, fitter, well-nourished girls begin to menstruate earlier (Graber, Brooks-Gunn, Paikoff and Warren, 1994). Although good diet and exercise seem to predict good health and thus earlier menstruation, there is also evidence that girls who engage in ballet, gymnastics and athletics at an advanced level menstruate later than their counterparts (Hopwood et al., 1990). Therefore, moderate levels of fitness reduce the age at which a young woman experiences menarche whilst extreme levels of fitness seem to delay the age at which a woman experiences menarche.

CRUCIAL STUDY

A study by Talpade and Talpade (2001) focused on early puberty occurring in African-American girls. The authors looked at 20 girls aged 5–7 years and 28 women aged 70–85 years. The diets of each group were compared. The older African-American women recalled eating two meals a day whilst the young girls were eating at least three meals a day. The young girls were also eating more fruit, bread and grains, vegetables, meat and milk than the older African-American women had at their age. The authors conclude that the different diet consumed by the young African-American girls accounted at least partly, for their experience of early signs of puberty.

Adolescence is a period of immense physical change and with that change comes a lot of psychological adjustment. Young women and young men are sensitive to the bodily changes they are experiencing and the onset of puberty can be a difficult time for them. For young women in particular, the onset of puberty is usually most distinctly defined by menarche, the first menstruation. Typically, most young women are informed about menstruation. They may be told by teachers in school or by parents at home. Many may read about menstruation in young women's magazines or hear about it from older siblings and friends. First menstruation is rarely a traumatic event to teenage girls, although it may still come as a surprise to many of them (Brooks-Gunn, 1988b). For teenage boys, their first ejaculation may also come as a surprise. Most young men are aware that ejaculations will occur from the penis, but few are told of what to expect by their teachers or parents, from magazines and their friends (Gaddis and Brooks-Gunn, 1985, cited in Berk, 1998). Young men are much less likely to tell their friends about their first ejaculation than young women are to tell their friends about menarche (Brooks-Gunn et al., 1986). As a result, young men have much less social support for the period of puberty than do young women.

The timing of puberty relative to your peers can have quite an effect on your sense of well-being. Young men who mature earlier than their peers are considered confident, independent and more physically attractive than their later maturing peers. Early maturing boys are also more likely to do well at school academically and athletically (Brooks-Gunn, 1988a). For young women however, the reverse seems to be true. Early maturing girls have worse self-esteem and seem less popular. They can appear depressed and lonely and are unlikely to do well at school during this time. The young women who matured later are seen to be much more popular with their peers and are rated much more physically attractive than their early maturing peers (Ge, Conger and Elder, 1996).

Evaluation

Physical attractiveness is an important issue at stake here. The young men who mature earlier are considered more physically attractive than their peers whilst the young women who mature later are considered more physically attractive than their peers. The feeling that you are physically attractive could account for the young person's self-confidence and hence their popularity. But why are physically more mature men considered more attractive than their less mature peers, whilst the physically immature women are considered more attractive? The answer could lie in our society's notion of beauty and attractiveness. If you are a man and are used as a model in an advertising campaign, you are more likely to be chosen if you have a rugged, muscular physique. The early maturing boy resembles that ideal. However, if you look at advertising campaigns with women as models, you will see that youth and beauty are the overwhelming messages being conveyed. The look is more of a pre-pubescent woman than a post-pubescent woman. Our early maturing woman does not fit the ideal notion of beauty conveyed. Youth and its connection to beauty has long been idolised in women in our society and there are arguments which suggest that the early maturing young woman's dissatisfaction with herself and her low self-confidence could be related to the idealised woman she sees in all forms of media (Alsaker, 1995). This finding is also supported by work by Hermes and Keel (2003). Hermes and Keel's study investigated the influence early puberty had on young women's awareness of and internalisation of this 'thin ideal'.

CRUCIAL CONCEPT

Internalisation is a term used by clinical psychologists to describe the learning (of values or attitudes etc.) that is incorporated within yourself. In this case, internalisation of the 'thin ideal' would mean that you absolutely believed that the 'thin ideal' was something you would want to try to be.

Hermes and Keel's study found that those young girls who were experiencing early puberty were more likely to have internalised the thin ideal. These girls too were more likely to show patterns of disordered eating, restricting their eating with the goal of losing weight.

Therefore, experiencing early puberty can be psychologically harmful for young women. It places them at a much greater risk of personal dissatisfaction, low self-confidence and internalisation of the 'thin ideal'. However, with the global trend being that women now are much more likely to experience menarche by age 12 years, are there any physical health implications for early puberty? A study conducted by Lavelle (1994) investigated the physical health of 1,578 women born between 1890 and 1950 who completed the Tecumseh Community Health Surveys. Lavelle found that women who experienced early menarche were significantly heavier and fatter than their 'normal-time' menarche counterparts. These women were subsequently more at risk of obesity-related diseases such as type 2 diabetes and coronary heart disease as well as breast cancer.

There are also important long-term psychological implications for the women experiencing early puberty. Young women who experience early puberty are more likely to experience psychopathology in the form of internalising symptoms and disorders (Hayward et al., 1997). Early sexually maturing women are also more likely to develop bulimic-type eating patterns.

CRUCIAL STUDY

A study by Kaltiala-Heino, Rimpela, Rissanen and Rantaneu (2001) looked at the pubertal experience of 19,321 boys and 19,196 girls aged 14–16 years. The authors' study concluded that girls who experienced early menarche, early sexual experiences and who were slightly older at the time of the study were more likely to express bulimic-type symptoms. Interestingly, boys experiencing early sexual maturation were **less likely** to express bulimic-type eating problems, although those experiencing early sexual experiences were more likely to have bulimic-type eating problems.

The Kaltiala-Heino study is supported by work by Stice, Presnell and Bearman (2001). The authors investigated the extent to which early menarche played a part in some psychological problems in 496 young women. Those young women who had experienced early menarche (typically before the age of 11½ years) were more likely to report worse depressive symptoms, substance abuse and psychological disorders than their later-maturing peers.

To summarise what we have learnt so far, adolescence is a time of physical and psychological change. As a distinct period of life it tends to occur during puberty, a time where the body physically changes from a child to one of a sexually mature adult. The timing of puberty relative to one's peers, however, has different psychological effects for young men and women. Evidence suggests that young men benefit from early sexual maturation. The young man who is physically developing ahead of most of his peers is considered confident and more physically attractive. In contrast, the young woman who experiences early menarche has less self-confidence and is more at risk for psychopathology than her later-maturing peers. The long-term effects of early maturation seem to be less obvious for the young men; however, for young women, the long-term effects can be much more significant. Evidence suggests that the early-maturing woman is at increased risk of long-term psychopathology (depression and bulimic-type eating problems in particular) and long-term chronic health problems such as diabetes and coronary heart disease. The next section of this chapter will look at three main areas of change experienced by adolescents. These are changes in adolescent sexuality, cognitive development and social relationships.

Quick test

1. What are the two main hormones responsible for puberty?

2. What is their effect on the body?

3. What are the implications of experiencing early onset of puberty in relation to your peers?

Section 3

Adolescent sexuality, cognitive and social development and social relationships

Now you know a little of the biology of puberty, this section will describe different aspects of adolescent life. First we will discuss adolescent sexuality and how that develops in relation to puberty. Then we will look at cognitive and social development during the period of puberty. Finally, we will discuss the development of social relationships during puberty and beyond.

Adolescent sexuality

Romantic and sexual behaviour in young people usually starts to occur when the young men are aged 14–15 years and the women are aged 13–14 years. It seems to be very much related to physical maturity. Those young people experiencing early puberty are more likely to engage in romantic relationships at an earlier age than their later-maturing peers. Often, however, these early relationships are based on stereotyped ritual patterns of behaviour. The young people have what looks on the surface like an adult romantic relationship but often report very little emotional intimacy (Simmons and Blyth, 1987). Sexual behaviour, like most behaviours, follows a developmental pattern. The first sexual behaviour most young people engage in is masturbation. Boys tend to begin to masturbate at an earlier age and report more frequent masturbation than do girls. Hass (1979) reported that two thirds of young men aged 16–19 years reported masturbating once or more times a week on average compared with only half the young women reporting similar masturbation frequency. By the time young people have matured sexually, they are beginning to consider relationships of a sexual nature. The average age that young men have full sexual intercourse is 15½ years, and for young women it is 16 years of age (Janus and Janus, 1993). The type of sexual encounter differs for young men and young women. Only one third of young men report repeating that sexual encounter with their first partner. In contrast, two thirds of young women report having many repeats with their first partner (Simon et al., 1972). The psychological experience of young people also varies by gender. Young men are more likely to experience positive feelings and receive positive reactions from their friends. Young women are much more likely to experience mixed feelings and to receive a mixed reaction from their friends (Carns, 1973). Interestingly, there are two times of the year when young people are more likely to become sexually active! A phenomenon called the **seasonality of sexual debut** has been reported by Levin, Xu and Bartkowski (2002). The authors used data from the National Longitudinal Study of Adolescent Health to investigate whether there were particular times during the year when young people were more likely to have first sexual intercourse. Levin, Xu and Bartkowski found that there were two peaks. Young people were more likely to have first sexual intercourse in the early summer months, a phenomenon called the 'summer effect'. Later in the year, young people who were romantically involved in relationships were more likely to have first sexual intercourse in December, a phenomenon called the 'holiday season effect'. The authors conclude that first intercourse during summertime was more likely to occur between non-romantic partners. For romantic partners, first intercourse was more likely to occur during December.

None of these studies, however, investigated what factors, if any, might predict which young people are at risk from unsafe sexual practice or why young people might abstain from sexual behaviour. Adolescents who are sexually active often do not use contraception or protection in the form of condoms. Indeed, 75% of sexually transmitted infections are seen in young people (Steinberg and Belsky, 1991). However, not all young people are sexually active and not all sexually active young people are experiencing sexually transmitted infections or unwanted pregnancy. The following studies provide evidence that attending school is a protective factor for sexually risky behaviour in young people.

CRUCIAL STUDY

A national survey conducted in Sweden provides evidence that longer periods of schooling have a health protective effect on young people. The study describes the sexual behaviour of 896 17-year-old young men (Edgardh, 2002). The group of young men was split into those who still attended school and those who did not. The findings were interesting and showed quite dramatic differences between the two groups: 54% of the young men still at school had experienced sexual intercourse compared with 74% of the non-attenders. Non-attenders at school were three times more likely to have incurred a sexually transmitted infection during sexual intercourse. They were also three times more likely to report partner's unwanted pregnancy occurring as a result of sexual intercourse. Irrespective of attendance at school, those young men who experienced early puberty were more likely to have first sexual intercourse at an earlier age and to experience more sexual partners. However, non-attendance at school indicated that the young man was at greater risk of infections and unwanted pregnancy in their partner.

This finding is supported by other research. A study conducted by Schvanveveldt, Miller, Berry and Lee (2001) has also uncovered a link between educational attainment and sexual activity. This was a longitudinal study conducted over 11 years. The authors found that those young people who had lower educational goals (did not expect to complete more than a standard level of education) were more likely to become sexually active at a younger age. Those young people who did become sexually active at a younger age than their peers also experienced a further reduction in academic goals and achievement. This study provides evidence that early sexual activity is associated with previous low educational expectations. It also suggests that early sexual activity results in a further lowering of those already low educational expectations.

Of course, not all sexual activity is heterosexual in nature. A lot of research has focused on unwanted pregnancy as a risk of adolescent sexual activity and all current health promotion material is geared towards this risk associated with heterosexual activity. However, unwanted pregnancy is not a factor implicated in homosexual activity, and sex education in schools and in adolescent-focused media often disregards homosexuality as a choice of sexual behaviour. Yet homosexual activity is fairly common in young people. It most often occurs before the age of 15 years and is most commonly reported by young men (Hass, 1979). Around 15% of young men and 10% of young women report homosexual contact in adolescence. However, only 3% of men and 2% of women report ongoing homosexual contact (Chilman, 1979). This suggests that a number of adolescents engage in homosexual contact as part of their drive to understand who they are. To call this period one of 'experimentation' seems to negate the positive aspects of homosexual activity that the young people may experience, but statistically few young people continue the contact (Hass, 1979). In particular, the low numbers of women continuing homosexual contact is surprising given the burgeoning level of acceptance of female homosexuality.

There are a number of theories of homosexuality, which we will touch on very briefly here. There is an argument that we decide to treat babies of each gender in a specific way and rear them to be 'girls' or 'boys'. During puberty the girls and boys become women and men and display their socially learned gender characteristics. However, anthropologists studying cultures in the Dominican Republic came across a sub-group called the Guevodoces. These were young people who were genetically male but as babies displayed the external genitals of a female. These children were raised as girls but at puberty testosterone was released and their bodies took on a more masculine appearance, their male genitals developed and they acted like boys. What is happening here? The male sexual maturation hormones are overriding the social learning process. The children who were raised as girls, taught to behave like girls and dressed as girls became boys as soon as puberty began. This suggests that gender characteristics are very much determined by gender-specific sexual maturation hormones. Perhaps gender is not so completely the social construct we have always thought it was.

There is evidence to suggest that testosterone has a large part to play in sexual orientation. If male animals are castrated they start to demonstrate same-sex preferences. If female animals receive injections of large doses of testosterone, they too will start to demonstrate same-sex preferences (Adkins-Regan, 1988). However, in humans there does not seem to be any obvious difference between the testosterone levels in either heterosexual or homosexual men or women. Indeed, even identical twins may not necessarily share the same sexual orientation. One may be heterosexual in her choice of partner and one may be homosexual in her choice of partner (Bailey and Bell, 1993).

Evaluation

During adolescence, the young person undergoes physical sexual maturation and develops a sense of sexuality. The young person begins to have romantic relationships and has to make decisions regarding their sexual behaviour. They have to decide what level of sexual risk behaviour is acceptable, a factor which appears to be influenced by their educational status and goals. A moderate proportion of young people engage in both homosexual and heterosexual acts but only 3% of young men and 2% of young women continue with homosexual contact. Social learning theory might suggest you learn your gender roles by the way you are brought up. The experience of the Guevodoces would suggest otherwise, that gender is hormonally driven. However, evidence from biological studies shows no heightened levels of testosterone in homosexual women or reduced levels of testosterone in homosexual men. Indeed, the results of twin studies reveal that people with identical genetic make-up can display very different sexual partner preferences. During adolescence, the young person also undergoes a number of cognitive and social developments. The next section will help you understand these.

Cognitive and social development

According to Piaget, young people develop the ability to think in abstract terms from the age of 11 years. This stage of cognitive development is called the formal operations stage.

─── CRUCIAL CONCEPT ───

Formal operations stage: the young person looks at situations, sees all possible outcomes and solves them by process of logical elimination. The young person can also think about abstract terms such as justice and peace or use symbols instead of numbers to solve mathematical problems.

During the formal operations stage the young person develops hypothetico-deductive reasoning and propositional thought. Hypothetico-deductive reasoning is the ability to solve problems in a specific way. Our young person may look at a situation and develop a general theory or hypothesis about why it has occurred. They might then weigh up all the possible reasons why this situation has occurred to then deduce how the outcome might be affected. The young person then will apply these hypotheses and see what the outcome actually is in the real world. By this process, the young person is developing the ability to look at events and consider a number of possible reasons for them occurring. For instance, a young person engaged in the formal operations stage might view a news report of a break-out of war in a region. They might form hypotheses explaining why war has occurred and have views on possible outcomes. By keeping up to date with news reports, the young person will see how the outcome of war is affected by certain actions and develop a personal view on the causes of war. During this stage, the young person is using unique cognitive skills. They are starting to solve problems by using possibilities to test realities. Children who have not engaged in the formal operations stage of cognitive processing are unable to do this.

The second characteristic of the formal operations stage of cognitive development is propositional thought. The young person develops an ability to evaluate logic without needing real-life example to back it up. For instance, the young person might develop the skills needed in mathematics to use symbols in place of numbers. They might also develop the ability to deduce truth from logical statements. For example, if Steve is taller than Carole and Kim is taller than Steve, who is the shortest person in the group? Children engaged in the concrete operations stage will not be able to do this task, but adolescents who have entered the formal operations stage of cognitive development will find this task relatively easy. Young people also develop an interest in philosophical discussions about abstract concepts such as truth and justice. Developing the ability of propositional thought is important for young people to be able to consider non-concrete concepts.

Evaluation

Although Piaget considered progression to the formal operations stage of cognitive development to be achieved by all, this just is not the case. Think about yourself, how able are you at logic puzzles or philosophical discussions? Are you better or worse at these tasks than your friends? A study by Keating (1979) indicated that only 40–60% of college students consistently use formal logic – which means that 40–60% of college students regularly fail Piaget's operational problems!

A key aspect of adolescence is something called adolescent egocentrism. The adolescent develops a crushing preoccupation with him or herself, a process that may involve abstract thought but is not necessarily open to formal reasoning. There is no evidence that young people are the centre of attention, but adolescents certainly feel they are. This over-whelming feeling encourages the adolescent to go to extreme lengths not to be embarrassed. This usually involves dressing the same as your peers, wearing your hair the same way and behaving in the same way.

> ──────────── CRUCIAL CONCEPT ────────────
>
> **Adolescent egocentrism**: the adolescent's preoccupation with himself or herself. This is likened to being on a permanent social stage where the adolescent is the focus of attention.

During adolescence, a number of changes occur in the adolescent's self-concept. It becomes more complex and differentiated. The young person begins to focus more on others' opinions. During early adolescence there is usually a drop in self-esteem as the young person's egocentrism makes them 'hyper-aware' of others' opinions. It suddenly becomes very important to look a certain way, to wear certain clothes, to style your hair in a particular fashion – even if you are just popping around to the shops for a pint of milk! This fall in self-esteem does, however, soon recover and self-esteem becomes generally stable (Simmons and Blythe, 1987).

Alongside the changes in self-esteem that occur during adolescence comes a period of identity searching. It is during adolescence that Erikson described the identity *vs.* identity-diffusion stage of development. Forming an identity is vital if the young person is to know who they are, what they value and what they want out of life. To successfully develop a strong sense of identity, Erikson argued that you need to successfully complete all the previous stages of social development. For instance, without developing a strong sense of trust, you are unlikely to find ideologies that you can believe in. If you have little autonomy then you are unlikely to be able to search out who you are and what you value from the mass of information around you. However, achieving success at the identity stage does not just involve successful completion of previous stages but also involves something called an identity crisis. During their identity crisis, the adolescent has to go through a temporary period of identity confusion before they are able to make choices on values and goals. The adolescent has to make active choices that involve narrowing their life options. This is a process of experimentation that may continue to adulthood.

Evaluation

This period of adjustment may depend on the timing of physical maturation. If the young person experiences early or late maturation relative to their peers then the adolescent may develop a strong sense of self-consciousness. In particular, young women who experience discordant sexual maturation often have the most problems with self-consciousness. There are also strong gender-role pressures on young people. Young women may feel they have to be sexually attractive and young men may feel they have to be independent and strong.

This need to fulfil certain gender roles may lead to conflict with other demands such as academic achievement (Stattin and Magnusson, 1990).

Therefore, the period of adolescence is a time of cognitive development. The young person is engaged in developing formal operational thought processes (Piaget, 1952). They are developing the ability to use hypothetical concepts to understand and predict the world and the ability to use and understand logic and abstract thought processes. The young person is also engaged in developing a sense of identity (Erikson, 1968). They have to decide who they are, what they value and what their life-goals are. Although this process continues into adulthood, it is during adolescence that this peaks and the young person experiences their identity crisis. As a result of these cognitive and social changes, conflict and the struggle for autonomy are key features of the adolescent's social relationships with their parents and peers. The next part of this section will help you understand this.

Social relationships

During adolescence there is a determined struggle for autonomy. Young people start to identify themselves as separate entities from their parents. This process involves de-idealising your parents and focusing on your ability to solve your own problems (Steinberg & Silverberg, 1986). This usually results in increased conflict, particularly during middle-adolescence. Young people begin to assert their independence in ways from refusing to tidy their rooms to negotiating to stay out late with their friends. Although the parents of teenagers may feel that they are no longer close to their children, most actually do not lose intimacy (Hill and Holmbeck, 1986). Indeed, those teenagers who display the most independence-seeking behaviour are often those who report being emotionally closest to their parents. In a lot of cases, most conflict tends to occur when parents do not allow for this developing autonomy (Grotevant and Cooper, 1985).

More important than parent–adolescent conflict is parent–parent conflict. To live with parents who are constantly arguing can be worse for adolescents than experiencing parental divorce. If their parents are in conflict, young men are more likely to express more aggression and delinquent behaviour than young men whose parents are not in conflict, whilst young women are more likely to display anxiety and depression than their peers whose parents do not argue (Hetherington, 1991).

Parent–parent conflict can also have an effect on the timing of puberty in young men and women. Young people who experience stress in family life, parental marital unhappiness, conflict with their mothers and rejection from their fathers throughout childhood experience earlier onset of puberty. They also experience first sexual intercourse at an earlier age. Young women are more likely to have that first sexual intercourse with a man much older than them, whilst young men are also likely to have more sexual partners than their peers from low-conflict families (Kim, Smith and Palermiti, 1997). Parental expectation can also have an influence on when adolescents start to engage in sexual behaviour. Adolescents of mothers who disapprove of sexual activity are much more likely to engage in first sexual intercourse at a later age, particularly if they feel highly connected to their mothers (Sieving, McNeely and Blum, 2000).

Whilst young people are engaged in gaining autonomy from their parents they are also placing greater emphasis on their peer or friendship groups. As mentioned in Chapter 6, adolescents tend to belong to one of two types of peer groups: the clique or the crowd. A clique is a group of about five or six young people, all the same age and sex who have similar interests and backgrounds. A crowd is a larger group of young people of both sexes with similar but also different interests and backgrounds (Steinberg and Silverberg, 1986). When an adolescent is a member of one of these two groups they will often look to that group for decisions on social matters (such as clothes, fashion and music choices) and for short-term decisions such as venue of choice for Saturday night's outing. However, the young person still looks to their parents for basic values and long-term choices. It is here that parents can impart a sense of morality and normative values, and encourage participation in education or choice of suitable career (Wintre et al., 1988).

Membership of a social group, either a clique or a crowd, serves a very important purpose. It allows the adolescent to develop a sense of identity within a safe, supportive environment. In particular, the type of groups to which young women often belong allow for self-disclosure and intimacy. Young women can, for example, express their preferences for pop idols, movie screen heroes and career choices within a group that is likely to have similar opinions. These groups allow young people to test their similarity to others and, during their period of egocentrism, provide boundaries whilst they are on their social 'stage' (Diaz and Berndt, 1982).

We have now discussed three key developmental factors in adolescence: sexual development, cognitive development and change in social relationships. We know that adolescence is related to puberty and we understand the impact non-peer synchronous onset of puberty can have on the psychological well-being of the young person. We know that the young person develops the ability to understand logic and abstract concepts. We know that adolescence is a time when the young person is searching for an identity, a process which often results in an identity crisis. We know too that young people develop an autonomy from their parents at this time, and that their relationship with their parents and their parents' relationship with each other are important for both the psychological well-being and the physical well-being of the adolescent. We also know that peer relationships are important, particularly as they provide a safe environment for identity-formation. The next section briefly touches on common psychological problems occurring in adolescence, why these psychological problems seem to occur and whether they persist into adulthood.

Quick test

1. What are the main factors influencing adolescent sexual behaviour?

2. What are the main changes in cognitive development in adolescence?

3. What are the main changes in social development throughout adolescence?

Section 4

Common psychological problems in adolescence

Although we have discussed the psychological impact of early-onset puberty in young people, we have not talked much about common psychological problems occurring in young people. Three problems will be briefly discussed here: depression and suicide, criminal behaviour and eating disorders.

Depression and suicide

Depression is a fairly common problem in adolescence. It usually stems from a sense of loss, from perhaps a lack of romantic relationship or relationship breakdown. Other causes might be family breakdown and moving house, or a blow to self-esteem such as failing tests or exams. Usually the depressive symptoms disappear in a few days but for about 3% of young people the depression is severe (Weiner, 1980). About 20–35% of young people experience some depression during puberty and 15% experience depression for long periods of time. There is a hormonal component to depression, young girls experience twice as many depressive episodes as young boys. For boys, depression is more common before puberty suggesting that higher levels of testosterone associated with puberty might provide young men with protection from depression. For girls, depression is more common after puberty. It is well documented that there is a link between the fluctuation of sex hormones during the menstrual cycle and experience of depressive symptoms (Brooks-Gunn and Petersen, 1991).

Severe depression carries with it a risk of suicidal thoughts and subsequently possible suicide attempts. In the USA, suicide is the third leading cause of death in young people, after motor vehicle accidents and murder (US Department of Health and Human Services, 1996c cited in Berk, 1998). In fact, the number of teenage suicide attempts and successful suicides has tripled over the past 30 years to one in 1000 young people attempting suicide. Interestingly, young men are four or five times more likely to succeed at suicide than young women. Considering the higher rates of depression among young women you would think that this statistic would be reversed. However, young women do make suicide attempts, but they are less successful than the young men. Young women are more likely to choose drug overdose as their method of suicide whereas young men are more likely to shoot or hang themselves. The method of choice of young women allows for revival by emergency services whereas the methods young men choose are much more rapid and effectual.

Criminal behaviour

In the USA, adolescents account for approximately one quarter of the population but constitute one third of arrests for crime. Most of the crimes involve petty theft, crimes against property and under-age drinking. Usually the young person does not commit the crimes alone but in groups of two, three or more teenagers. Often, committing the crimes is a necessary part of membership of the social group and once the adolescent becomes more independent and his peers less influential, the criminal behaviour stops. For a few, the criminal behaviour continues, but usually from late teens to adulthood the petty crimes cease.

So who commits the crimes? Currently young men are the greatest offenders, out-numbering women offenders by seven to one. Although young men from low-income and ethnic minority groups are more often arrested for crime, there is no evidence that young men from other backgrounds engage in criminal behaviour any less (Fagan, Slaughter and Hartstone, 1987). More convincing factors related to criminality are low levels of education, peer rejection and membership of groups where criminal behaviour is highly rated. Young people reared in families where conflict was common, discipline was inconsistent and parenting lacked warmth are more likely to engage in criminal behaviour (Feldman and Weinberger, 1994). Criminal behaviour is also more likely to be shown by young people who have low career goals, are isolated from their friends and engage in illegal drug use (Greenberger and Steinberg, 1986).

Eating disorders

Eating disorders are essentially the manipulation of eating habits. There are two main eating disorders shown in adolescence: anorexia nervosa and bulimia nervosa. Anorexia nervosa occurs in about 0.5% of the population and might be characterised by restricting food intake or eating then vomiting and exercising excessively. Young people with anorexia nervosa have low body weight and an intense fear of putting on weight. They might have perceptual disturbance and think they are fatter than they really are. They usually have low self-esteem but are usually very intelligent and high academic achievers. The people most at risk of anorexia nervosa are women (90% of sufferers are women) aged 16–21 years, middle class and intelligent.

Bulimia nervosa is different from anorexia. The person does not starve themselves but has episodes of rapid consumption of vast quantities of food followed by vomiting, fasting or excessive exercise to prevent weight gain. Characteristically, a person with bulimia nervosa may consume 2,000–4,000 calories of food in less than two hours in a binge (Mitchell, Hatsukami, Eckert and Pyle 1985). The binges are usually conducted in secret and can be triggered by stress and negative emotions. The person prefers being alone when eating and might be uncomfortable in social eating situations. During the binge the person feels that they are not in control, that they cannot control their food intake. After the binge the person feels ashamed at their lack of control and feels disgust and discomfort and has a fear of weight gain. This feeling of disgust and the fear of weight gain then increases the likelihood that the person will purge their food. People with bulimia nervosa will force vomiting and or take laxatives to purge their body of the vast quantities of food they have just consumed. Most people with bulimia nervosa are teenagers or young adults and, again, 90% are women. Approximately 1–2% of the population is affected (Gotesdam and Agras, 1995) and many start the binge–purge behaviour as a result of failed dieting.

As a group, young people with eating disorders are malnourished and show deficiencies in iron, vitamins, protein and high sugar levels (McGarrity, 1976). The high proportion of women with eating disorders is a reflection of their concerns over body weight and body shape. Many young women want to be thinner, whereas most young men want to be larger. However, eating disorders are related to low levels of self-esteem and are more likely to occur in young women with early onset puberty who have high levels of body dissatisfaction (Smolak, Levine and Gralen, 1993). Most young women do not go on to develop eating disorders. Only 1–3% of young women develop bulimia nervosa whilst one in 25,000 will develop anorexia nervosa (Steinberg and Levine, 1990).

To summarise this chapter, adolescence is an important time in our lives. As a result of industrialisation we have developed the capacity as a society to allow our teenagers to attend school for a much longer period of time than ever before and as a result young people are spending ever increasing amounts of time in same-age company. This has encouraged the development of youth culture and changed social expectations of young people. There are specific developmental changes that occur in adolescence. The young person develops an ability to critically evaluate information based on logic and to defend abstract notions, perhaps of justice or freedom. The young person seeks autonomy from his or her parents at this stage and works towards creating a personal identity. Sexual maturation occurs during the teen years and most young people engage in sexual activity. This sexual behaviour can bring with it a number of risk factors, especially sexually transmitted infections and unwanted pregnancy, but some adolescents cope with this step to adulthood fairly well. Young people are not just at high risk of STI's and unwanted pregnancy however, they are much more likely to experience depression and possibly suicidal thoughts. Suicidal behaviour is a common cause of death in the USA for young people, with young men more at risk of death than young women. Young people are high offenders in criminal behaviour although their acts are usually pretty minor violations of the law and the majority of young people grow out of this delinquent behaviour. Young women are, however, at high risk of developing eating disorders during their teen years, a problem that unfortunately extends into adulthood. The next section of this chapter sets you an example examination question and shows you how to go about answering it.

Quick test

1. What are the risk factors for a young person to experience depression?

2. Why do some young people engage in criminal behaviour?

3. What are eating disorders and who is most likely to experience them?

Section 5

End of chapter assessment

How will you be assessed?

You will be expected to understand how the period of adolescence developed within a changing, industrialised society and how this has created the distinct person, the adolescent. You will need to understand the changes in physical and psychological development that occur during this time and the importance of this to modern society. You need to understand the importance of sibling and friend social relationships during adolescence and how the focus changes from family relationships to friend relationships. You will also need to be aware of some key developmental issues in adolescence and be able to discuss them, perhaps with particular reference to one. You might need to refer to how a young person's sexuality develops for instance, or perhaps to refer to the development of eating disorders during adolescence.

Question

Briefly describe the historical development of the concept of adolescence. What are the key social and cognitive changes during adolescence? Discuss with reference to one psychological problem encountered by some adolescents.

Answer

This question is composed of three parts. First you are being asked to provide a quick overview of how the notion of adolescence has developed. Second you are being asked to consider the contributions of Piaget and Erikson to our understanding of adolescence. Third, you are being asked to refer your answer to one (and only one) psychological problem. We have talked about depression, delinquency and eating disorders and you might want to choose one of those areas. There is a lot of information required for this question and you will have to decide which parts of the question are worth more marks and which parts of the question are worth only a few marks. A clue to this is present in the way the question is written. It starts with 'Briefly describe the historical development of the concept of ''adolescence'''. This suggests that you should only dedicate one or two paragraphs of your essay to this part of the question. The next part 'What are the key social and cognitive changes during adolescence?' suggests that a good portion of the essay should be devoted to answering this part of the question. The last part of the question ('Discuss with reference to one psychological problem encountered by some adolescents') suggests that you should illustrate your essay answer with studies reporting the adolescent experience of one psychological problem. Decide which problem you are going to refer to before you start writing.

The first paragraph should therefore be a general overview of adolescence, including a definition of adolescence as well as the adolescent. You should include in this paragraph a statement showing which psychological problem you are going to use throughout your essay to illustrate your answer. You should also mention that you will refer to Piaget's theory of cognitive development and Erikson's theory of social development. Now move on to the next paragraph.

Here you should describe the history of adolescence. You need to have an understanding of the role industrialisation has had to play in the changing structure of society. You need to say that this changing structure allowed for periods of extended education of the young which in turn created something new, youth culture. Talk about what it means to be a teenager in a cultural context as well as a biological context. You do not need to go in to detail about non-synchronous puberty for this essay unless you are going to need this information later when you discuss psychological problems. Remember, you do not have to relate everything you know about adolescence – always answer the question!

Now move on to Piaget's theory of cognitive development. You need to say that successful completion of previous childhood stages of cognitive development is considered necessary before the adolescent can successfully progress to the formal operations stage. Think about what a person can do during the formal operations stage. Discuss the burgeoning ability of the adolescent to think logically and abstractly. How does that reflect current education practices?

The next part of the essay will tackle Erikson's theory of social development. What does it mean to be searching for an identity? How does the young person cope with an identity crisis? Now is the time to bring in the psychological problem you have chosen. Whether you choose depression or delinquency, eating disorders or something else entirely, you must be specific and keep to this problem throughout the essay. Take depression, for example: how does this relate to social development? How might a young man or woman come to experience depressive symptoms? Think about peer acceptance, belonging to social groups, change at home, family discord and so on. All the life-events that can happen during adolescence may have a part to play in depression. Now think about cognitive development. How might this be related to depression? Think about what characterises the formal operations stage of cognitive development and relates to our understanding of the causes of depression.

When you have discussed cognitive and social development with reference to your chosen psychological disorder, it is time to conclude the essay. Always go back to the beginning of the essay and answer any questions you posed at the start. Think back to the essay question and make sure you have answered it fully. Then pull the whole essay together with a few concluding sentences.

Section 6

Further reading

A recent large-scale study of the adolescent experience has been written into a book and is well worth reading for an insight into teenage lives:

Schucksmith, J. and Hendry, L. B. (1998). *Health Issues and Adolescents: Growing Up, Speaking Out*. London: Routledge.

Review

(Rachel Gillibrand)

At the start of this book we said that to study developmental psychology is to study how we all develop from the basic raw materials of human life to happy, healthy, fully functioning adults living in a complex social world. As you now know, we begin life as a matter of a few cells and after about nine months are born into a world where all our instincts are driven towards survival. We need to eat, to be warm and to be safe and all our activities in our early years are focused on that. As we develop biologically we also develop the ability to think, to talk and to reason. We develop strong bonds with the people who care for us, and form deep, long-lasting relationships with our sisters and brothers, our aunts and uncles, our parents and grandparents. As we grow older we play with friends and family and learn rules about social living that will stay with us into adulthood. Each chapter in this book has been written to help you to understand the processes and stages of growing up from infancy to early adulthood. You should now be able to comment knowledgeably on anything from the biology of conception to birth, the formation of attachments in infancy or the development of different cognitive abilities in children. You should also be able to discuss the use of sarcasm and metaphor by adolescents, teen sexual activity or indeed the social construction of the period of adolescence.

Chapter 1 introduced you to the nature versus nurture debate. We asked the question, how much of who we are is determined by our genes (nature) or by our environment (nurture)? You were introduced to the study of genetics and know now that you are a mix of your mother's and your father's genes. Genes are our raw materials for life, they are what we start with and what influences most of our physical characteristics. However, as you also learnt from the chapter, the environment a person lives in also has an enormous effect on the adult you become. You might have the genes to be a tall person, but without the right diet and living conditions, you might not grow to be tall. Without the right environment, you cannot realise your full biological potential. So which is more important, nature or nurture?

Chapter 2 discussed in more detail how the genetic material from the mother and father is combined to form a child. Although having children might seem the most natural thing on earth, look at the dangers. For a process which is so essential for the survival of the species, it seems riddled with complications. First, there are only a very few days when a woman is fertile each month. Then the sperm have to be of sufficient quality to fertilise the woman. Next the fertilised egg has to adhere successfully to the uterine wall before the pregnancy is even viable and even then the pregnancy can be wrought with problems. The developing foetus might be bombarded with pollutants like cigarette smoke or alcohol. The mother might get an infection which could be passed on to the child and which might harm development in some way. With all the risks of conception and pregnancy taken into account, it is astonishing that so many children are born at all!

Having reached the stage of birth, Chapter 3 seeks to discover what the child is aware of. Are they surrounded by a blooming buzzing confusion of sensory information or are children born with the ability to make fundamental sense of the sensory world? Although Piaget believed children were not able to distinguish colours, shapes or objects at birth, current research suggests that they can. Not only does the parent enjoy colourful mobiles for cots and prams but the child enjoys them too! And, yes, the child recognises her mother's voice and her father's smell and loves the taste of sweet things.

One thing you are bound to have noticed if you have close contact with children, is how fast they grow. Clothes you bought for your child last month are already looking a little small and shoes that you thought would last a school term are already starting to pinch! Chapter 4 detailed how quickly everything develops in the child, from the developing brain to bones, muscle and weight. Children grow extremely quickly in the first five to six years. Children develop many synaptic connections in the brain which allow them to develop complex behaviours such as language, thought and the ability to grasp and use objects. When children are born they have quite a high fat-to-weight ratio, but as they grow older they become leaner and develop heavier bones and more muscle. Again, this chapter referred back to the nature versus nurture debate. The child's genes indicate that they will grow to be tall and slim like their parents, but in the current environment of fast, fatty foods, many children are growing tall yet heavier and fatter than their parents. The environment is affecting the height/weight ratio of the growing child over and above what is defined by the child's genetic make-up.

We discussed the development of cognitive abilities in Chapter 5. We learnt about the ability to think and reason, to fantasise and problem-solve. How do we remember the telephone number we have just been given? Memory and attention. How do we remember a birthday we had as a child? Long-term memory. Without developing complex cognitive abilities we would not be able to function very well in a busy world. We would not be able to remember facts and figures from one day to the next. We would not be able to write creative prose or to daydream about our next vacation.

From birth onwards, humans are engaged in a social world. Parents, sisters and brothers may form a family unit that the child is born in to and it is to these people that the child learns to relate. As we know, newborn children are unable to fend for themselves. Human children are extremely reliant on others for their survival needs and Chapter 6 discussed how attachment behaviours encourage caring behaviours from parents towards their child. We looked at many theories of attachment ranging from biological-drive theories to ethological theories. We looked at different styles of attachment and what they mean for the parent and child. Is there a critical period when attachments can only form? Review the literature to form your own ideas.

Chapter 7 introduced us to the notion of the sense of the self. How we recognise ourselves in the mirror or in photographs is a complex process that takes a few years to perfect. However, it takes much longer to accept that the person in the mirror is a true reflection of ourselves, especially when we do not like what we see! Yet, being able to identify yourself as different to others is an important skill to develop. With it comes the realisation that there are others around you and that you need to interact with them. Children become social creatures fairly quickly and the skills they learn during play with others are vital for successful social living. How do you know when the person opposite you is having a bad day? Theory of mind tells us how.

Whilst humans are busy forming attachments to each other, they are also trying to communicate with each other. Parents smile at their babies and babies smile back. As the child gets older they develop more complex forms of communicating. Copying their parents' speech and developing expertise with their parents' help, children soon learn to chatter away quite happily! Are we born with the ability to acquire language? Many theorists think so, but have we any proof? Throughout this book, the nature versus nurture debate continues. How can we possibly learn everything we need to say if we do not have any biological predisposition to learn language? How do we learn words for things that did not exist yesterday if we only have a set amount of vocabulary available to us? Language is an important part of developmental psychology and the debate will continue for a long time yet.

Finally, we moved away from childhood and into the period of adolescence. Without the pretty luxurious way we live today, we could not support this period of extended education and childhood. We encourage our teenagers to study and work hard with the goal of them entering the adult world much later than their grandparents or great-grandparents did. As a result, teenagers have developed their own culture and expectations, much of it completely alien to their adult parents. With it too have come problems. Our teenagers experience a lot of pressure to conform to the societal ideal delaying adulthood and when they display adult-like behaviours are often criticised for it. We want teenagers to develop rewarding relationships but do not like it when they form sexual relationships. We want them to show they are more grown-up than their younger child siblings, but are shocked when the teenager gets pregnant or goes joyriding. The world of the teenager is a difficult one, but most get through this time and become happy successful adults.

Where do we go from here? As we have said, developmental psychology is all about human life from conception to childhood, from adolescence to adulthood. After reading this book you are now aware of the biological processes during this time and the cognitive changes that occur. You now understand the development of social relationships and the sense of the self. You know about the development of language and how it is used to full effect. You also understand the period of adolescence and what this means to the developing young person. Make sure you take the quick tests throughout and attempt the questions at the end of each chapter. Once you feel you have covered everything in this book you should feel perfectly placed to understand why you are and you are.

References

Adams, R. J. (1987). An evaluation of colour preference in early infancy. *Infant Behavior and Development,* 10: 143–150.

Adams, R. J. and Courage, M. C. (1998). Human newborn colour vision: measurements with chromatic stimuli varying in excitation purity. *Journal of Experimental Child Psychology*, 68: 22–34.

Adamson, L. (1995). *Communication Development During Infancy.* Madison Brown.

Adkins-Regan, E. (1988). Sex hormones and sexual orientation in animals. *Psychobiology,* 16 (4): 335–347.

Adolph, K. E. (2000). Specificity of learning: why infants fall over a veritable cliff. *Psychological Science,* 11: 290–295.

Ainsworth, M. and Bell, S. (1969). Some contemporary patterns of mother–infant interaction in the feeding situation. In A. Ambrose (ed.), *Stimulation in Early Infancy*, 133–170. London and New York: Academic Press.

Ainsworth, M. D. S., Blehar, M. C., Waters. E. and Wall, S. (1978). *Patterns of Attachment: A Psychological Study of the Strange Situation*. Hillsdale, NJ: Erlbaum.

Alsaker, F. D. (1995). Timing of puberty and reactions to pubertal changes. In M. Rutter (ed.), *Psychosocial Disturbances in Young People*. New York: Cambridge University Press.

Anglin, J. M. (1993). Vocabulary development: a morphological analysis. *Monographs of the Society for Research in Child Development,* 58 (10) (Serial No. 238).

Apgar, V. (1953). A proposal for a new method of evaluation in the newborn infant. *Current Research in Anaesthesia and Analgesia*, 32: 260–267

Atkinson, J. (2000). *The Developing Visual Brain*. Oxford: Oxford University Press.

Atkinson, J. and Braddick, O. (1981). Acuity, contrast sensitivity and accommodation in infancy. In R. N. Aslin, J. R. Alberts and M. R. Petersen (eds.), *Development of Perception: Psychobiological Perspectives: Vol. 2: The Visual System*, 245–277. New York : Academic.

Atkinson, R. C. and Shiffrin, R. M. (1968). Human memory: a proposed system and its central processes. In K. W. Spence and J. T. Spence (eds.), *The Psychology of Learning and Motivation. Advances in Research and Theory*, 2. New York: Academic.

Austin, J. L. (1962). *How To Do Things with Words*. Oxford: Oxford University Press.

Baddeley, A. (1990). *Human Memory: Theory and Practice*. London: Allyn and Bacon.

Bailey, J. M. and Bell, A. P. (1993) Familiality of female and male homosexuality. *Behavior Genetics,* 23(4): 313–322.

Baillargeon, R. and DeVos, J. (1991). Object permanence in young infants: further evidence. *Child Development*, 62: 1227–1246.

Bancroft, J., Sanders, D., Davidson, D. and Warner P. (1983). Mood, sexuality, hormones and the menstrual cycle. III. Sexuality and the role of androgens. *Psychosomatic Medicine*, 45: 509–516.

Bandura, A. (1989). Social cognitive theory. In R. Vasta (ed.), *Annals of Child Development,* 6. *Theories of child development: revised formulations and current issues*, 1–60. Greenwich, CT: JAI Press.

Bandura, A. and Walters, R. H. (1963). *Social Learning and Personality Development*. New York: Holt, Rinehart and Winston.

Banich, M. T. (2003). *Neuropsychology: The Neural Bases of Mental Function*. New York: Houghton Mifflin.

Baron-Cohen, S. (1995). Theory of mind and face-processing: how do they interact in development and psychopathology? In D. Cicchetti and D. J. Cohen (eds) *Developmental Psychopathology, Vol. 1: Theory and Methods*. Oxford: John Wiley & Sons.

Barsalou, L.. W. (1983). Ad hoc categories. *Memory and Cognition,* 11: 211–227.

Bates, E., O'Connell, B. and Shore, C. (1987). Language and communication in infancy. In J. D. Osofsky (ed.), *Handbook of Infant Development,* (2nd edn.). New York: Wiley.

Baumrind, D. and Black, A. E. (1967). Socialization practices associated with dimensions of competence in preschool boys and girls. *Child Development,* 38: 291–327.

Bayley, N. (1993). *Bayley Scales of Infant Development*. (2nd edn.). New York: Psychological Corporation.

Bell, M. A. and Fox, N. A. (1996). Crawling experience is related to changes in cortical organization during infancy: Evidence from EEG coherence. *Developmental Psychology,* 29: 551–561.

Belsky, J., Steinberg, L. and Draper, P. (1991). Childhood experience, interpersonal development and reproductive strategy: an evolutionary theory of socialisation. *Child Development, 6,* 2(4): 647–670.

Berger, K. S. (2001). *The Developing Person Through the Lifespan,* (5th edn.). New York: Worth Publishers.

Berk, L. E. (2003). *Child Development*. London: Allyn and Bacon.

Birnholz, J. C. and Benacerraf, B. R. (1983). The development of human foetal hearing. *Science,* 222: 516–518.

Bjorklund, D. F. and Pelligrini, A. D. (2000). Child development and evolutionary psychology. *Child Development,* 71: 1687–1708.

Blakemore, C. (1976). The conditions required for the maintenance of binocularity in the kitten's visual cortex. *Journal of Physiology,* 261: 423–444.

Bohannon, J. N. and Stanowicz, L. (1988). The issue of negative evidence: adult responses to children's language errors. *Developmental Psychology,* 24: 684–689.

Borke, H. (1975). Piaget's mountains revisited: changes in the egocentric landscape. *Developmental Psychology,* 11: 240–243.

Bouchard Jr, T. J. (1994). Genes, environment and personality. *Science,* 264: 1700–1701.

Bowlby, J. (1969). *Attachment and Loss: Vol. 1. Attachment.* New York: Basic Books.

Braungart, J. M., Plomin, R., DeFries, J. C. and Fulker, D. W. (1992). Genetic influence on tester-rated infant temperament as assessed by Bayley's infant behaviour record: non-adoptive and adoptive siblings and twins. *Developmental Psychology,* 28: 40–47.

Bremner, J. (1998). *Infancy*. Oxford: Basil Blackwell.

Broerse, J., Peltola, C. and Crassini, B. (1983). Infants' reactions to perceptual paradox during mother–infant interactions. *Developmental Psychology,* 19: 310–316.

Bronfenbrenner, U. and Evans, G. W. (2000). Developmental science in the 21st century: emerging theoretical models, research designs and experimental findings. *Social Development,* 9: 115–125.

Brooks-Gunn, J. (1988a). Antecedents and consequences of variations in girls' maturational timing. *Journal of Adolescent Health Care,* 9: 365–373.

Brooks-Gunn, J. (1988b). The impact of puberty and sexual activity upon the health and education of adolescent girls and boys. *Peabody Journal of Education,* 64: 88–113.

Brooks-Gunn, J., Gross, R. T., Kraemer, H. C., Spiker, D. and Shapiro, S. (1992). Enhancing the cognitive outcomes of low-birth-weight, premature infants: for whom is the interaction most effective? *Pediatrics,* 89: 1209–1215.

Brooks-Gunn, J. and Peterson, A. C. (1991). Studying the emergence of depression and depressive symptoms during adolescence. *Journal of Youth and Adolescence,* 20: 115–119.

Brooks-Gunn, J., Warren, M. P., Samelson, M. and Fox, R. (1986). Physical similarity of and disclosure of menarcheal status to friends: effects of grade and pubertal status. *Journal of Early Adolescence,* 6: 3–14.

Brown, R. (1973). *A First Language: The Early Stages*. Cambridge, MA: Harvard University Press.

Brown, R. and Hanlon, C. (1970). Derivational complexity and the order of acquisition in child speech. In J. Hayes, *Cognition and the Development of Language*. New York: Wiley.

Bruner, J. S. (1983). *Child's Talk: Learning to Use Language*. Oxford: Oxford University Press.

Bullock, M. and Gelman, R. (1979). Preschool children's assumptions about cause and effect: temporal ordering. *Child Development*, 59: 26-37.

Campos, J. J., Hiatt, S., Ramsay, D., Henderson, C. and Svejda, M. (1978). The emergence of fear on the visual cliff. In M. Lewis and L. Rosenblaum (eds.), *The Origins of Affect*. New York: Plenum

Carlson, N. R. (2001). *Physiology of Behaviour*. London: Allyn and Bacon.

Carlsson, S. G., Fagerberg, Horneman, Hwang, Larson, Rodholm and Schaller (1978). Effects of amount of contact between mother and child on the mother's nursing behavior. *Developmental Psychobiology*, 11(2): 143–150.

Casaer, P. (1993). Old and new facts about perinatal brain development. *Journal of Child Psychology and Psychiatry*, 34: 101–109.

Case, R. (1992). Neo-Piagetian theories of intellectual development. In H. Beilin and P. B. Pufall (eds.), *Piaget's Theory: Prospects and Possibilities*. Hillsdale, NJ: Erlbaum.

Cashon, C. H. and Cohen, L. B. (2000). Eight-month-old infants' perception of possible and impossible events. *Infancy*, 1: 429–446.

Catherwood, D., Cramm, A. and Foster, H. (2003). Asymmetry in infant hemispheric readiness after exposure to a visual stimulus. *Developmental Science*, 6: 62–66.

Catherwood, D., Skoien, P., Green, V. and Holt, C. (1996). Assessing the primal moments in infant encoding of compound visual stimuli. *Infant Behavior and Development*, 19: 1–11.

Cernoch, J. M. and Porter, R. H. (1985). Recognition of maternal axillary odours by infants. *Child Development*, 56: 1593–1598.

Chen, Z., Sanchez, R. P. and Campbell, T. (1997). From beyond to within their grasp: the rudiments of analogical problem-solving in 10- to 13-month-olds. *Developmental Psychology*, 33: 790–801.

Chi, M. T. H. (1978). Knowledge structures and memory development. In R. S. Siegler (ed.), *Children's Thinking: What Develops?*, 73–96. Hillsdale, NJ: Erlbaum.

Chi, M. T. H. and Ceci, S. J. (1987). Content knowledge: its role, representation and restructuring in memory development. *Advances in Child Development and Behavior*, 20: 91–142.

Chi, M. T. H. and Koeske, R. (1983). Network representation of a child's dinosaur knowledge. *Developmental Psychology*, 19: 29–39.

Chilman, C. S. (1979). *Adolescent Sexuality in a Changing American Society: Social and Psychological Perspectives*. Bethesda: US Department of Health, Education and Welfare.

Chomsky, N. (1959). A review of B. F. Skinner's 'Verbal Behaviour'. *Language*, 35: 26–129.

Chomsky, N. (1968). *Language and Mind*. San Diego, CA: Harcourt Brace Jovanovich.

Christianson and Loftus, M (1991). Remembering emotional events: the fate of detail information. *Memory and Cognition*, 5: 81–108.

Coie, J. D., Dodge, K. A. and Cappotelli, H. (1982). Dimensions and types of social status: a cross-age perspective. *Developmental Psychology*, 18: 557–570.

Cole, M. and Cole, S. (2001). *The Development of Children*. New York: Worth.

Cooley, C. H. (1902). *Human Nature and the Social Order*. New York: Scribners.

Cooper, R. M. and Zubek, J. P. (1958). Effects of enriched and restricted early environments on the learning ability of bright and dull rats. *Canadian Journal of Psychology*, 12: 159–164.

Crews, F. (1996). The verdict on Freud (Review of Freud evaluated: the complete arc). *Psychological Science*, 7: 63–68.

Crook, C. (1987). Taste and olfaction. In P. Salapatek and L. Cohen (eds.), *Handbook of Infant Perception: Vol.1: From Sensation to Perception*. New York: Academic.

Csibra, G., Davis, G., Spratling, M. W. and Johnson, M. H. (2000). Gamma oscillations and object processing in the infant brain, *Science*, 290: 1582–1585.

Curtiss, S. (1977). *Genie: A Psycholinguistic Study of a Modern Day 'Wild Child'*. New York: Academic Press.

Damon, W. and Hart, D. (1988). *Self Understanding in Childhood and Adolescence*. New York: Cambridge University Press.

Darnell Jr, J. E. (1997). STATS and gene regulation. *Science,* 173: 1630–1635.

Davidson, R. J. (1994). Asymmetric brain function: affective style and psychopathology: the role of early experience and plasticity. *Development and Psychopathology,* 6: 741–758.

de Schonen, S. and Bry, I. (1987). Interhemispheric communication of visual learning: a developmental study in 3- to 6-month-old infants. *Neuropsychologia,* 25: 601–612.

de Schonen, S. and Mathivet, E. (1990). Hemispheric asymmetry in a face discrimination task in infants. *Child Development,* 61: 1192–1205.

DeCasper, A. J. and Fifer, W. P. (1980). Of human bonding: newborns prefer their mothers' voices. *Science,* 208: 1174–1176.

DeCasper, A. J. and Spence, M. (1986). Newborns prefer a familiar story over an unfamiliar one. *Infant Behavior and Development,* 9: 135–150.

DeCasper, A., Leccnuet, J-P., Busnel, M-C., Granier-Deferre, C. et al. (1994). Foetal reactions to recurrent maternal speech. *Infant Behaviour and Development,* 17: 159–164.

Deloache, J. S. and Brown, A. L. (1983). Very young children's memory for the location of objects in a large-scale environment. *Child Development,* 54: 888–897.

Descartes, R. (1637, reprinted 1972). *Treatise of Man*. Cambridge, MA: Harvard University Press.

DeVilliers, P. A. and DeVilliers, J. G. (1979). *Early Language*. Cambridge, MA: Harvard University Press.

DeVilliers, P. A. and DeVilliers, J. G. (1992). Language development. In M. H. Bornstein and M. E. Lamb (eds.), *Developmental Psychology: An Advanced Textbook* (3rd. edn.). Hillsdale, NJ: Erlbaum.

Diamond, A., Prevor, A., Callender, G. and Druin, D. P. (1997). *Prefrontal Cortex Cognitive Deficits in Children Treated Early and Continuously for PKU*. Chicago: University of Chicago Press.

Diaz, R. M. and Berndt, T. J. (1982). Children's knowledge of a best friend: fact or fancy? *Developmental Psychology,* 18(6): 787–794.

DiPietro, J. A., Hodgson, D. M., Costigan, K. A. and Johnson, T. R. B. (1996). Foetal antecedents of infant temperament. *Child Development,* 67: 2568–2583.

Dobson, V. and Teller, D. Y. (1978). Assessment of visual activity in infants. In J. C. Armington, J. Krauskopf and B. R. Wooten (eds.), *Visual Psychophysics and Physiology*. New York: Academic.

Donaldson, M (1978). *Childrens' Minds*. Glasgow: Fontana.

Dunn, J. (1988). *The Beginnings of Social Understanding*. Cambridge, MA: Harvard University Press.

Eder, R. A. (1989). The emergent personalogist: the structure and content of 3½, 5½ and 7½ year olds' concepts of themselves and other persons. *Child Development,* 60: 1218–1228. Cited in D. Shaffer (1999). *Developmental Psychology: Childhood and Adolescence* (5th edn.). Pacific Grove, CA: Brooks/Cole.

Eder, R.A. (1990). Uncovering young children's psychological selves: individual and developmental differences. *Child Development,* 61: 849–863. Cited in D. Shaffer (1999) *Developmental Psychology: Childhood and Adolescence* (5th edn). Pacific Grove, CA: Brooks/Cole.

Edgardh, K. (2002). Sexual behaviour and early coitarche in a national sample of 17-year-old Swedish boys. *Acta Paediatrica,* 91: 985–991.

Eichorn, D. (1979). Physical development: current foci for research. In J. D. Osofsky (ed.), *Handbook of Infant Development*. New York: Wiley.

Eimas, P. D. (1975). Auditory and phonemic coding of the cues for speech: discrimination of the [r-l] distinction by young infants. *Perception and Psychophysics,* 18: 341–347.

Eimas, P. D., Siqueland, E. R., Jusczyk, P.W. and Vigorito, J. (1971). Speech perception in infants. *Science,* 171: 303–306.

Eisenberg, L. (1999). Experience, brain and behaviour: the impact of a head start. *Pediatrics,* 103: 1031–1035.

Elder, G. H., Liker, J. K. and Cross, C. E. (1984). Parent–child behavior in the Great Depression: life course and intergenerational influences. In P. B. Baltes and O. G. Brim (eds.) *Life-span Development and Behaviour*, 6. New York: Academic Press.

Emory, E. K. and Toomey, K. A. (1988). Environmental stimulation and human foetal responsibility in late pregnancy. In W. P. Smotherman and S. R. Robinson (eds.), *Behaviour of the Foetus*. 141–161. Caldwell, NJ: Telford.

Enkin, M., Keirse, M. J. N. G. and Chalmers, I. (1989). *Effective Care in Pregnancy and Childbirth*. Oxford: Oxford University Press.

Epelbaum, M., Millerett, C., Buisseret, P. and Dufier, J. L. (1993). The sensitive period for strabismus amblyopia in humans. *Ophthalmology*, 100: 323–327.

Erikson, E. H. (1963). *Childhood and Society* (2nd edn.). New York: Norton.

Erikson, E. H. (1968). *Identity, Youth and Crisis*. New York: Norton.

Espy, K. A., Molfese, V. J. and DiLalla, L. F. (2001). Effects of environmental measures on intelligence in young children: growth curve modelling of longitudinal data. *Merrill-Palmer Quarterly*, 47: 42–73.

Fagan, J., Slaughter, E. and Hartstone, E. (1987). Blind justice? The impact of race on the juvenile-justice process. *Crime and Delinquency*, 33: 259–286.

Falkner, F. and Tanner, J. M. (1986). *Human Growth: A Comprehensive Treatise* (2nd edn), 3. New York: Plenum.

Fantz, R. (1964). Visual experience in infants: decreased attention to familiar patterns relative to novel ones. *Science*, 146: 668–670.

Feldman, S. S. and Weinberger, D. A. (1994). Self-restraint as a mediator of family influences on boys' delinquent behaviour: a longitudinal study. *Child Development*, 65: 195–211.

Fernald, A. (1989). Intonation and communicative intent in mothers' speech to infants: is the melody the message? *Child Development*, 60: 1497–1510.

Finlay, D. and Ivinskis, A. (1984). Cardiac and visual responses to moving stimuli presented either successively or simultaneously to the central and peripheral visual fields in 4-month-old infants. *Developmental Psychology*, 20: 29–36.

Flavell, J. H., Green, F. L. and Flavell, E. R. (1986). Development of knowledge about the appearance-reality distinction. *Monographs of the Society for Research in Child Development*, 51 (1, Serial No. 212).

Flavell, J. H. and Miller, P. H. (1998). Social cognition. In D. Kuhn and R. S. Siegler (eds.), *Handbook of Child Psychology, Vol. 2: Cognition, Perception and Language*. 851–898. New York: Wiley.

Freeman, W. H. (1999). *How Brains Make Up Their Minds*. London: Weidenfeld & Nicolson.

Freud, S. (1935). *A General Introduction to Psychoanalysis*. Translated by J. Riviare. New York: Modern Library.

Friedman, S. (1972). Habituation and recovery of visual response in the alert human newborn. *Journal of Experimental Child Psychology*, 13: 339–349.

Gaddis, A. and Brooks-Gunn, J. (1985). The male experience of pubertal change. *Journal of Youth and Adolescence*, 14: 61–69. Cited in L. E. Berk (1998) *Development Through the Life-span*. Needham Heights: Allyn & Bacon.

Garner, D. M. and Garfinkel, P. E. (eds.) (1997). *Handbook of Treatment for Eating Disorders*. New York: Guildford Press.

Ge, X., Conger, R. D. and Elder Jr, G. H. (1996). Coming of age too early: pubertal influences on girls' vulnerability to psychological distress. *Child Development*, 67: 3386–3400.

Gelman, S. A. and Markman, E. M. (1986). Categories and induction in young children. *Cognition*, 23: 183–209.

Genome International Sequencing Consortium (2001). Initial sequencing and analysis of the human genome. *Nature*, 409: 860-921.

Gibson, E. and Walk, R. D. (1960). The 'visual cliff'. *Scientific American*, 202: 64–71.

Giedd, J. N., Blumenthal, J., Jeffries, N. O., Rajapaske, J. C., Vaituzis, C. and Liu, H. (1999). Development of the corpus callosum during childhood and adolescence: a longitudinal MRI study. *Progress in Neuro-Psychopharmacology and Biological Psychiatry*, 23: 571–588.

Gleitman, L.R. (1990). The structural sources of verb meanings. *Language Acquisition,* 1: 3–55.

Goldfield, E. C. and Wolff, P. H. (2002). Motor development in infancy. In A. Slater and M. Lewis (eds.) *Introduction to Infant Development*. Oxford: Oxford University Press.

Goodfellow, P. N. and Lovell, B. R. (1983). SRY and sex determination in mammals. *Annual Review of Genetics*, 27: 71–92.

Goodman, C. (1979). Isogenic grasshoppers: genetic variability and development of identified neurons. In X. O. Breakefeld (ed.), *Neurogenetics.* New York: Elsevier.

Gopnik, A. and Astington, J. W. (1988). Children's understanding of representational change and its relation to the understanding of false belief and the appearance-reality distinction. *Child Development,* 59: 26–37.

Gotesdam, K. G. and Agras, W. S. (1995). General population-based epidemiological survey of eating disorders in Norway. *International Journal of Eating Disorders,* 18: 119–126.

Graber, J. A., Brooks-Gunn, J., Paikoff, R. L. and Warren, M. P. (1994). Prediction of eating problems: an 8 year study of adolescent girls. *Developmental Psychology,* 28: 731–740.

Graham, F. K. and Clifton, R. K. (1966). Heart rate change as a component of the orienting response. *Psychological Bulletin,* 65: 305–320.

Grattan, M. P., De Vos, E., Levy, J. and McClintock, M. K., (1992). Asymmetric action in the human newborn: sex differences in patterns of organization. *Child Development,* 63: 273–289.

Greenberger, E. and Steinberg, L. (1986). *When Teenagers Work*. New York: Basic Books.

Grice, P. (2001). *Aspects of Reason*. Oxford: Oxford University Press.

Grotevant, H. D. and Cooper, C. R. (1985). Patterns of interaction in family relationships and the development of identity exploration in adolescence. *Child Development,* 56: 415–428.

Guerri, C. (1998). Neuroanatomical and neurophysiological mechanisms involved in central nervous system dysfunctions induced by prenatal alcohol exposure. *Alcoholism:Clinical and Experimental Research,* 22: 304–312.

Gwiazda, J. and Birch, E. E. (2001). Perceptual development: vision. In E. B. Goldstein (ed.) *Handbook of Perception*. 636–668.

Hainline, L. (1998). The development of basic visual abilities. In A. Slater (ed.), *Perceptual Development: Visual, Auditory and Speech Perception in Infancy*, 5–50. Hove: Psychology.

Haith, M. M. (1980). *Rules That Babies Look By*. Hillsdale, NJ: Erlbaum.

Haith, M. M. (1999). Some thoughts about claims for innate knowledge and infant physical reasoning. *Developmental Science,* 2: 153–156.

Halliday, J. L., Watson, L. F., Lumley, J., Danks, D. M. and Sheffield, L. S. (1995). New estimates of Down syndrome risks at chorionic villus sampling, amniocentesis and live birth in women of advanced maternal age from a uniquely defined population. *Prenatal Diagnosis,* 15. 455–465.

Harlow, C. M. (ed.) (1986). *From Learning to Love: The Selected Papers of H. F. Harlow*. New York: Praeger.

Harlow, H. F. (1958). The nature of love. *American Psychology,* 13: 673–685.

Harris, G. (1997). Development of taste perception and appetite regulation. In G. Bremner, A. Slater and G. Butterworth (eds.), *Infant Development: Recent Advances*, 9–30. Hove: Psychology Press.

Hartung, B. and Sweeney, K. (1991). Why adult children return home. *Social Science Journal,* 28: 467–480.

Hass, A. (1979). *Teenage Sexuality*. New York: MacMillan.

Hawkins, J., Pea, R. D., Glick, J. and Scribner, S. (1984). 'Merds that laugh don't like mushrooms': evidence for deductive reasoning by preschoolers. *Developmental Psychology,* 20: 584–594.

Hayward, C., Killen, J. D., Wilson, D. M., Hammer, L. D., Litt, I. F., Kraemer, H. C., Haydel, F., Varady, A. and Taylor, C. B. (1997). Psychiatric risk associated with early puberty in adolescent girls. *Journal of the American Academy of Child and Adolescent Psychiatry,* 36: 255–262.

Held, R. and Hein, A. (1963). Movement produced stimulation in the development of visually guided behaviour. *Journal of Comparative and Physiological Psychology,* 56: 872–876.

Hepper, P. G. (June 1988). Foetal 'soap' addiction. *Lancet,* 1347–1384.

Hepper, P. G. (1996) Foetal memory does it exist? *Acta Paediatrica*, supplement 416, 16-20.

Hermes, S. F. and Keel, P. K. (2003). The influence of puberty and ethnicity on awareness and internalization of the thin ideal. *International Journal of Eating Disorders,* 33: 465–467.

Hetherington, E. M. (1991) The role of individual differences and family relationships in children's coping with divorce and remarriage. In P. A. Cowan and E. M. Hetherington (eds.), *Family Transitions*. Hillsdale, NJ: Erlbaum.

Hill, J. P. and Holmbeck, G. N. (1986). Attachment and autonomy during adolescence. In G. Whitehurst (ed.), *Annals of Child Development*, 3. Greenwich, CT: JAI Press.

Hodapp, R. M. (1996). Down syndrome: developmental, psychiatric and management issues. *Child and Adolescent Psychiatric Clinics of North America,* 5: 881–894.

Hoff-Ginsberg, E. (1997). *Language Development*. Pacific Grove, CA: Brooks/Cole.

Holyoak, K. J., Junn, E. N. and Billman, D. O. (1984). Development of analogical problem-solving skill. *Child Development*, 55: 2042–2055.

Hopkins, B. and Westra, T. (1988). Maternal handling and motor development: an intracultural study. *Genetic, Social and General Psychology Monographs,* 14: 377–420.

Hopwood, N. J., Kelch, R. P., Hale, P. M., Mendes, T. M., Foster, C. M. and Beitins, I. Z. (1990). The onset of human puberty: biological and environmental factors. In J. Bancroft and J. M. Reinisch (eds.), *Adolescence and Puberty*. New York: Oxford University Press.

Hughes, M. and Grieve, R. (1980). On asking childrern bizarre questions. *First Language,* 1: 149–160.

Huttenlocher, P. R. (1990) Morphometric study of human cerebral cortex development. *Neuropsychologia,* 28: 517–527.

Ingram, D. (1989). *First Language Acquisition*. Cambridge: Cambridge University Press.

Jacobson, A. G. (1966). Inductive processes in embryonic development. *Science,* 152: 25–34.

James, W. (1890). *The Principles of Psychology*. New York: Holt.

Janus, S. and Janus, C. (1993). *The Janus Report on Sexual Behaviour*. New York: Wiley.

Johnson, J. and Newport, E. (1989). Critical period effects in second language learning: the influence of maturational state on the acquisition of English as a second language. *Cognitive Psychology,* 21: 60–99.

Johnson, M. H. (1993). Cortical maturation and the development of visual attention in early infancy. In M. H. Johnson (ed.), *Brain Development and Cognition: A Reader*. Oxford: Blackwell.

Johnson, M. H. (1998). The neural basis of cognitive development. In D. Kuhn and S. Siegler (eds.), *Handbook of Child Psychology, Vol 2: Cognition, perception and language*, 1–49. New York: Wiley.

Johnson, M. H. and Morton, J. (1991). *Biology and Cognitive Development*. Oxford: Blackwell.

Jusczyk, P. N. (1995). Language acquisition: speech sounds and phonological development. In J. L. Miller and P. D. Eimas (eds.), *Handbook of Perception and Cognition, Vol 11: Speech, Language and Communication*, 263–301. Orlando, Fl: Academic.

Jusczyk, P. N. (2002). Language development: from speech perception to first words. In A. Slater and M. Lewis (eds.) *Introduction to Infant Development*. Oxford: Oxford University Press.

Jusczyk, P. N., Friederici, A. D. and Svenkerud, V. Y. (1993) Infants' sensitivity to the sound patterns of native language words. *Journal of Memory and Language,* 32: 402–420.

Juul, A. (2001). The effects of oestrogen on linear bone growth. *Human Reproduction Update,* 7: 303–313.

Kaltiala-Heino, R., Rimpela, M., Rissanen, A. and Rantanen, P. (2001). Early puberty and early sexual activity are associated with bulimic-type eating pathology in middle adolescence. *Journal of Adolescent Health,* 28: 346–352.

Karmiloff-Smith, A. (1992). *Beyond Modularity: A Developmental Perspective on Cognitive Science.* Cambridge, MA: MIT Press.

Karmiloff-Smith, A (1995). Annotation: the extraordinary cognitive journey from foetus through infancy. *Journal of Child Psychology and Psychiatry,* 36: 1293–1313.

Karmiloff-Smith, A. (1999). The connectionist infant: would Piaget turn in his grave? In A. Slater and D. Muir (eds.), *The Blackwell Reader in Developmental Psychology,* 43–52. Oxford: Blackwell.

Keating, D. (1979). Adolescent thinking. In J. Adelson (ed.), *Handbook of Adolescent Psychology.* New York: Wiley.

Kett, J. F. (1977). *Rites of Passage: Adolescence in America, 1790 to the Present.* New York: Basic Books.

Kim, K., Smith, P. K. and Palermiti, A. L. (1997). Conflict in childhood and reproductive development. *Evolution and Human Behavior,* 18: 109–142.

Klaus, M. H. and Kennell, J. H. (1976). *Maternal-infant Bonding: The Impact of Early Separation or Loss on Damily Development.* St. Louis: Mosby.

Klaus, M. H. and Kennell, J. H. (1982). *Parent-infant Bonding.* St. Louis: Mosby.

Klaus, M. H., Kennell, J. H., and Klaus, P. H. (1995*). Bonding: Building the Foundations of Secure Attachment and Independence.* Reading, MA: Addison-Wesley.

Kuhn, D. (1995). Microgenetic study of change: what has it told us? *Psychological Science,* 6: 133–139.

Lagerkrantz, H., and Slotkin, T. A. (1986). The 'stress' of being born. *Scientific American,* 280: 68–75.

Lavelle, M. (1994). Are there long-term health consequences of secular trend in early menarche? *Collegium Anthropologicum,* 18: 53–61.

Levin, M. L., Xu, X.H. and Bartkowski, J. P. (2002). Seasonality of sexual debut. *Journal of Marriage and the Family,* 64: 871–884.

Lewis, M. and Brooks-Gunn, J. (1979). *Social Cognition and the Acquisition of Self.* New York: Plenum Press.

Lewontin, R. C. (1976). Race and intelligence. In N. J. Block and C. Dworkin (eds.), *The I.Q. Controversy.* New York: Pantheon.

Li, Z., van Aelst, L. and Cline, H. T. (2000). Rho GTPases regulate distinct aspects of dendritic arbor growth in Xenopus central neurons in vivo. *Nature Neuroscience,* 3: 217-225.

Libet, B., Wright, E. W., Feinstein, B. and Pearl, D. K. (1979). Subjective referencing of the timing for a conscious experience. *Brain,* 102: 193–224.

Liley, A. W. (1972). The foetus as a personality. *Australian and New Zealand Journal of Psychiatry,* 6: 99–103.

Lorenz, K. (1952). *King Soloman's Ring.* New York: Crowell.

Louis, J., Cannard, C., Bastuji, H. and Challamel, M. J. (1997). Sleep ontogenesis revisited: a longitudinal 24-hour home polygraphic study on 15 normal infants during the first 2 years of life. *Sleep,* 20: 323–333.

MacFarlane, A. (1975). Olfaction in the development of social preferences in the human neonate. In *Parent-infant Interaction.* (CIBA Foundation Symposium No. 33). Amsterdam: Elsevier.

Mandler, J., Bauer, P. J. and McDonough, L. (1991). Separating the sheep from the goats: differentiating global categories. *Cognitive Psychology,* 23: 263–298.

Manktelow, K. (1999). *Reasoning and Thinking.* Hove: Psychology Press.

Mareschal, D. (1998). To reach or not to reach: that is the question. *Developmental Science,* 1: 198–199.

Margulis, L. and Sagan, D (1997). *What is Sex?* New York: Simon & Schuster.

Mayes, L. C. and Bornstein, M. H. (1997). Attention regulation in infants born at risk: prematurity and prenatal cocaine exposure. In J. A. Burack and J. T. Enns (eds.), *Attention, Development, and Psychopathology,* 97–122. New York: Guildford.

McCarty, M. E. and Ashmead, D. H. (1999). Visual control of reaching and grasping in infants. *Developmental Psychology,* 35: 620–631.

McGarrity, W. C. (1976). Nutritional deficits in adolescents with eating disorders. Guest lecture, Department of Nutrition, Oxford University.

Mead, G. H. (1934). *Mind, Self and Society.* Chicago: University of Chicago Press.

Mehler, J., Jusczyk, P. W., Lambertz, G., Halsted, N., Bertoncini, J. and Amieltison, C. (1988). A precursor of language acquisition in young infants. *Cognition,* 29: 143–178.

Mitchell, J. E., Hatsukami, D., Eckert, E. D. and Pyle, R. L. (1985). Characteristics of 275 patients with bulimia. *American Journal of Psychiatry,* 142(4): 482–485.

Moffitt, A. R. (1973). Intensity discrimination and cardiac reaction in young infants. *Developmental Psychology,* 8: 357–359.

Moon, C., Cooper, R. P. and Fifer, W. P. (1993). Two-day-old infants prefer their native language. *Infant Behaviour and Development,* 16: 495–500.

Moore, K. L. and Persaud, T. V. N. (1998). *Before We Are Born.* Philadelphia: Saunders.

Morgane, P. L., Austin-La France, R., Bronzino, J., Tonkiss, J., Diaz-Cintra, S., Cintra, L., Kamper, T. and Galler, J. R. (1993). Prenatal malnutrition and development of the brain. *Neuroscience and Biobehavioural Reviews,* 17: 91–128.

Morrongiello, B. A., Fenwick, K. D., Hillier, L. and Chance, G. (1994). Sound localization in newborn human infants. *Developmental Psychobiology,* 27: 519–538.

Morton, J. and Johnson, M. H. (1991). Conspec and Conlearn: a two-process theory of infant face recognition. *Psychological Review,* 98: 164–181.

Muir, D. and Clifton, R. K. (1985). Infants' orientation to the location of sound sources. In G. Gottlieb and N. A. Krasnegor (eds.), *Measurement of Audition and Vision in the First Year of Postnatal Life: A Methodological Overview.* Norwood, NJ: Ablex.

Nazzi, T., Floccia, C. and Bertoncini, J. (1998). Discrimination of pitch contours by neonates. *Infant Behavior and Development,* 21: 779–784.

Nelson, C. A. and Bosquet, M. (2000). Neurobiology of foetal and infant development: implications for infant mental health. In C. H. Zeanah Jr (ed.), *Handbook of Infant Mental Health,* 37–59. New York: Guildford.

Nelson, K. (1973). Structure and strategy in learning to talk. *Monographs of the Society for Research in Child Development,* 38 (Serial No. 149).

Newman, C., Atkinson, J. and Braddick, O. (2001). The development of reaching and looking preferences in infants to objects of different sizes. *Developmental Psychology,* 37: 561–572.

Nilsson,L. and Hamberger, L. (1990). *A Child Is Born.* New York: Delacorte.

Niswander, K. R. and Evans, A. T. (1996). *Manual of Obstetrics.* Boston: Little Brown.

Olson, R. K., Forsberg, H. and Wise, B. (1994). Genes, environment and the development of orthographic skills, In V. W. Berninger (ed.), *The Varieties of Orthographic Knowledge I: Theoretical and Developmental Issues.* Dordrecht: Kluwer Academic Publishers.

Parke, R. D. and Beitel, A. (1986). Hospital-based intervention for fathers. In M. E. Lamb (ed.), *The Father's Role: Applied Perspectives.* New York: Wiley.

Parten, M. (1932) Social participation among preschool children. *Journal of Abnormal and Social Psychology,* 27: 242–269.

Pascalis, O. and Slater, A. (eds.) (2003). *The Development of Face Processing in Infancy and Early Childhood.* New York: Nova Science.

Peters, R. H., Koch, P. C. and Blythe, B. L. (1988). Differential effects of yohimbine and naloxone on copulatory behaviors of male rats. *Behavioral Neuroscience,* 102: 559–564.

Piaget, J. (1929). *The Child's Conception of the World.* London: Routledge & Kegan Paul.

Piaget, J. (1952). *The Origins of Intelligence in Children.* New York: International Universities Press. (Original work published in 1932.)

Piaget, J. (1958). *The Growth of Logical Thinking from Childhood to Adolescence.* New York: Basic Books.

Pinel, J. J. (2000). *Biopsychology.* London: Allyn and Bacon.

Plomin, R. and Dunn, J. (eds.) (1986). *The Study of Temperament: Changes, Continuities and Challenges.* Hillsdale, New Jersey: Erlbaum.

Plomin, R. (1994). The Emmanuel Miller Memorial Lecture 1993: genetic research and identification of environmental influences. *Journal of Child Psychology and Psychiatry*, 35: 817–834.

Porter, R. H. and Winberg, J. (1999). Unique salience of maternal breast odours for newborn infants. *Neuroscience and Biobehavioral Reviews*, 23: 439–449.

Posner, M. I. (1992). Attention as a cognitive and neural system. *Current Directions in Psychological Science*, 1: 11–14.

Posner, M. I. and Rothbart, M. K. (1981). The development of attentional mechanisms. In J. H. Flowers (ed.), *Nebraska Symposium on Motivation*, 28: 1–52. Lincoln, NE: University of Nebraska Press.

Poulin-Dubois, P. and Heroux, G. (1994). Movement and children's attribution of life properties. *International Journal of Behavioural Development*, 17: 329–347.

Prechtl, H. F. R. (1988). Developmental neurology of the foetus. *Clinical Obstetrics and Gynaecology*, 2: 21–36.

Quinn, P. C. (2002). Categorization. In A. Slater and M. Lewis (eds.), *Introduction to Infant Development*, 115–130. Oxford: Oxford University Press.

Quinn, P. C. and Eimas, P. D. (1998). Evidence for global category representation for humans by young infants. *Journal of Experimental Child Psychology*, 69: 151–174.

Read, M. (1968). *Children of Their Fathers: Growing up Among the Ngoni of Malawi*. New York: Holt, Rinehart and Winston.

Reich, P. A. (1986). *Language Development*. Englewood Cliffs, NJ: Prentice-Hall.

Reznick, J. S. and Goldfield, B.A. (1992). Rapid change in lexical development in comprehension and production. *Developmental Psychology*, 28: 406–413.

Rice, C., Koinis, D., Sullivan, K. and Tager-Flusberg, H. (1997). When 3-year-olds pass the appearance-reality test. *Developmental Psychology*, 33: 54–61.

Richards, C. A. and Sanderson, J. A. (1999). The role of imagination in facilitating deductive reasoning in 2-, 3- and 4-year-olds. *Cognition*, 72: B1–B9.

Rosch, E. (1978). Principles of categorization. In E. Rosch and B. B. Lloyd (eds.), *Cognition and Categorization*, 27–48. Hillsdale, NJ: Erlbaum.

Rose, S. A., Gottfried, A. N. and Bridger, W. H. (1981). Cross-modal transfer and information processing by the sense of touch in infancy. *Developmental Psychology*, 17: 90–98.

Rosenstein, D. and Oster, H. (1988). Differential facial responsiveness to four basic tastes in newborns. *Child Development*, 59: 1555–1568.

Rosenzweig, M. R., Leiman, A. L. and Breedlove, S. M. (1999). *Biological Psychology: An Introduction to Behavioural, Cognitive, and Clinical Neuroscience*. Sunderland, MA: Sinauer.

Rovee-Collier, C. K. and Fagen, J. W. (1981). The retrieval of memory in early infancy. In L. P. Lipsitt (ed.), *Advances in Infancy Research*, 1: 225–254. Norwood, NJ: Ablex.

Rovee-Collier, C. K. and Boller, K. (1995). Interference or facilitation in infant memory? In F. N. Dempster and C. J., Brainerd (eds.), *Interference and Inhibition in Cognition*. San Diego CA: Academic.

Rubin, K. H., Hastings, P. C., Xinyen S. and McNichol, K. (1998). Intrapersonal and maternal correlates of aggression, conflict, and externalizing problems in toddlers. *Child Development*, 69(6): 1614–1629.

Ruff, H. A. and Rothbart, M. E. (1996). *Attention in Early Development: Themes and Variations*. Oxford: Oxford University Press.

Rummelhart, D. E., McClelland, J. L., and the PDP Research Group (1986). *Parallel Distributed Processing: Explorations in the Microstructure of Cognition, 1: Foundations*. Cambridge, MA: M.I.T. Press.

Russell, M. J. (1976). Human olfactory communication. *Nature*, 260: 520–522.

Sadler, T. W. (2000). *Langman's Medical Embryology*. Baltimore: Williams & Wilkins.

Samuels, C. (1986). Bases for the infant's development of self-awareness. *Human Development*, 29: 36-48.

Saxe, G. B. (1988). Candy-selling and math learning. *Educational Researcher*, 17: 14–21.

Scarr, S. (1997). Behaviour-genetic and socialization theories of intelligence: truce and reconciliation.In R. J. Sternberg and E. L. Grigorenko (eds.), *Intelligence, Heredity and Environment.* 3–41. New York: Cambridge University Press.

Scarr, S. and Weinberg, R. A. (1983). The Minnesota Adoption Studies: genetic differences and malleability. *Child Development,* 54: 260–267.

Schaffer, H.R. (1971). *The Growth of Sociability.* Baltimore: Penguin Books.

Schaffer, H. R. and Emerson, P. E. (1964) The development of social attachments in infancy. *Monographs of the Society for Research in Child Development,* 29(94).

Schneider, W. and Bjorklund, D. F. (1998). Memory. In D. Kuhn and R.S. Siegler (eds.), *Handbook of Child Psychology 2: Cognition, Perception and Language* (5th edn.), 467–522. New York: Wiley.

Schneider, W., Gruber, H., Gold, A. and Opwis, K. (1993). Class expertise and memory for chess positions in children and adults. *Journal of Experimental Child Psychology,* 56: 328–349.

Schneider, W. and Pressley, M. (1997). *Memory Development Between Two and Twenty.* Mahwah, NJ: Erlbaum.

Schvaneveldt, P. L., Miller, B. C., Berry, E. H. and Lee, T. R. (2001). Academic goals, achievement, and age at first sexual intercourse: Longitudinal, bidirectional influences. *Adolescence,* 36: 767–787.

Searle, J. R. (1969). *Speech Acts: An Essay in the Philosophy of Language.* Cambridge, Cambridge University Press.

Searle, L. V. (1949). The organization of hereditary maze-brightness and maze-dullness. *Genetic Psychology Monographs,* 39: 279–325.

Shaffer, D. R. (1999). *Developmental Psychology: Childhood and Adolescence.* Pacific Grove, CA: Brooks/Cole.

Siegal, M. (1997). *Knowing Children: Experiments in Conversation and Cognition.* Hillsdale, NJ: Erlbaum.

Siegler, R. S. (1996). *Emerging Minds: The Process of Change in Children's Thinking.* New York: Oxford University Press.

Siergovel, R. M., et al., (2000). Annual changes in total body fat and fat-free mass in children from 8 to 18 years in relation to changes in body mass index: the Fels Longitudinal Study. *Annals of the New York Academy of Science,* 904: 420–423.

Sieving, R. E., McNeely, C. S. and Blum, R. W. (2000). Maternal expectations, mother–child connectedness, and adolescent sexual debut. *Archives of Pediatrics and Adolescent Medicine,* 154: 809–816.

Simmons, R. G. and Blyth, D. A. (1987). *Moving into Adolescence.* New York: Aldine De Gruyter.

Simon, W., Berger, a. S. and Gagnon, J. H. (1972). Beyond anxiety and fantasy: The coital experiences of college youth. *Journal of Youth and Adolescence,* 1(3): 203–222.

Simons, K. (1993). *Early Visual Development, Normal and Abnormal.* New York: Oxford University Press.

Skinner, B. F. (1957). *Verbal Behaviour.* East-Norwalk, CT: Appleton-Century-Crofts.

Skinner, B. F. (1966). The ontogeny and phylogeny of behaviour. *Science,* 153: 1205–1213.

Slater, A. (1998). *Perceptual Development: Visual, Auditory and Speech Perception.* Hove: Psychology Press.

Slater, A. and Johnson, S. P. (1999). Visual sensory and perceptual abilities of the newborn: beyond the blooming, buzzing confusion. In A. Slater and S. P. Johnson (eds.), *The Development of Sensory, Motor and Cognitive Capacities,* 121–141. Hove: Sussex Press.

Slater, A. and Lewis, M. (2002). *Introduction to Infant Development.* Oxford: Oxford University Press.

Slater, A. M., Mattock, A. and Brown, E. (1990). Size constancy at birth: newborn infants' reponses to retinal and real size. *Journal of Experimental Child Psychology,* 49: 314–322.

Slater, A. M. and Morison, V. (1985). Shape constancy and slant perception at birth. *Perception,* 14: 337–344.

Slater, A., Morison, V. and Rose, D. (1983). Perception of shape by the newborn baby. *British Journal of Developmental Psychology,* 1: 135–142.

Slobin, D. I. (1979). *Psycholinguistics*. Glenview, IL: Scott, Foresman.

Smith, R. (1999). The timing of birth. *Scientific American, 280*: 68–75.

Smolak, L., Levine, M. P. and Gralen, S. (1993). The impact of puberty and dating on eating problems among middle school girls. *Journal of Youth and Adolescence, 22*: 355–368.

Sokolov, E. N. (1963). *Perception and the Conditioned Reflex*. Oxford: Pergamon.

Spelke, E. (2000). Core knowledge. *American Psychologist, 55*: 1233–1242.

Spelke, E. S. (1979). Perceiving bimodally specified events in infancy. *Developmental Psychology, 15*: 626–636.

Stattin, H. and Magnusson, D. (1990). *Pubertal Maturation in Female Development*. Hillsdale, NJ: Erlbaum.

Steinberg, L. and Levine, A. (1990). *You and Your Adolescent: A Parent's Guide for Ages 10–20*. New York: Harper & Row.

Steinberg, L. and Silverberg, S. (1986). The vicissitudes of autonomy in early adolescence. *Child Development, 57*: 841–851.

Stice, E., Presnell, K. and Bearman, S. K. (2001). Relation of early menarche to depression, eating disorders, substance abuse, and comorbid psychopathology among adolescent girls. *Developmental Psychology, 37*: 608–619.

Stipek, D., Gralinski, H. and Kopp, C. (1990). Self-concept development in the toddler years. *Developmental Psychology, 26*: 972–977.

Streri, A., Lhote, M. and Dutilleul, S. (2000). Haptic perception in newborns. *Developmental Science, 3*: 319–327.

Streri, A. and Spelke, E. S. (1988). Haptic perception of objects in infancy. *Cognitive Psychology, 20*, 1–12.

Subbotsky, E. V. (1994). Early rationality and magical thinking in preschoolers: space and time. *British Journal of Developmental Psychology, 12*: 97–108.

Sullivan, H. S. (1953). *The Interpersonal Theory of Psychiatry*. New York: Horton.

Sullivan, K., and Winner, E. (1993). Three-year-olds' understanding of mental states: the influence of trickery. *Journal of Experimental Child Psychology, 56*: 135–148.

Svejda, M. J., Campos, J. J. and Emde, R. N. (1980). Mother–infant 'bonding': failure to generalize. *Child Development, 51*(3): 775–779.

Talpade, M. and Talpade, S. (2001). Early puberty in African-American girls: nutrition past and present. *Adolescence, 36*: 789–794.

Tanner, J. M. (1990). *Foetus Into Man: Physical Growth from Conception to Maturity*. Cambridge, MA: Harvard University Press.

Taylor, M. and Gelman, S. A. (1988). Incorporating new words into the lexicon: preliminary evidence for language hierarchies in two-year-old children. *Child Development, 60*: 625–636.

Teller, D. Y. (1998). Spatial and temporal aspects of colour vision. *Vision Research, 38,* 3275-3282.

Teller, D. Y. and Bornstein, M. H. (1987). Infant colour vision and colour perception. In P. Salapatek and L. Cohen (eds.), *Handbook of Infant Perception, Vol. 2: From Perception to Cognition*, 185–236. Orlando: Academic.

Thatcher, R. W. (1991). Maturation of human frontal lobes: physiological evidence for staging. *Developmental Neuropsychology, 7*: 397–419.

Thatcher, R. W., Lyon, G. R., Rumsey, J. and Krasnegor, J. (1996). *Developmental Neuroimaging*. San Diego, CA: Academic.

Thelen, E. (1995). Motor development: a new synthesis. *American Psychologist, 50*: 79–95.

Thelen, E. and Smith, L. (eds.) (1994). *A Dynamic Systems Approach to the Development of Cognition and Action*. Cambridge, MA: MIT Press.

Thompson, P. M., Giedd, J. N., Woods, R. P., MacDonald, D., Evans, A. C. and Toga, A. W. (2000). Growth patterns in the developing brain detected by using continuum mechanical tensor maps. *Nature, 404*: 190–192.

Trehub, S. E., Schneider, B. A., Morrongiello, B. A. and Thorpe, L. A. (1988). Auditory sensitivity in school-aged children. *Journal of Experimental Child Psychology,* 46: 273–285.

Tryon, R. C. (1934). Individual differences. In F. A. Moss (ed.), *Comparative Psychology.* 409–448. New York: Prentice-Hall.

Tuchmann-Duplessis, H. (1975). *Drug Effects on the Foetus.* Acton, MA: Publishing Science Group Inc.

Turner, A. M. and Greenough, W. T. (1985). Differential rearing effects on rat visual cortex synapses 1. Synaptic and neuronal density and synapses per neuron. *Brain Research,* 329: 195–203.

Tversky, A. and Kahneman, D. (1973). Availability: a heuristic for judging frequency and probability. *Cognitive Psychology,* 4: 207–232.

US Department of Health and Human Services (1996c). Vital statistics of the United States. Washington DC: US Government Printing Office. In L. Berk (1998). *Development Through the Life-span.* Needham Heights, MA: Allyn & Bacon.

Vasta, R., Haith, M. M. and Miller, S. A. (1992). *Child Psychology: The Modern Science.* New York: Wiley.

Von Hofsten, C. (1979). Development of visually-guided reaching: the approach phase. *Motor Behaviour,* 5: 160–178.

Vygotsky, L. S. (1987). Thinking and speech. In R. W. Rieber, A. S. Carton (eds.), and N. Minick (trans.), *The Collected Works of L. S. Vygotsky, Vol. 1: Problems of General Psychology.* 37–285. New York: Plenum (original 1934).

Wachs, T. D. (2000). *Necessary but Not Sufficient: The Respective Roles of Single and Multiple Influences on Individual Development.* Washington, DC: American Psychological Association.

Wahlsten, D. (1994). The intelligence of heritability. *Canadian Psychology,* 35: 244–259.

Watson, J. B. and Rayner, R. (1920). Conditioned emotional reactions. *Journal of Experimental Psychology,* 3: 1–14.

Weiner, I. B. (1980). Psychopathology in adolescence. In J. Adelson (ed.), *Handbook of Adolescent Psychology.* New York: Wiley.

White, B. and Held, R. (1966). Plasticity of sensori-motor development in the human infant. In J. F. Rosenblith and W. Allinsmith (eds.), *The Causes of Behaviour,* 60–70. Boston, MA: Allyn and Bacon.

Wilkin, P. E. (1979). Prenatal and postnatal responses to music and sound stimuli: a clinical report. *Canadian Music Education (Research edition),* 33: 223–232.

Wilkin, P. E. (1993). Prenatal and postnatal repsonses to music and sound stimuli. In T. Blum (ed.) *Prenatal Perception, Learning and Bonding.* Berlin: Leonardo.

Wilson, R. S. (1986). Growth and development of human twins. In F. Falkner and J. M. Tanner (eds.), *Human Growth: A Comprehensive Treatise.* New York: Plenum.

Wintre, M. G., McVey, R. and Fox, G. (1988). Age and sex differences in choice of consultant for various types of problems. *Child Development,* 59(4):1046–1055.

Wolff, P. H. (1966). The causes, controls and organization of behaviour in the neonate. *Psychological Issues,* 5(17).

Index